1984

GREEK VEGETARIAN COOKING

Artfully adapted starters, main meals, side dishes and
sweets from traditional Greek cuisine, making
imaginative use of fresh fruit, vegetables and other
wholefood ingredients.

D0376431

By the same author

RAISING A CHILD NATURALLY

GREEK VEGETARIAN COOKING

Colorful Dishes from the Eastern Shores of the Mediterranean

by

Alkmini Chaitow

Illustrated by Clive Birch

THORSONS PUBLISHERS INC.
New York

Thorsons Publishers Inc.
377 Park Avenue South
New York, New York 10016

First U.S. Edition 1984

LIBRARY OF CONGRESS CATALOGING IN
PUBLICATION DATA

Chaitow, Alkmini.
    Greek vegetarian cooking.
    Includes index.
    1. Vegetarian cookery.   2. Cookery, Greek.
    I. Title.
TX837.C437 1982   641.5'636   83-24245
ISBN 0-7225-0725-9

Printed and bound in Great Britain

Thorsons Publishers Inc. are distributed to the trade by
Inner Traditions International Ltd., New York

Contents

I dedicate this book to my husband Leon
and our daughter Sasha,
with love.

Acknowledgements

I would like to thank Simon Martin, Editor of *Here's Health* for "pulling the trigger" and encouraging my writing.

I thank my mother, Antigoni Metallinou, for her influence in my cooking.

Finally, I thank my husband Leon for his constant help and support.

Introduction

Some people eat to live; in the West, most people seem to live to eat. Whichever group you fall into, the food described in this book will be found to be ideal. For those who see food as a simple matter of providing the body with its raw materials for the day, these balanced recipes of health-promoting wholefoods will provide many interesting variations. For those to whom the preparing, serving and eating of exciting foods is an important part of their lives, the unique "Greekness" of these recipes will open new vistas. For myself, I can say that the eating of such dishes as *Skordalia* and *Stuffed Squash Blossoms*, to name but two of the recipes included here, have been experiences I will always remember and cherish.

For a variety of reasons more and more people are following a vegetarian pattern of eating, and there is an even greater swing away from over-refined convenience and "junk" foods and towards foods which have undergone a minimum of processing. Such foods have become known as wholefoods, and the advantages of a balanced wholefood and vegetarian diet are now so evident that many nutritionists have ceased to label those that eat this way as cranks or faddists, and instead openly recommend this eating pattern. From a health maintenance point of view, a diet such as this, with its abundance of complex carbohydrates, vegetable proteins, minerals, vitamins, enzymes, fiber and minimum of refined carbohydrates and saturated fats, is demonstrably superior to a "normal" Western diet.

From an ecological standpoint, the vegetarian way of eating, with the emphasis on whole grains, legumes, vegetables and fruits, is one which imposes far less strain on the earth's resources in terms of land and energy requirements for food production. Also, from an aesthetic or humanitarian viewpoint, such a diet is the logical result of compassion for animals and a desire to minimize or end the suffering endured by billions of animals for the sake of a flesh-consuming society.

Since eating and its associated social aspects are an integral part of life, it is important to ensure that a change to a different dietary pattern does not create more problems than it solves. The new diet should provide nutritious and delicious food which, ideally, is not too difficult to prepare or too expensive. Most of the food in this book qualifies in these respects.

I have been a vegetarian for some twenty-five years and have seen my health improve from a reasonable average to a much higher level, despite the slide into middle age. Much of the credit for this must go to the delicious and often inspired culinary gifts of my wife, Alkmini. Born and bred on the magical island of Corfu, she has utilized her knowledge of Mediterranean cooking to add variety and interest to the basic ingredients of vegetarian whole-food cooking. Some of her recipes have been taken from the traditional meatless meals eaten during the Greek Orthodox Lenten period. Others have been adapted from commonly eaten dishes by substituting wholefood vegetarian ingredients for their fish or meat contents. Still others are purely her own invention based on her knowledge of the characteristics of the various ingredients used in a wholefood diet.

Having had no formal culinary training, her instinctive awareness of which foods blend together, both in taste and texture, has been enhanced by her knowledge of the nutritional value of the foods available to a vegetarian. Knowing of the many individuals who are unable to eat dairy products, Alkmini has successfully experimented with alternatives such as soy milk. As a result, such dishes as Millet Pie, for example, can be enjoyed by anyone with a milk allergy by using soy milk to make the delicious Béchamel Sauce (see page 42).

The recipes in this book will open new horizons for many vegetarians whose meals may have become less than exciting. For those who are feeling their way towards this vegetarianism, the recipes will provide meals, the enjoyment of which will soon blot out past habits in a deluge of new flavors and textures.

The basic pattern of eating that I have found most conducive to the promotion and maintenance of health is one in which one of the two main meals, midday or evening, is a raw salad-type meal and the other a cooked protein savory-type meal. With the salad meal it is essential, I believe, to maintain interest by including a variety of textures and tastes. The salad recipes will enhance these aspects of anyone's raw food intake. The protein (cooked) meal, which should be accompanied by cooked or raw vegetables, can contain animal protein in the form of eggs, cheese or milk, or consist completely of vegetable foods. If no animal protein is present in the ingredients of such a meal (and, personally, this is the ideal I would aim for) then in order that the body gets its necessary protein there must be a combination of legumes and cereals. Legumes such as lentils, chickpeas and lima beans, and cereals such as millet, wholegrain wheat, brown rice, etc., will provide all the required protein and amino acids when eaten at the same meal.

My own breakfast recommendation is a wholegrain cereal, seeds (sunflower, pumpkin etc.) and fruit (fresh and dried) mixture with natural yogurt.

In this book Alkmini has not only provided recipes, but also some menu suggestions and patterns of eating which should help guide the newcomer towards a balanced intake of these lovely foods. Food should be fun, and what a bonus if it is also good for you! The Mediterranean people enjoy their food, and mealtimes are pleasant family or social gatherings. By adding the extra dimension of wholeness to the food and by adapting many of the region's delicacies to meet the needs of vegetarians, I believe many people will enjoy new and exciting mealtime experiences, while also building and maintaining healthier bodies.

Western civilization owes much to Greece in terms of its heritage, whether it be language, ideas or morals. With this contribution to the culinary arts, the debt to her is just a little bit greater.

LEON CHAITOW
N.D., D.O., M.B.N.O.A.

1. General Instructions

Cooking should not be drudgery. Perhaps it is repetitive, in that day follows day and meal follows meal, seemingly without end. When thinking about cooking, therefore, it helps to consider the creative aspect of the art, as well as the pleasure and nourishment which the effort will bring to family or friends. The environment in which the food is prepared and cooked should be pleasant. This will be helped by organizing a clean and tidy kitchen. Such details as a colorful apron, a small vase with one or two flowers, a little background music, and so on, all help to make the humblest kitchen into a pleasant little kingdom in which to create the alchemy of good cooking.

After selecting the recipe, the next step is to gather together all the ingredients on the working surface. Individual plates and containers should hold the various prescribed quantities. This may seem obvious, but it is surprising how many recipes go wrong because halfway through the preparation, something essential is found to be missing. It pays to be methodical and to work slowly. For example, washing each dish and saucepan as it is used saves a great deal of effort later.

Once the food is prepared and cooking, it should not be left for more than a minute or two. This time can be spent tidying up and cleaning, all the while keeping an eye on the food. The result will be a tidier kitchen, and the cooking food will not be in danger of burning.

Results may, from time to time, be disappointing. This is unlikely to be the fault of the recipe, but more probably a result of too much water having been used, or the wrong amount of seasoning (too much or too little), or the heat used may have been too high or too low. The best advice is to use your common sense and try again, adapting and experimenting by all means, but only when the basic recipe has been successfully mastered.

It is certainly a good idea, when guests are expected, to use only recipes that you have previously mastered. This helps to avoid tension, aggravation, disappointment, and embarrassment.

Cooking Vegetables the Greek Way

The advantage of cooking vegetables the Greek way (boiling until soft) is that they can be served cold. This means that preparation can take place some hours prior to serving them. The flavor of cooked vegetables, served cold, is superior to that of hot vegetables, but they will have lost something of their nutritive value. Cooking vegetables for cold serving is simply a matter of bring a saucepan of salted water to the boil, adding the vegetables and cooking until tender. These should be drained, placed on a serving dish, and dressed with olive oil and lemon juice before serving, cold, when required. Garnish with black olives for additional flavor.

Steaming Vegetables (Not the Greek Way)

When hot cooked vegetables are needed for a meal, they should be prepared just prior to serving. In Greece, the majority of people boil vegetables until they are very soft. This method might be traditional, but is not ideal for retaining nutritional value or for producing really tasty vegetables. If the aim is to achieve tasty dishes, full of nutritional goodness, which retain their freshness, crispness and color, then the ideal cooking method is steaming.

Place the vegetables in a steamer. Depending upon the type of vegetable, more or less time will be required. Cauliflower and zucchini, for example, require five to seven minutes, whereas globe artichokes, carrots, Brussels sprouts, etc., need a few minutes more. For a delicious flavor-enhancer, add a dressing of olive oil and lemon juice (two parts oil to one part lemon, and a little salt) to the cooked vegetables just before serving.

The *Skordalia* dish (page 18) complements any cooked vegetable. If *Skordalia* is not available, then one or two cloves of raw garlic sliced thinly on the vegetables makes for a fantastic, flavorsome experience; this is real "peasant" style food. As for the odor, friends might not appreciate the garlic, but your heart certainly will. It is worth noting that *the lowest incidence of heart disease in the world occurs in Corfu*. The use of olive oil and garlic in large amounts is thought to be the main reason for this.

A Few Tips

- When preparing globe artichokes, the fingers tend to discolor to a dirty brown shade. Rubbing your hands with half a lemon will remove this.

- After eating garlic brush your teeth and chew some parsley. This should help to remove, or at least to reduce, the odor.

- To give a brown color to vegetable soup or broth, add to the cooking contents in the saucepan some outer leaves of onion. These should be removed before serving.

- Lemon juice can be available all year round by freezing it, as ice cubes, and storing in plastic bags in the freezer.

- Bread keeps fresh when kept in the refrigerator.

- When lemons are very fresh or not terribly juicy, they may be hard. It is much easier to squeeze the juice out of them if they are first rolled and pressed on a hard surface before cutting.

- In Greece, we use a bowl of cow's milk to remove undesirable smells from the refrigerator. Place the bowl with the milk in it and leave for a day or so, before discarding.

- In order to minimize the sharpness of some varieties of onions, the onion slices should be placed in a bowl containing water and a little cider vinegar. These should soak for half an hour to an hour. The taste of the onion should then be sweeter.

- To avoid 'crying' when peeling onions, leave the root untouched until the rest of the onion has been sliced. Amazing as it seems, this simple measure does prevent this common kitchen discomfort.

- When wishing to thaw something from the freezer, do so by transferring it to the refrigerator. Thawing in a hurry spoils the flavor and might result in the idea that the particular food does not freeze well.

- Potatoes are widely used in Greek cooking. Apart from the obvious ways, there are several specialities such as Potato Salad and Skordalia (mashed potatoes with garlic and lemon), which are uniquely Greek. When the intention is to make either Potato Salad or Skordalia, it is recommended that they first be boiled in salted water. The quality of the potatoes can, of course, affect the quality of the resulting dish.

    If you wish to find out which potatoes are particularly starchy (and therefore better for the purpose of mashing or mixing, as in Skordalia), then cut a potato in half and rub the two halves together. If, in doing so, a lot of juice is evident then this indicates that the potatoes contain a lot of water and would probably split in cooking. If, on the other hand, a frothy, thick, liquid is produced by rubbing the two halves together, this indicates a higher starch content, and therefore a "better" potato. (This useful little trick was shown to me by my very old-fashioned grandmother some twenty-five years ago).

- Never use any potatoes that are green. These are dangerous in any quantity and can cause upsets, even in small amounts. Avoid using sprouting potatoes and never use any potato tops or their flowers.

2. Mezze Dishes (Appetizers)

Mezze in the Greek language means "bits and pieces" of appetizing foods. By the time a guest has finished the "appetizers", so much has usually been eaten that the appetite is fully satisfied. This type of "meal" would be ideal for a party or as a variation from the normal – perhaps eaten outdoors on a summer evening.

On individual little plates serve the following:

Tjatjiki (page 18)
Roasted Lima Beans (page 95)
Stuffed Squash Blossoms (page 79)
Potato Salad (page 103)
Beet Salad (page 104)
Hummus (page 23)
Eggplant Dip (page 22)
Chickpea Croquettes (page 101)
Cheeses
Black olives
Radishes and radish tops
Scallions
Lettuce leaves
Cucumber sticks
Wholewheat bread

GARLIC POTATO
Skordalia

(Enough for several meals) *Gluten and Dairy-free*
This is a tasty relish or side dish. The virtues of garlic are
well known – it is credited with anti-catarrhal qualities, it
is said to lower the blood-pressure, to be anti-rheumatic
and to lower cholesterol levels; it is often cited as a "blood
purifier". These valuable assets added to the nutritive
value of lemon juice (vitamin C) and olive oil make this
dish a real health food. Keep surplus refrigerated.

3½ pounds potatoes
2 large heads of garlic, about 1½ ounces each in weight,
    peeled and crushed
Sea salt to taste
4 lemons
1½ cups olive oil
A little parsley
6 black olives
2-3 slices of lemon

Boil the unpeeled potatoes in salted water. Crush the
garlic into an empty mixing bowl. Peel the potatoes and
add them to the bowl *while still hot*. Add a pinch of salt. A
mixer should be used to reduce the potato and garlic
mixture to a pulp. Alternately, add the lemon juice and
olive oil bit by bit until all the ingredients are totally
blended into a smooth mixture. This procedure can be
(and was in the past) carried out by mixing the ingredients
in a mortar and pestle. Such a method has the same result
but is, of course, very hard work.

Place the creamy mixture into a bowl and garnish with
parsley, olives and slices of lemon. This has a very strong
garlic flavor and more or less garlic can be used, according
to taste.

Note:
(a) Skordalia may be served cold as a side dish. It goes
    very well with any vegetable, especially beets.

(b) If the mixture is not creamy (since the quality of potatoes vary) add one to two tablespoons warm water and a little more lemon juice to the mixture.

GARLIC WITH BREAD AND NUTS
Skordalia me Karydia

Dairy-free

This wholesome dip has the nutritive value of nuts with their high mineral content as well as the health-giving qualities of garlic and olive oil. It is ideally used as a dip with salad sticks (carrot, cucumber, celery, radishes).

1 head of garlic, peeled and crushed
2 cups wholewheat bread, soaked and well squeezed
Sea salt
2½ cups olive oil
1 cup walnuts or almonds, well grated
⅓ cup wine vinegar

Place the crushed garlic in the mixing bowl with the bread. Add a little salt and mix well. Then add alternately, a little at a time, the soaked bread, the oil, nuts and vinegar. If you find that the mixture is too thick, add a little warm water. This is a side dish and is served cold.

Note: The texture will, to a large extent, depend on whether an electric mixer or mortar and pestle is used. In both cases, the nuts must be ground first.

YOGURT AND CUCUMBER DIP
Tjatjiki

Gluten-free

This delicious and refreshing summer dip has the nutritive value of yogurt (vitamin B, etc.) as well as the health-giving qualities of garlic and cucumber. Wholewheat bread, cucumber and celery are ideal for dipping into Tjatjiki.

2 cloves crushed garlic (or more to taste)
Sea salt and freshly ground black pepper
2 teaspoonsful olive oil
1 teaspoonful wine vinegar
8 ounces goat's or sheep's milk yogurt
½ a cucumber, coarsely grated

Mix the crushed garlic with the salt and pepper. Add the oil and vinegar and mix well. Place the yogurt in a serving bowl. Add the oil and vinegar mixture in stages, stirring gently with a wooden spoon. Then add the grated cucumber and mix well. Chill before serving.

Note: If the yogurt is very fresh and therefore runny, I suggest that you place the grated cucumber on absorbent paper towels in order to get rid of excess juice before adding it to the yogurt.

TAHINI DIP

Gluten and Dairy-free

This uniquely flavorsome dip has great nutritive value, not only through the proven health-giving properties of olive oil, garlic, parsley and lemon juice, but also in the calcium, iron and thiamin content of sesame seed paste (tahini).

5-6 tablespoons lemon juice
2 cloves of garlic, crushed
3 tablespoons very finely chopped parsley
4 heaped tablespoons tahini (sesame paste from health food stores)
Sea salt

Place all the ingredients together and mix well to a smooth, creamy texture. Serve with toast or fresh whole-wheat bread, celery, and tomatoes.

Note: If the above mixture does not produce a smooth, creamy texture, add a little water.

EGGPLANT DIP
Melitzanosalata

Gluten-free

This tasty dip is ideally served with salad vegetables cut into strips, such as carrots, celery, and cucumber, or with wholewheat bread. The goat's or sheep's cheese and goat's milk make this a protein-rich dish.

2 large eggplants
1½ cups pure olive oil
1 cup goat's milk
Lemon juice to taste
½ cup féta cheese
Sea salt and freshly ground black pepper

Wash, dry and place the eggplants in the oven at 350°F for 1-1½ hours. When cooked, remove and discard the skins. Place the flesh in a mixing bowl and reduce to a creamy texture. This mixture should be worked with a pestle in a mortar, adding alternately the oil, milk and a little lemon. When the mixture is frothy, add the cheese which should already have been crumbled by hand. Season with salt and pepper. Place the mixture in a glass bowl and decorate with small slices of tomato, parsley and black olives.

HUMMUS DIP

Gluten and Dairy-free
Chickpeas (garbanzo beans) have a high protein content (13 per cent) and are rich in potassium, magnesium and iron.

½ cup chickpeas
2 tablespoons tahini (sesame paste from health food stores)
4 tablespoons olive oil
2 cloves of garlic
Sea salt
Lemon juice and lemon slices
Black olives

Soak the chickpeas overnight. Empty the water, add fresh water and then cook before changing the water again. (This eliminates enzymes which can produce flatulence). Allow the chickpeas to cook until tender. Place the chickpeas in a blender or a bowl. Add the tahini, oil, garlic, salt, lemon and 4 tablespoons of warm water. Mix until creamy. If the texture is too thick, add 1-2 tablespoons of water to thin it down. Place in a serving bowl and refrigerate until needed. You may sprinkle a little paprika onto the mixture and decorate with lemon slices and black olives.

3. Raw Salads

When thinking in terms of preparing a raw salad, bear in mind that the following items can be eaten raw, either individually or as a combination. A little imagination regarding color and taste will give you a dish which will not only look attractive and taste delicious, but will provide value in the form of vitamin C and most minerals. A salad should constitute one of the main meals each day, or at least a major part of it.

The following items can be eaten raw:
Tomatoes
Onions
Scallions
Carrots
Garlic
Cauliflower
Watercress
Radishes
Radish tops (young)
Turnips, grated
Beets, grated
Parsnips, grated
Brussels sprouts
Fennel

Sea kale
Nasturtiums
Dandelions
Peas   } when young and tender
Lima beans
String beans
Cucumber
Parsley
Endive
Lettuce
Chicory
Mint
Red Cabbage
White Cabbage
Chives
Leeks
Mushrooms
Zucchini
Sprouted seeds such as:
Fenugreek
Alfalfa
Mung beans
Aduki beans
Soy beans
Lentils
Chickpeas

Chemicals seem to be used more and more in the commercial growing of vegetables and so be sure to thoroughly wash your salad ingredients before preparing the meal.

Ideally, any raw salad should be served as soon as it is prepared. In this way, such important ingredients as vitamin C will be retained instead of being lost. If, however, you have guests and wish to prepare the salad some time before the meal, then keep the prepared salad sealed in the refrigerator and add the dressing just before serving. If the dressing is added too long before serving then the salad will lose its crispness and will look "tired".

CUCUMBER SALAD
Agourosalata

(Serves 2 as a side dish)

½ a cucumber
1 large or 2 small tomatoes
4 thin slices onion
6 black olives

For the dressing:
1⅔ tablespoons oil (ideally, olive oil)
2 teaspoons cider or wine vinegar
½ teaspoon oregano
Sea salt

Wash the cucumber, tomato and onion well. Cut the cucumber in half, lengthwise, and then into slices. Cut the tomato in half and then into slices. If the tomato is large you should get 12 slices, if small, eight. Place them in a salad bowl. Add the slices of onion and olives. Mix the ingredients for the dressing thoroughly and pour this onto the salad. Mix gently but thoroughly.

TOMATO SALAD
Domatosalata

(Serves 2 as a side dish)

4 small tomatoes
⅓ green pepper
2 tablespoons finely chopped parsley
6 black olives

For the dressing:
3 tablespoons olive oil
1 teaspoon vinegar
⅓ teaspoon oregano

Wash the vegetables. Slice the tomatoes and pepper. Mix the dressing. Place the vegetables on a plate, sprinkle with parsley, pour over the dressing and decorate with the olives.

Note: The tomato slices should be generous and chunky rather than slivers. The pepper should be sliced more thinly.

CARROT AND CABBAGE SALAD
Lahano me Carota

(Serves 4 as a side dish)

½ a small white cabbage
3 carrots, coarsely grated
8 ounces canned corn, drained
3 tablespoons lemon juice
4 tablespoons olive oil
Sea salt
Dash of black pepper

Slice the cabbage *thinly*. Add to this the carrots, corn, lemon juice, olive oil and seasoning, just prior to serving. Ingredients should be well mixed.

*Note:*Red cabbage could be used as well and also some celery, if desired.

PEASANT SALAD
Salata Horiatiki

(Serves 2-3 as a side dish)

2-3 radishes
2 tomatoes, thinly sliced
8 slices cucumber
½ a green pepper, finely chopped
2 lettuce leaves, thinly shredded
2 scallions, thinly sliced
½ an onion, thinly sliced
4 teaspoons chopped parsley
4 teaspoons chopped mint

For the dressing:
½ teaspoon oregano
3⅓ tablespoons olive oil
4 teaspoons cider or wine vinegar
4 ounces féta or other white cheese
8 black olives

When all the salad ingredients are washed and prepared, place them in a bowl, prepare the dressing and pour it over the salad. Mix gently with a wooden serving set. Add the cheese (which should have been cut into small pieces) and the olives.

Note: This would be an ideal lunch to serve with jacket potatoes and/or wholewheat bread.

LETTUCE SALAD
Salata Marouli

(Serves 3-4 as a side dish, according to the size of the lettuce)

1 fresh, firm lettuce
4 scallions
5 mint leaves (if available) and/or
⅓ cup chopped parsley

For the dressing:
3 tablespoons olive oil
2 tablespoons lemon juice
Sea salt

Wash the salad ingredients well and tear the lettuce by hand into small pieces. Chop the scallions and mint leaves and place them in a bowl with the parsley. Add the dressing; mix thoroughly but gently and serve.

CABBAGE AND TOMATO SALAD
Salata Lahano-Domates

(Serves 4 as a side dish)

¼ small white cabbage ⎫
¼ small red cabbage   ⎬ finely sliced and chopped
                       ⎭
3 celery stalks, finely chopped
2 firm tomatoes, sliced
8 black olives

For the dressing:
3⅓ tablespoons olive oil
1⅓ tablespoons cider or wine vinegar or lemon juice
Sea salt

Place all the prepared vegetables in a bowl. Add the dressing and mix thoroughly but gently (i.e., avoid bruising the vegetables), and serve.

DANDELION, RADISH AND RADISH TOPS
Prikalida me Rapania

(Serves 2 as a side dish)

15 dandelion leaves, chopped
6 radishes and radish tops, chopped
1 small onion, sliced
8 black olives
2 small tomatoes, sliced

For the dressing:
2 tablespoons olive oil
1 tablespoon cider vinegar or lemon juice
Sea salt

Place the ingredients in a bowl; add the dressing, mix thoroughly but gently, and serve.

Note: Watercress may be added, if desired. For use in salad, the inner, tender dandelion leaves are preferable.

SALAD LETTUCE WITH EGGS
Salata Marouli me Avga

(Serves 3-4 as a side dish)

2 hard-boiled eggs
1 firm lettuce
4 scallions, chopped
A little chopped parsley and/or mint
8 black olives

For the dressing:
2⅔ tablespoons olive oil
4 teaspoons wine or cider vinegar or lemon juice
Sea salt
Freshly ground black pepper

Peel and slice the eggs. Wash all the vegetables well. In a salad bowl place the lettuce which has been hand shredded, the sliced eggs, scallions, parsley and mint. Mix the oil, vinegar, salt and pepper; add this dressing to the salad and serve.

RAW ARTICHOKE SALAD
Agginares Omes Salata

Gluten and Dairy-free

Artichokes can be eaten raw. They are very nourishing, rich in minerals and are reputed to aid liver function. They may be used raw in salad, in which case they should be prepared as described on page 60 and then diced. The rubbing of the surface with lemon is very important to delay discoloration and oxidation.

(Serves 1-2 as a side dish)

1 artichoke, diced
1 celery stalk, skinned and diced
1 tomato, sliced
6 tender dandelion leaves, chopped
2 scallions, chopped
A few olives

Dress with a generous amount of olive oil, lemon juice and a little sea salt.

4. Soups

Soups are widely used in Greece all the year round, but especially during the winter months. Soups may serve as a starter or as a main course. Frequently, a nourishing, thick vegetable soup is augmented by the addition of wholewheat pasta. This turns a simple dish into a delicious meal in itself. The wonderful range of legumes provides a large variety of choices with which to prepare soups. Red kidney beans should, if used, be boiled for at least 10 minutes prior to being added to any recipe.

The recipes given here are those I remember being prepared by my grandmother and my mother. These recipes are very easy to make, very nourishing, very tasty and very Greek.

Féta cheese, black olives and wholewheat bread (or toast) are the ideal accompaniments for any of the following soups.

POTATO SOUP

(Serves 4-5 as a starter) *Gluten-free*

2½ pounds potatoes, peeled and diced
1 large onion, chopped
1-2 pints water (according to quality of potatoes –
   see page 16)
1½ cups goat's milk or skimmed milk
Sea salt and freshly ground black pepper
3 tablespoons polyunsaturated margarine

Place the potatoes and onion in a saucepan and cover with water. Simmer over a medium heat until the potatoes are tender. Reduce these to a creamy consistency in a food processor, then empty into a saucepan, bring to the boil and add the hot milk, salt and pepper. Stir and allow to simmer until you have a thick creamy texture. Remove from the heat and add the margarine.

LENTIL SOUP
Soupa Fakes

(Serves 4 as a main course)   *Gluten and Dairy-free*

¾ pound lentils
1 large carrot
8 cloves of garlic, halved lengthwise
½ an onion, chopped
½ teaspoon oregano
½ cup olive oil
14 ounces canned peeled tomatoes, sieved
Sea salt and black pepper to taste

Boil the lentils for 5 minutes. Empty this water and add 2 pints water; bring to the boil and allow to simmer for a further 10 minutes. Add all the other ingredients and allow to cook on a low heat until all the ingredients are tender (approximately 1 hour). When ready, the soup should be thick, but not solid. A little more water can be added, if required.

Note: This soup, eaten with wholewheat bread or toast, fresh celery and black olives is a nourishing, satisfying and extremely tasty meal in itself. This soup also freezes well.

DRIED PEA SOUP
Soupa Bizeli

(Serves 4 as a starter) *Gluten and Dairy-free*

¾ pound dried peas
3 celery stalks, chopped
1 medium-sized onion, sliced
3 carrots, chopped
4 teaspoons polyunsaturated margarine
⅔ cup olive oil
Sea salt
Black pepper

Soak the peas overnight. Wash them well and place in a saucepan with fresh water. Simmer the peas until well cooked. In the meantime, sautée the onion with the margarine. When the onion is soft, add it to the peas and add the rest of the ingredients. Allow to simmer until the consistency is fairly thick. Blend the resulting soup into a smooth liquid prior to serving.

CHICKPEA SOUP
Soupa Revithia

(Serves 3-4 as a main course) *Gluten and Dairy-free*

1 pound chickpeas
2 teaspoons rosemary
Sea salt
Black pepper
¾ cup olive oil
Lemon juice

Soak the chickpeas for at least 24 hours, and change the water at least twice. Simmer them for 30 minutes, then change the water; resume the cooking and change the water again 20 minutes later. Add the rosemary, salt, pepper and oil and allow to simmer until the chickpeas are *very* tender. Add a squeeze of lemon juice (according to taste), prior to serving.

BEAN SOUP
Fasoulada

(Serves 4 as a main course)   *Gluten and Dairy-free*

¾ pound navy beans
1 leek
3 carrots   } chopped or diced
2 onions
3 celery stalks
1 pound canned tomatoes
¾ cup olive oil
Sea salt
Black pepper
¼ teaspoon paprika

Soak the beans overnight. Rinse well and place in a saucepan with water. Bring to the boil and allow to cook for 15 minutes before changing the water again. Bring to the boil and allow to simmer until the beans show signs of splitting; add all the ingredients. (The tomatoes should have been passed through a sieve). Add more water if necessary and allow to simmer until the vegetables and beans are tender.

Note: The thickness of the soup is a matter of personal taste; by varying the amount of water, this can be controlled. As a winter meal, the thicker and more chewy it is, the better. Serve with olives and wholewheat bread.

TOMATO SOUP WITH SPAGHETTI
Domatosoupa me Spaghetti

(Serves 2-3 as a main course)   *Dairy-free*

1 pound canned tomatoes
2 celery stalks, chopped
1 onion, chopped
1 large carrot, chopped
½ cup olive oil
Sea salt
Black pepper
1 cupful wholewheat spaghetti, broken into
    approximately 1-inch lengths.

Place the sieved tomatoes in a saucepan. Add 3 pints of water and the celery, onion, carrot, oil, salt and pepper. Allow to simmer for 30 minutes, then add the spaghetti. Serve when the spaghetti is cooked (about 10-15 minutes).

Note: Various shapes of wholewheat pasta can be used in soups, e.g., short-cut macaroni or pasta shells. When using pasta, the resulting soup may be on the thick side. Just add some more water and another pinch of salt and bring to the boil for a minute or so before serving. Freezing any pasta soup is not recommended.

VEGETABLE SOUP
Hortosoupa

(Serves 4 as a main course)   *Gluten and Dairy-free*

1½ pounds fresh tomatoes, chopped
2 medium-sized potatoes, diced
2 carrots, diced
1 cupful red or white cabbage, finely chopped
3 celery stalks, chopped
½ cup fresh string beans, chopped
1 large onion, chopped
¾ cup olive oil
Sea salt
Black pepper

Place the tomatoes in a saucepan with 2 pints of cold water. Simmer for 30 minutes, then add all the well washed and chopped vegetables, the oil and salt and pepper and cook for approximately 45 minutes to 1 hour until the vegetables are tender.

5. Sauces

There are numerous sauces in Greek cooking, many with impressive names and even more impressive colors. Most of them, however, are meant to accompany non-vegetarian dishes. There are two basic sauces from which most others derive. These are tomato sauce and béchamel sauce.

The tomato sauce described below is the one widely used in Corfu, and it is a versatile sauce, used to accompany many pasta and rice dishes. This can be made in large quantities, as it does freeze well.

Béchamel sauce is, of course, the same the world over. I would not say its origin is Greek, but we make it "Greek style" by adding extra cheese and eggs for greater taste and nourishment. Béchamel sauce is widely used, as in moussaka dishes and Macaroni Pie, for example.

The "milk-free" béchamel, using plant milk, still contains cheese. This is usually well tolerated by individuals who are sensitive to milk itself. The soy milk used in this béchamel sauce affects the texture of the sauce, but the flavor is still delicious. It is possible that goat's cheese or cottage cheese could be used or even tofu (soy "cheese"), but the texture of the resulting sauce will obviously differ from that produced by a hard cheese. Bearing this in mind, the adventurous cook can play around with the basic ingredients and methods to produce unique creations.

TOMATO SAUCE (CORFU-STYLE)
Saltsa dae Domata

A basic ingredient of a number of dishes

Gluten and Dairy-free

3 pounds canned tomatoes (including the liquid)
1 cup parsley, chopped
1 teaspoon basil or 3 bay leaves
1 tablespoon dark brown sugar
1¼ cups olive oil
1½ large onions, chopped
⅓ cup garlic, chopped not crushed
Sea salt to taste

Place all the ingredients in a non-stick saucepan over medium heat, so that the contents are not boiling, but just gently bubbling. Stir periodically and continue for 1½ to 2 hours until all the liquid has evaporated. The result will be a thick tomato sauce.

This should be used in the preparation of vegetarian Pastitsio (Macaroni Pie), page 55, or Millet Pie, page 78 or spaghetti.

Note: Do not worry about the amount of garlic used – once cooked, most of its odor disappears. As it freezes very well you can make larger quantities for future use.

BÉCHAMEL SAUCE WITH MILK (Goat's or Cow's)
Saltsa Bessamel

Quantities given in this recipe are for Macaroni, Moussaka or Millet Pies (see pages 55, 75 and 78).

Because I consider these dishes to be a little complicated, it is better to make a larger quantity than for just one meal. Therefore, the quantities given below are intended to make 12 portions of one of these dishes, most of which can be frozen.

1½ cups wholewheat pastry flour
8 tablespoons butter or polyunsaturated margarine
3½-4 cups warm milk
1 whole egg and 5 yolks
Sea salt and freshly ground black pepper to taste
¾ pound hard cheese, grated (preferably Kefalotyri)

Place the flour and butter in a large non-stick frying pan over medium heat. Stir gently with a wooden spoon until smooth. Gradually add the milk, stirring constantly. The sauce should be thick, but not solid. (Add a little more milk if too thick.) Remove from the heat and add the egg, egg yolks, salt and pepper and cheese. Mix well and use immediately.

BECHAMEL SAUCE WITH SOY MILK
Saltsa Bessamel me Soyia

10 tablespoons wholewheat pastry flour
8 tablespoons butter or polyunsaturated margarine
1 pint soy milk ⎫
1 pint hot water ⎭ mixed together
3 whole eggs and 1 yolk
6 tablespoons grated hard cheese
Sea salt and freshly ground black pepper

Place the flour and butter in a non-stick frying pan over a medium heat. Mix to a smooth consistency and add all the milk substitute, stirring continuously. The final consistency should be thick but not solid (add a little more of the soy milk and hot water mixture if necessary). Remove from the heat and add the eggs, cheese, salt and pepper and mix well.

Note: The above quantities will make a pie or moussaka to serve 4-6, depending on what else you are serving with it.

MAYONNAISE
Mayoneza

Gluten and Dairy-free

This homemade mayonnaise contains no preservatives and should always be kept refrigerated and used within a few days of its preparation.

1 teaspoon mustard powder
1 teaspoon raw sugar
1 teaspoon sea salt
Dash of freshly ground black pepper
2 egg yolks
2 teaspoons white wine vinegar
1 cup olive oil
Juice of 1 lemon

In a bowl, mix together the mustard powder, sugar, salt and pepper. Add the egg yolks and the vinegar and mix until these and the previous ingredients are well blended. Add the oil drop by drop, stirring constantly. When the mayonnaise begins to become thick, thin it with a little lemon. Add the rest of the lemon and oil little by little until they are both fully blended. Refrigerate for 2 hours before serving.

6. Rice Dishes

Rice is a very important staple food, originating in India and brought to Europe by Alexander the Great. It is appropriate, therefore, that it should be so much a part of Greek cooking.

Whichever variety (long grain, short grain, etc.) of rice is used it is nutritionally essential to use the whole (so-called 'brown) unpolished rice and not devitalized white or polished rice. Whole rice is a valuable complex carbohydrate containing limited, but good quality protein (about 8 per cent). It also contains vitamins B_1, riboflavin (B_2), niacin and pyridoxine (B_6), in good quantities – most of these being reduced to negligible amounts by the polishing or refining process. The main mineral content of rice is potassium, magnesium and iron.

Rice is an excellent food, being easy to digest and placing little strain on the digestive system. It is particularly suitable for people with diabetic tendencies as it has been shown to be gradually absorbed (in comparison, for example, to potatoes) thus keeping the blood sugar levels stable.

Cooking instructions are difficult with rice as different varieties can require quite different timing. Rice should be rinsed in tepid water and covered in the saucepan by about $1\frac{1}{2}$ inches of water. More water may be added during the cooking (in which case, carefully pour a little

boiling water onto the cooking rice, trying not to disturb
it). Once it is boiling, the heat should be reduced to allow
a gentle simmering until all the water is absorbed. To
avoid a gooey, sticky consistency, the rice should not be
stirred. About 45 minutes is needed to complete the
cooking process for whole rice. Cooked as described, the
rice should have a fluffy quality.

As a vegetable accompaniment to a main course, a few
herbs, spices or onions may be mixed with the rice prior
to cooking.

Note: All rice dishes are delicious if served with plain
goat's yogurt.

RICE WITH TOMATOES
Domatoryzo

(Serves 2 as a main course)   *Gluten-free*

1 large onion, chopped
2 cloves garlic, sliced not crushed
8 tablespoons polyunsaturated margrine
1 pound ripe tomatoes, chopped
2 cupsful brown rice
1 cube clear vegetable stock (from health food stores)
Sea salt
Black pepper
Grated cheese to garnish

Place the onion, garlic and margarine in a saucepan and
cook until the onion is golden. Add the chopped tomatoes
and allow to cook slowly over gentle heat for about 40
minutes. Add the rice and 2 to 3 cups of warm water (the
quantity of water varies according to the quality of rice),
and the stock, salt and pepper. Cover and allow to simmer
until all the water has evaporated. Serve with the grated
cheese.

Note: Wholewheat toast, tomato salad with onions, and
goat's yogurt with nuts and honey as a dessert would make
this a perfectly nourishing meal.

RICE WITH BUTTER AND CHEESE
Ryzi me Voutyro ke Tyri

(Serves 2 as a main course or 4-5 as a side dish) *Gluten-free*

2 cups brown rice
1 cube clear vegetable stock (from health food stores),
    dissolved in hot water
½ cup olive oil or polyunsaturated margarine
Sea salt and freshly ground black pepper
A pat of butter
Grated cheese to taste

Wash the rice well in a sieve under running tepid water.
Place the rice in a saucepan with 4-5 cups of water and the
stock. Bring to the boil. Add the olive oil, salt and pepper
and allow to simmer until all the water has evaporated, by
which time the rice should be ready (fluffy, not sticky).
Remove from the heat and add a little butter. Use a side
dish, having sprinkled grated cheese over it just prior to
serving.

BOILED RICE WITH LEMON
Rizonero me Lemoni

Gluten and Dairy-free
This recipe is widely used in Greece for medicinal purposes – digestive upsets and diarrhea.

Brown rice
Sea salt
Olive oil
Lemon juice

Wash the rice well with tepid water. Place in a saucepan covering it with cold water, bring to the boil and then simmer until very soft. Make sure that all the water is absorbed. A few minutes before removing from the heat, add a little salt.

Quantities will, of course, vary with needs but 1 cup of uncooked rice should make an adequate serving when cooked. Serve the rice when no longer hot, adding 2 to 4 teaspoons olive oil and the juice of one lemon.

Note: For small quantities of rice, say ½ cup or less, use 2½ to 3 parts water to 1 part rice.

RICE WITH GOLDEN RAISINS
Ryzi me Soultanes

(Serves 2-3 as a main course)   *Gluten-free*

2 cups brown rice
½ cup olive oil or polyunsaturated margarine
1 cube clear vegetable stock
½ cup golden seedless raisins
3 scallions, chopped
½ cup sweet corn
Grated hard cheese to garnish

Prepare rice as in the recipe Rice with Butter and Cheese (page 46), omitting the grated cheese at this stage. When cooked, mix in the raisins, the chopped scallions and the corn. Grated cheese may then be added if desired. Serve hot, this makes an ideal side dish or, served cold, may be part of a salad meal. As a main course, serve with black olives, tomato salad, cheese and wholewheat toast.

Note: Using the same recipe, the corn and raisins may be replaced with peas.

RICE WITH SPINACH
Spanakoyrzo

(Serves 3-4 as a main course) *Gluten and Dairy-free*

1 medium-sized onion, chopped
1 cup vegetable oil
3 pounds spinach, well washed and cut into large pieces
1 tablespoon tomate purée
4 cloves of garlic, sliced not crushed
2 or 3 scallions
3 tablespoons parsley
Sea salt and freshly ground black pepper
1 cup brown rice

Place the chopped onion with the oil in a wide saucepan and simmer. When the onion is golden brown, add the spinach. Continue stirring until all the spinach is lightly cooked. Then add the tomato purée to which has been added 2 cups of warm water, the garlic, scallions, parsley, salt and pepper. Allow to simmer for ¾ hour, stirring occasionally. In the meantime, precook the rice and then mix it in with the spinach. Add a little more water, if necessary, and allow to simmer until all the water has evaporated.

Note: The use of tomato is optional. If you don't use tomato though, a little lemon juice squeezed onto the dish, before serving, will improve the flavor.

LEEKS WITH RICE
Prasoryzo

(Serves 2 as a main course)   *Gluten and Dairy-free*

6 medium-sized leeks
2 pound canned tomatoes
1 cup brown rice (soaked overnight)
¼ cup olive oil
1 large onion, chopped
Sea salt and freshly ground black pepper

Clean the leeks and chop them into 1½-inch length pieces. Place these together with all the other ingredients in a saucepan. Cover (only just) with water. Simmer over a gentle heat (do not bring to the boil), until all the liquid has evaporated. Serve hot or cold.

LEEKS WITH POTATOES
Prassa me Patates

In the above recipe, the rice may be replaced by potatoes. Instead of a cup of rice add 4 medium-sized potatoes (cut into 3-4 portions each). A little less water should be used. Add a little paprika during cooking. Serve with wholewheat bread, white cheese and olives. Scallions, fresh firm tomatoes and especially watercress go well with this dish.

RICE WITH TOMATO SAUCE
Ryzi me Saltsa

Gluten-free
(As a main dish, the following quantities make 1 serving)

1 cup brown rice
¾ cup Tomato Sauce (page 40)
Grated cheese to taste

Cook the brown rice as described on page 44. Serve with the tomato sauce and a generous amount of grated cheese.

RICE CROQUETTES
Kroketes me Ryzi

(Serves several as a side dish)

1⅓ tablespoons polyunsaturated margarine
1½ cups short grain brown rice
1 cup grated hard cheese
1 small onion, grated
1½ tablespoons pine nuts
Sea salt and freshly ground black pepper
1 heaped tablespoon chopped parsley
3 eggs
12 rye crispbreads, powdered
Extra polyunsaturated margarine or vegetable oil for
    frying

In a saucepan, place 3 cups of water and 1⅓ tablespoons of margarine. Bring to the boil and add the washed rice. Stir, cover and allow to simmer until the water has completely evaporated. (If the rice is not completely cooked, add some more water and cook a little longer). Remove from the heat and add the cheese, onion, pine nuts, salt and pepper, parsley, one egg and two yolks (beat them before adding them to the mixture). Mix thoroughly and allow to stand (covered) for 30 minutes.

The rye crispbreads should be reduced to a powder with a food processor or pestle and mortar. Prepare the croquettes one by one, forming them into uniform shapes. Dip them in the rye powder, then the beaten egg whites and then again into the powder before frying in the margarine or oil. Serve hot or cold.

STUFFED ZUCCHINI WITH RICE
Kolokythakia Gemista me Ryzi

(Serves 6 as a main course)   *Gluten-free*

4 pounds medium-sized to large zucchini
1¼ pounds canned tomatoes
1 large onion, chopped
5 cloves of garlic, chopped
1½ cups olive oil
¾ cup parsley, chopped
Sea salt and freshly ground black pepper
1½ cups parboiled brown rice
½ cup grated cheese
2 tablespoons currants
¾ cup ground almonds
¼ cup pine nuts

With an instrument such as an apple corer empty the pulp of each zucchini into a saucepan, after washing them thoroughly. Add the tomatoes, onion, garlic, 1 cupful of oil, parsley, salt and pepper. Simmer until only a little liquid remains; add the rice and simmer until all the water has evaporated.

When cool, add the cheese, currants, almonds and pine nuts. Stir with a wooden spoon until all the ingredients are well mixed. Stuff the zucchini carefully with this mixture. Place them in an ovenproof container. Pour the rest of the oil over them and add salt and pepper to taste. Cook for 1 hour in a hot oven at 425°F before serving, hot or cold.

Note: Skordalia and freshly chopped salad or cold cooked vegetables (see pages 102-110) are ideal accompaniments for this traditional Greek dish, which also freezes well.

Rice is also used in the following recipes:

For children:

7. Pasta Dishes

The following general advice on cooking pasta will help in the creation of delicious dishes. Wholewheat pasta is nourishing and contains the nutritional benefits of 100 percent of the grain. Typical analysis indicates around 10 percent total dietary fiber, considered important for a sound healthy digestion, 13 percent protein, as well as all the other nutrients of the whole grain. Being a minimally refined, complex carbohydrate, its value in the diet is considerable. It is also quick to prepare, inexpensive, and is enjoyed by most people.

Place the pasta (spaghetti or macaroni or any shapes such as pasta shells) in a saucepan and cover with boiling salted water. To avoid having to add more water during cooking, which can affect the quality of the final result, it is as well to be generous with the water in the first place. Once the pasta has been placed in the boiling water, it should be stirred gently to ensure that it does not stick together. When the pasta is tender (after about 15-20 minutes), remove from the heat and add 2 cups of cold water and allow to stand for half a minute. Drain in a colander before returning to the saucepan. Mix gently with 2-4 tablespoons of butter, polyunsaturated margarine or olive oil. Add a little black pepper and a small amount of grated cheese (quantities of these depend on the amount of pasta used). Wholewheat pasta may be served on its own or with wholewheat bread, black olives and a green side salad to make a perfect light meal.

When cooking pasta for children, various shapes may be used; for example, alphabet shapes, numbers or shells are often an exciting alternative to spaghetti or macaroni.

MACARONI PIE
Pastitsio

(Serves 12 – this recipe also freezes well)

Tomato Sauce (page 40)
¾ pound wholewheat macaroni (short-cut)
4 tablespoons butter
1 cup grated hard cheese
Béchamel Sauce (page 41 or 42)

Prepare the tomato sauce. Place the macaroni in boiling, slightly salted water. When cooked (after about 20 minutes), remove from the heat and add 1 quart of cold water, strain immediately through a colander. Return the cooked marcaroni to the saucepan and add the butter, grated cheese and a little pepper. Mix thoroughly but gently and cover. Prepare the béchamel sauce. Mix 1½ cups of the béchamel sauce with the macaroni. Place half of this in an ovenproof dish. Cover with a generous layer of tomato sauce and then place the remainder of the macaroni on top of this. Finally, cover with the rest of the béchamel sauce. Place in a hot oven and leave until the surface is a golden color (approximately 1 hour).

Note: This dish is delicious served hot or cold and goes well with Skordalia (page 18), broad beans and fresh salad or steamed vegetables.

MACARONI WITH BÉCHAMEL SAUCE
Macaroni me Bechamel

(Serves 12)

12 ounces wholewheat macaroni (long- or short-cut)
4 tablespoons butter
1 cup grated hard cheese
Sea salt and freshly ground black pepper
Double quantity of Béchamel Sauce (page 41 or 42)

Cook the macaroni according to the instructions given on page 54. Prepare the béchamel sauce. In a large bowl or saucepan, place the macaroni, some pepper, the butter, grated cheese, and 2 cups of the béchamel sauce. Mix these well but gently. Place half this mixture in an ovenproof dish, followed by a layer of the remaining béchamel. Then add the rest of the macaroni mixture, finishing with a layer of the remaining béchamel. Level the contents and place in a hot oven at 425°F until the surface has a golden color. Allow it to cool before cutting it into portions.

Note: This recipe should make 12 portions. What is not used can be frozen. Smaller quantities can, of course, be made by scaling down all the ingredients; however, the effort required in its preparation is doubly rewarded, not only by the pleasure the dish brings, but by having a large reserve for future use.

BAKED MACARONI
Makaronaki Cofto Sto Fourno

(Serves 4-5 as a main course)

1½ pounds very ripe fresh tomatoes
½ cup polyunsaturated margarine or butter or
  vegetable oil
4 celery stalks, chopped
Sea salt and freshly ground black pepper
1 pound wholewheat macaroni (short-cut)
Grated cheese

Peel the tomatoes (this will be made easier if the tomatoes have been placed in hot water for a few minutes). Cut them into small pieces and place in an ovenproof dish. Add the shortening or oil, celery, salt and pepper. Add 2 cups of warm water and stir. Place in a hot oven at 425°F and bake for 20 minutes. Remove from the oven and add the macaroni, stirring with a fork to make sure that it does not stick together. Return to oven. It should be ready when the water has evaporated. If the macaroni is not soft, add a little more water and cook for a little longer. Serve with a generous amount of cheese (e.g., Parmesan).

SPAGHETTI WITH TOMATO SAUCE
Spaghetti me Domata

(Serves 4-5 as a main course)

1 pound wholewheat spaghetti
Butter or polyunsaturated margarine
Sea salt and freshly ground black pepper
Tomato Sauce (page 40)
Grated hard cheese (according to taste)

Cook the spaghetti according to the instructions given on page 54. Serve with tomato sauce and a generous quantity of grated cheese (e.g., Parmesan).

SPAGHETTI WITH PEAS
Spaghetti me Bizi

(Serves 4-5 as a main course)

¾ cupful olive oil
1 medium-sized onion, chopped
2 celery stalks, chopped
½ cup parsley, chopped
1 clove of garlic, chopped
1 pound fresh peas, shelled and washed
Sea salt and freshly ground black pepper
1 pound wholewheat spaghetti
3 tablespoons butter
Grated hard cheese

Heat the olive oil in a saucepan over medium heat and add the onion, celery, parsley and garlic. Stir constantly until golden and then add the peas, salt, pepper and a cup of water. Allow to simmer over slow heat until the water has evaporated. Break the spaghetti into shorter lengths (roughly into thirds) and cook in boiling, slightly salted water. When cooked, place the saucepan under cold running water. Shake and drain through a colander. When drained, add the butter and some pepper and ½ cup of grated cheese. Mix well but gently over low heat. Add the sauce with the peas and mix carefully. Serve immediately after sprinkling with some more grated cheese.

Note: As an alternative, a little of the warmed tomato sauce may be added prior to the final grated cheese dressing.

TAGLIATELLE WITH EGGPLANT
Tayiatela me Melitzanes

(Serves 12)

Tomato Sauce (page 40)
12 ounces wholewheat tagliatelle
5 tablespoons butter, melted
1 cup grated hard cheese
2 very large or 3 medium-sized eggplants
Olive oil for frying
Béchamel Sauce (page 41 or 42)

Prepare the tomato sauce. Cook the pasta according to the instructions given on page 54. Toss gently with the butter and cheese. In the meantime, cut the eggplants lengthwise into thick slices and place them in very salty water, using sea salt. (This will draw the bitterness out of them.) Let them soak for at least 30 minutes, then dry with paper towels. Fry the slices in olive oil and place on paper towels to drain.

Prepare the béchamel sauce. In an ovenproof dish, arrange alternate layers of tagliatelle, eggplant and tomato sauce. Finish with a layer of the remaining tagliatelle before spreading the béchamel sauce on top. Place in a hot oven at 425°F, and remove when the surface is golden brown.

Note: Serve with Skordalia (page 18), steamed vegetables or fresh salad. Any remaining portions freeze well.

8. Main Meals and Side Dishes

Globe Artichokes

These are rich in vitamin A, the B vitamins and vitamin C. They contain good quantities of calcium, potassium and iron. Many health-giving properties are ascribed to artichokes, including being of use in digestive complaints, anemia and rheumatism.

In the following recipes using artichokes, the most difficult part is the preparation of the artichoke prior to cooking. Good and speedy results will be achieved if the following instructions are followed: Cut away the stem close to the head and take away most of the leaves until the tender ones are reached. Cut the artichoke into two pieces (from top to bottom) and, with a grapefruit knife, remove all the choke (hairy covering over the heart). Squeeze half a lemon into a saucepan with 1 quart cold water and, with the other half, rub the surface of the artichoke before placing it in the lemon water. This will prevent the artichokes from oxidizing and turning brown. The very tender white leaves may be included with the artichoke heart. The stem of the artichoke is also edible if the outer layer is first peeled off.

Note: For Artichokes Vinaigrette any type or shape of artichokes may be used. For all other recipes it would be preferable to obtain artichokes that are longish in shape rather than round, as these are usually more tender and easier to prepare.

Any artichoke dish tastes particularly good when served with cheese, olives and brown bread.

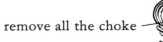remove all the choke

FRIED ARTICHOKES
Agginares Tiyianites

(Use this recipe as a side dish or mezze)   *Dairy-free*

4 artichokes
1½ cups wholewheat pastry flour
1 cup warm water
1 egg
Sea salt
Olive oil for frying

Prepare the artichokes according to the instructions on page 60 and cut them in quarters if small, in eighths if large. Boil them in salty water and a little lemon juice for 10 minutes. Allow them to cool, drain them, and gently wipe them with a paper towel. Dip each piece of artichoke in a mixture of the flour and water and place into the hot oil to fry. Remove when golden. Serve hot for crispness, or cold for greater flavor.

ARTICHOKES VINAIGRETTE
Agginares Vinegrette

Gluten and Dairy-free

1 firm, well rounded artichoke per person

For the Vinaigrette:
Quantities vary according to the number of artichokes. Always use twice as much oil as vinegar. Just before serving blend the vinaigrette ingredients well.

Olive oil
Vinegar
Mustard
Sea salt
Black pepper
Raw cane sugar

Remove the stems and very small outer leaves of the artichokes. Wash well under running water, opening the leaves gently with the fingertips. Place the artichokes in a deep saucepan with plenty of slightly salted water and boil until tender (approximately 30 minutes, according to size). The artichoke is cooked when one of the central leaves can be pulled from the head with relative ease. Remove from the heat, drain and serve, warm or cold, with vinaigrette sauce.

Only the tender tip of each leaf is eaten, the leaves being removed, one by one, by hand until the heart is exposed. This part may also be eaten if the choke is first cut away. Finger bowls should be available as the process is a little oily – but delicious.

ARTICHOKES WITH POTATOES AND PEAS
Agginares me Patates Ke Bizi

(Serves 3 as a main course or 6-8 as a side dish)
Gluten and Dairy-free

4 artichokes (see preparation instructions on page 60)
1 bunch of scallions, chopped
2 cups parsley, chopped
5 cloves of garlic, chopped
1 pound frozen peas or 2 pounds fresh peas in their
   pods
2 large potatoes, peeled and cut into 5 pieces each or
6-8 small new potatoes, whole
½ cup olive oil
Sea salt
Black pepper

When all the vegetables are washed, place them in a large non-stick saucepan. Add the olive oil, salt and pepper and cover with water. Simmer over medium heat, stirring gently from time to time until the warm water has evaporated. Serve hot or warm.

Note: If served as a main course, serve with cottage or féta cheese, wholewheat bread and olives. Skordalia would also complement this dish.

COOKED ARTICHOKE SALAD
Agginares Salata

Gluten and Dairy-free
This is a side dish to accompany any main dish. Quantities of ingredients depend upon the number of servings required.

Artichokes
Onion juice
Tomatoes
Boiled potatoes   }   optional
Hard-boiled eggs)
Salad dressing

For the Salad Dressing:
Lemon juice }   Use twice as much oil as lemon juice
Olive oil   {
Sea salt
Black pepper

For this recipe small young artichokes, cooked whole, are ideal; if large, see the instructions for preparation on page 60. Boil the washed and trimmed artichokes in lightly salted water until tender. Drain, allow to cool and then cut into small pieces (about ½-inch cubes), and place in a salad bowl. Add a few drops of onion juice, if liked, the sliced tomatoes, boiled potatoes and hard-boiled eggs. Pour a dressing of oil and lemon juice over the salad.

ARTICHOKES À LA POLITA
Agginares à la Polita

(Serves 4 as a main course)   *Dairy-free*

4 large artichokes
8 new potatoes, scrubbed and left whole
6 small onions, peeled and left whole
2 medium-sized carrots, sliced
8 scallions, chopped
1 cup olive oil
Juice of 1 lemon
1½ cups parsley, chopped
1 cup fresh dill, if available
Sea salt
Black pepper
1 tablespoon wholewheat pastry flour

Prepare the artichokes according to the instructions on page 60. Place in a saucepan and add the potatoes, the whole onions, sliced carrots, scallions, olive oil, lemon juice, parsley, dill, salt and pepper. Mix the flour with a cup of water and add to the above ingredients. Cover with warm water and allow to simmer over medium heat, uncovered, for approximately 1 hour. When all the water has evaporated, the ingredients should be ready. Remove from the heat and place a double piece of parchment paper between the lid and the saucepan (being careful not to touch the contents). This will absorb the steam, when removed from the heat, prior to serving.

Note: Serve with cottage cheese (or, ideally, féta), wholewheat bread and black olives.

ARTICHOKES WITH BROAD BEANS
Agginares me Koukia

(Serves 4 as a main course)   *Gluten and Dairy-free*

6 artichokes
2½ pounds broad beans
8 whole new potatoes or
2 large old potatoes, cut into 4 pieces each (scrubbed if
   new, peeled if old)
1 bunch of scallions, chopped
4 cloves of garlic, chopped
1½ cups parsley, chopped, and fresh dill
   (if no dill available, just use parsley)
⅔ cup olive oil
Sea salt
Black pepper

Prepare the artichokes according to the instructions on page 60. To prepare the broad beans, remove the shells if they are large ones, but for any small tender ones, use the shells as well, having removed any stringy fibers. Place all the ingredients in a non-stick saucepan; only just cover with water. Allow to simmer over medium heat until all the water has evaporated (approximately 1½ hours).

Remove from the heat and place parchment paper between the saucepan and the lid. This will absorb the steam. Allow to stand until ready to serve, hot or cold. Serve with cheese, wholewheat bread and black olives.

ARTICHOKES WITH BÉCHAMEL SAUCE
Agginares me Saltsa Bechamel

(Serves 4 as a main course)

8-10 artichokes
Juice of 1 lemon
½ cup polyunsaturated margarine or butter, melted
Sea salt
Black pepper
Béchamel Sauce (page 41 or 42)
2 cups grated hard cheese
Wholewheat breadcrumbs

Prepare the artichokes according to the instructions on page 60. Place them in a saucepan with boiling water to which has been added a little salt and the lemon juice. Cover and simmer for no more than 10 minutes. Drain and allow to cool. Dice the artichokes and sauté gently with half of the margarine or butter and add salt and pepper to taste.

Prepare the béchamel sauce. Into an ovenproof dish pour a layer of the sauce and sprinkle this with half each the grated cheese and breadcrumbs. Then place a layer of the diced artichokes, also sprinkled with cheese and breadcrumbs. Cover this with the remainder of the béchamel; level the surface and carefully sprinkle the rest of the cheese on top. Pour the rest of the margarine or butter onto the surface. Place in a pre-heated hot oven at 425°F and remove when golden.

Note: Serve this meal with lima beans, potato salad and steamed zucchini. Cottage cheese and olives would also go well with it.

ARTICHOKE MOUSSAKA
Agginares Moussakas

(Serves 12)

8 artichokes
14 ounces canned tomatoes
1 large onion, chopped
½ cup chopped parsley
3 cloves of garlic, chopped
¾ cup olive oil
2 bay leaves or ⅓ teaspoon dried basil
Sea salt
Black pepper
2¼ cups long grain brown rice, cooked
½ cup sunflower seeds and/or pine nuts or ground
    almonds
1 tablespoon raisins
Béchamel Sauce (page 41 or 42)

Prepare the artichokes in the usual way (see page 60). Boil them in lightly salted water for 10 minutes. Drain, allow to cool and cut into slices. In a non-stick saucepan, heat the tomatoes, having added the onion, chopped parsley, garlic, oil, bay leaves, salt and pepper. Allow to simmer until all the water has evaporated.

Remove from the heat. Add the rice which should have been pre-cooked in water with a little salt added. Remove the bay leaves. Add to this mixture the sunflower seeds and the raisins. Mix well. In an ovenproof dish, place a layer of sliced artichokes and then cover with all the contents of the tomato-rice mixture. Level this out before placing the remaining sliced artichokes on top.

Prepare the béchamel sauce. Cover the dish with a generous layer of this and place in a 425°F oven until the surface is golden brown.

Note: The moussaka may be started with a layer of potato slices (simply boil and slice several large potatoes in advance). Also, for extra nourishment, 2 tablespoons of grated cheese may be added to the rice mixture. This dish should be accompanied by steamed vegetables (carrots and peas), and/or potato and beet salad, wholewheat bread and olives.

JERUSALEM ARTICHOKES WITH TOMATOES
Karkiofoles me Domato

(Serves 2-3 as a side dish)   *Gluten and Dairy-free*

1 pound Jerusalem artichokes
8 ounces canned whole tomatoes
¾ cup parsley and/or fresh dill, chopped
Sea salt
Black pepper
½ teaspoon dark brown sugar
8 scallions, chopped
3-4 cloves of garlic, chopped
½ cup olive oil

Scrub the artichokes to remove any dirt and soil. If they are large, cut in two to three pieces, otherwise cook them whole. Put all the ingredients, except the artichokes, into a non-stick saucepan. Add 1 cup of water and bring to the boil. When half of the liquid has evaporated, add the artichokes. Partially cover and simmer until all the water has evaporated.

Note: This side dish can be served with any meal.

STUFFED CABBAGE LEAVES
Lahanodolmades

(Serves 4 as a main course)

1 cup brown rice
1 tablespoon currants
4 scallions, chopped
2 teaspoons pine nuts, if available
Sea salt and pepper
2⅔ tablespoons olive oil
1 egg white
2 teaspoons ground almonds
1 tablespoon grated cheese
2 tablespoons chopped parsley
1 large Savoy cabbage
1 cup lemon juice

For the sauce:
3⅓ tablespoons wholewheat pastry flour
4 tablespoons butter
2 cups milk
2 egg yolks
2 tablespoons grated hard cheese

Boil the rice for about 8 minutes. Strain and place in a mixing bowl. Add the currants, scallions, pine nuts, salt, pepper, half the oil, the egg white (lightly beaten), the almonds, grated cheese and parsley. Mix to blend well.

Boil the cabbage for 2-3 minutes to soften the outer leaves. Separate the cabbage leaves and place about a tablespoon of the stuffing in the center of each leaf, folding to enclose the mixture. Place the envelope in a non-stick saucepan. When the stuffing has all been used, chop any remaining leaves and spread on top of the stuffed leaves. Place two small plates over the leaves (this is to keep the contents firmly in place). Add the remaining olive oil, salt, pepper and the lemon juice and enough water to cover the contents of the saucepan. Simmer very gently over medium-low heat for 30 to 40 minutes until, by tipping the saucepan, you can see only about a cup of liquid remaining. Remove from the heat and remove the plates covering the cabbage.

Prepare the sauce as follows:
Pour the remaining liquid from above into a cup. Place the flour and butter together in a frying pan on medium heat. Stir continuously until these are all well mixed. Add, alternately, a little milk and cabbage water, until these are used, stirring continuously. Remove the pan from the heat. Add the two egg yolks and mix well and then add the cheese and a touch of salt and pepper. Pour this sauce into the saucepan containing the stuffed leaves. Encourage this to permeate between the stuffed cabbage leaves by shaking the container fairly vigorously. Bring back to the boil for half a minute. Remove and serve. This is delicious hot or cold, and also freezes well.

Note: This dish tastes particularly good with Skordalia (page 18), potatoes and steamed zucchini or beans.

JERUSALEM ARTICHOKES WITH PEAS
Karkiofoles me Bizi

(Serves 2-3 as a side dish)   *Gluten and Dairy-free*

1 pound Jerusalem artichokes
1 10-ounce carton frozen peas
¾ cup parsley, chopped
Sea salt
Black pepper
8 scallions, chopped
3-4 cloves of garlic, chopped
½ cup olive oil

Scrub the artichokes to remove any dirt and soil. If they are large, cut in two to three pieces, otherwise cook them whole. Put the ingredients, except artichokes and peas, into a non-stick pan. Add 1 cup of warm water and bring to the boil. When half of the liquid has evaporated add the artichokes and the peas. Partially cover and simmer until all the water has evaporated.

STUFFED VINE LEAVES
Dolmades

(Serves 4-6)   *Gluten-free*

1 onion, chopped
¾ cup olive oil
1½ cups long grain brown rice
4 teaspoonsful dill and/or parsley
2 scallions, chopped
Sea salt and freshly ground black pepper
½ cup currants
½ cup pine nuts or ground almonds
1 egg white
50 vine leaves
Juice of 1½ lemons

Place the onion in a saucepan with half of the oil over medium heat. Stir the onion until only very light brown and then remove from the heat. In the meantime, boil the rice in slightly salted water for 10 minutes before draining and adding it to the onion. Add the dill, the scallions, salt and pepper, 2 teaspoons of the olive oil, the currants, pine nuts and the egg white. Mix them gently together.

To prepare the vine leaves:
If picked from the garden, pick tender but good-sized leaves. Wash them well and remove the stems with scissors. Boil the leaves in salted water for 15 minutes. Drain and place on a clean surface to cool. If the leaves are shop bought, then rinse well and boil in plain water for 15 minutes.

Cover the bottom of a non-stick saucepan with a layer of leaves. Then take the leaves one by one, placing 2 teaspoons of the mixture onto each, before folding carefully into an envelope shape. Place these in the saucepan. When all the leaves have been used, pour the lemon juice and the rest of the olive oil over them. Add a touch of salt and pepper, and before covering with warm water, place one or two plates over them to keep the piles of stuffed vine leaves in place during the cooking process.

Cook over medium heat until the water evaporates; remove from the heat, remove the plates and allow to cool for about 10 minutes. Then gently place the stuffed vine leaves on a serving dish. These may be served hot or cold.

Note: If served hot, they may be accompanied by Hummus (page 23) or Skordalia (page 18), lima beans and other steamed vegetables. If served cold, Tjatjiki (page 20) or even plain goat's yogurt, with any fresh salad would be an ideal accompaniment.

STUFFED VINE LEAVES WITH BÉCHAMEL
Dolmades me Bechamel

Prepare the vine leaves exactly as in the previous recipe for Stuffed Vine Leaves. Ensure that there is one teacupful of liquid left from the cooking process. Then prepare the Béchamel Sauce as follows:

3⅓ tablespoons wholewheat pastry flour
4 tablespoons butter
2 cups milk (cow's, goat's or soy)
2 egg yolks
1⅓ tablespoons grated hard cheese (optional)
Sea salt and freshly ground pepper

Put the flour and butter together in a frying pan and place over a medium heat. Stir continuously until well mixed. Add, alternately, a little milk and a little liquid from cooking the vine leaves, until all is used up – stirring all the time. Remove the pan from the heat. Add the two egg yolks and mix well, then add the cheese and a touch of salt and pepper.

Pour this sauce into the saucepan containing the stuffed vine leaves, and encourage it to permeate the vine leaves by shaking the container fairly vigorously.

Bring back to the boil for half a minute. Remove from heat and serve. This is delicious hot or cold.

MOUSSAKA WITH EGGPLANT
Moussakas me Melitzanes

This is a traditional dish. In Greece it is cooked with minced meat, which I have replaced with brown rice, a little grated cheese, currants and seeds for taste and nourishment. Many people who eat meat, after sampling this recipe have preferred it to the orthodox one.

(Serves 8-12) (dimension of container 10 in. x 12 in. and 2 in. depth)

3-4 large eggplants
Olive oil for frying
1¼ cups short-grain brown rice
1 pound canned tomatoes
1 large onion, chopped
3 tablespoons chopped parsley
½ cup olive oil
3 cloves of garlic, chopped
Sea salt and freshly ground pepper
2 tablespoons sunflower seeds
3 tablespoons pine nuts and/or
½ cupful currants
3 tablespoons grated cheese
Béchamel Sauce (page 41 or 42)

Cut each eggplant lengthwise into slices (just under half an inch thick). Place these in a container with plenty of water and sea salt – 1 teaspoon of sea salt to 1 pint of water. Allow them to soak for a minimum of 30 minutes to remove the bitter juices. Rinse well, dry with paper towels and then fry in olive oil.

Wash the rice well, cover by about 1½ inches of cold water and simmer for 20 minutes. Add the tomatoes, with their juice (having first sliced the tomatoes with a sharp knife); also add the onion and parsley, the olive oil and garlic, salt and pepper. Bring to the boil and simmer, stirring occasionally. When all the water has evaporated, remove from the heat and add the seeds, pine nuts, currants and the grated cheese.

Make the béchamel sauce according to the instructions

on page 41 or 42. Take one eggplant at a time and form a layer in the ovenproof container with half of them. (They should cover the surface). The second layer should then be made with the rice mixture. Spread it gently and evenly. With the remaining eggplant, make another layer on top of the rice. Finally spread a thick layer of béchamel evenly on the top. Place in a 425°F oven and cook until the surface turns golden brown. Allow it to cool before cutting into portions.

Note: The color of the sliced eggplant might change to brown but this does not affect the taste. This dish also freezes well.

MOUSSAKA WITH POTATOES AND ZUCCHINI
Moussakas me Patates ke Kolokithia

Ingredients as on page 74, replacing eggplants with potatoes and zucchini.

The method of preparing the dish is the same as for the Moussaka with Eggplant. Simply replace the eggplants with 4 large potatoes washed well, sliced and fried (cut them into circular slices), and 6 zucchini, cut lengthwise and also fried. The bottom layer must be made with potatoes, followed by the rice, then the zucchini and finally the béchamel.

MOUSSAKA WITH POTATOES
Moussakas me Patates

Prepare in the same way as Moussaka with Eggplant (page 74). Replace the eggplants with 3 pounds potatoes, cut into circular slices and fried. Cover the surface of an ovenproof container with a little oil, as the potatoes might stick. In the container form a bottom layer of potatoes, followed by the rice mixture, a second layer of potatoes and then the béchamel sauce.

Note: Either dish can be served with Skordalia and lima beans, and does freeze well.

STUFFED EGGPLANT PAPOUTSAKIA
Melitzanes Papoutsakia ('Little Shoes')

(Serves 4 as a main course)

8 small eggplants
1¾ cups short-grain brown rice
2 cups canned tomatoes
1 large Spanish onion, chopped
4 cloves of garlic, chopped
½ cup chopped parsley
¾ cup olive oil
3-4 tablespoons pine nuts and/or sunflower seeds or
  ground almonds
Sea salt and freshly ground black pepper
2 tablespoons currants
3 tablespoons grated cheese
Béchamel Sauce (page 41 or 42)

Remove a thin lengthwise section from each eggplant.
Gently, with the help of a grapefruit knife and a small
spoon, scrape out the flesh. Allow the empty eggplants to
soak for up to 30 minutes in salted water. In the meantime,
wash the rice and place it in a saucepan covered with 1½
cups of cold water. Simmer for 20 minutes and then add
the tomatoes with their juice. Add the eggplant flesh, the
onion, garlic, parsley, olive oil, salt and pepper. Bring to
the boil and simmer for approximately 1 hour, stirring
occasionally. When all the water has evaporated, remove
from the heat and add the pine nuts, seeds, currants and
the grated cheese and mix well.

Boil the eggplant shells in slightly salted water for 5
minutes. Drain, season the inside with a little pepper, and
then stuff them with the mixture. Place in an ovenproof
casserole.

Prepare the béchamel sauce, half the quantity given on
page 41. Divide it on top of each stuffed eggplant. Place
in a hot oven 425°F until the béchamel is golden brown.
Serve with Skordalia and steamed vegetables.

Note: This dish can be prepared without béchamel, in
which case, replace the section previously removed,
season and pour a few drops of olive oil on top of each
eggplant. Cook in the oven for approximately 1 hour. It
also freezes well.

LENTIL AND NUT LOAF
Fakes me Amygdala Lefti

(Serves 6-8) *Dairy-free*

8 ounces lentils
1 large onion, chopped
8 cloves of garlic, whole
3 tablespoons olive oil
1 cup ground walnuts or almonds and/or pine nuts
3 cups wholewheat breadcrumbs
2 tablespoons tomato purée
1½ teaspoons oregano
3 tablespoons chopped parsley
2 eggs
Sea salt and freshly ground black pepper

To serve:
Garnish with tomato, onion, parsley

Soak the lentils for several hours, rinse, place in a saucepan and cover with cold water. Simmer gently for 20 minutes, by which time they should be tender. Any surplus liquid should be drained. Fry the onion and garlic in oil in a large saucepan until lightly brown. Remove from the heat and add the nuts, lentils, breadcrumbs, tomato purée, oregano, parsley and eggs. After mixing well, season with salt and pepper.

Place a strip of foil on the bottom and up the sides of a loaf pan. Grease it with butter. Place the mixture in the loaf pan and cover it with greased foil. Bake in the oven at 350°F for about 1 hour. After removing from the oven, leave the loaf in the pan for a few minutes. Run a knife around the edge of the pan and turn out the loaf. Serve in thick slices with salad or a cooked vegetable salad (page 106).

MILLET PIE
Korakiana

This is a nourishing and extremely tasty dish. It has a high protein content and is rich in minerals such as calcium, iron, phosphorus and most of the B-complex vitamins. The recipe provides 12 good portions which can be individually stored in a freezer. Portions should be defrosted at room temperature. If placed in an oven to warm, prior to serving, cover with foil to avoid dryness. Ideally, serve with lima beans or lentils as a side dish as well as steamed vegetables or with a raw salad.

(Serves 12)

2½ cups millet
5 cups water
2 vegetable bouillon cubes
½ large or 1 small onion, chopped
5-6 scallions, chopped
¾ cup parsley, chopped
½ cup pine nuts and/or
½ cup almonds, peeled and ground
¾ cup golden raisins
5 heaped tablespoons butter or polyunsaturated
    margarine
Sea salt and freshly ground black pepper
Tomato Sauce (page 40)
Béchamel Sauce (page 41 or 42)

Add the millet to boiling salted water containing the bouillon cubes. Simmer until the millet is tender, by which time all the water should have evaporated. Add all the remaining ingredients except the sauces and mix well, having removed the saucepan from the heat. Place half of the mixture in an ovenproof container and cover with the tomato sauce. Add the rest of the millet mixture and pour the béchamel sauce over the top. Place in a preheated, very hot oven at 450°F and cook until the surface is golden brown, about 1 hour.

Note: Using the same method, individual pies can be

prepared in ovenproof containers. These can also be frozen or served direct from the oven.

STUFFED SQUASH BLOSSOMS
Kolokytholoulouda Gemista

(Serves 2 as a side dish)

16 squash blossoms
½ cup cottage cheese or féta cheese
1 egg
2 scallions, finely chopped
1⅓ tablespoons chopped parsley (optional)
Sea salt and freshly ground black pepper
Vegetable oil for frying (preferably olive oil)

For the batter:
Mix thoroughly 1½ cups wholewheat pastry flour, 1 cup of water, 1 egg, a little sea salt and 1 tablespoon of olive oil

Wash the flowers very gently as they are fragile, taking care not to break them. Mix the cheese (having removed some of its liquid by gently squeezing it in cheesecloth or a kitchen towel), with the beaten egg, the scallions, parsley, salt and pepper. Put a spoonful of the mixture in each flower, dip in the batter and fry in hot oil until golden. Serve this delicacy hot or cold as an appetizer or side dish.

WHOLE MUSHROOMS PLAIN
Oloklira Manitaria Sketa

(Serves 3-4 as a side dish)   *Gluten-free*

1 pound button mushrooms
2 tablespoons butter or polyunsaturated margarine or
   ½ cup olive oil
Sea salt and freshly ground black pepper

Wash the mushrooms well and place them in a saucepan, together with the butter or oil, sea salt and pepper. Simmer on a medium to low heat for 20 minutes. At this stage, turn the heat high and stir constantly until all the liquid has evaporated. Serve warm.

Note: Non-button mushrooms can be cooked in the same way. With button mushrooms, however, freshness can be ensured with more tasty results.

MUSHROOMS WITH TOMATOES
Manitaria me Domata

(Serves 3-4 as a side dish)   *Gluten-free*

1 pound canned tomatoes or 5 fresh tomatoes
2 tablespoons butter or ½ cup olive oil
1 large Spanish onion, finely chopped
Sea salt and freshly ground black pepper
1 pound button mushrooms

In a saucepan, place the tomatoes which have been finely chopped (if canned tomatoes are used add the juice, if fresh tomatoes are used, add 1 cup of water), the butter or oil, the onion, sea salt and pepper. Bring to the boil and simmer (covered) for 20 minutes. Then add the well washed and sliced mushrooms. Cover and simmer for a further 15-20 minutes and then uncover the saucepan, turn the heat up to maximum and stir constantly until all the liquid has evaporated. Serve warm.

MUSHROOMS IN BUTTER A LA FLOSSI
Manitaria me Voutyro

(Serves 3-4 as a side dish) *Gluten-free*

1 pound button mushrooms
1 large Spanish onion, chopped
2-3 small carrots, sliced
Sea salt and freshly ground black pepper
2 tablespoons butter

Wash the mushrooms thoroughly and slice them across into two, three or four slices (according to mushroom size). Add the onion, carrots, salt, pepper and butter to the saucepan. Place on a medium heat (add no water) and simmer for approximately 20 minutes, stirring occasionally. Then turn the heat full on, stirring constantly until all the juice has evaporated. Serve warm.

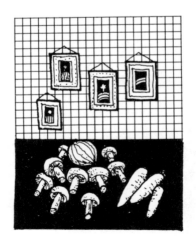

STUFFED TOMATOES WITH EGGS
Domates Gemistes me Ayga

(Serves 2 as a main course)

1 pound new potatoes
4 very large tomatoes
Sea salt and freshly ground black pepper
8 ounces hard cheese
¼ cup chopped parsley
1 cup olive oil
4 eggs
2 teaspoons powdered whole-rye crispbread
1¼ cups brown rice
2 teaspoons butter or polyunsaturated margarine

Scrub the potatoes well, removing all the skin and then boil for 20 minutes. Wash the tomatoes well, remove the tops and carefully scoop out the pulp. Season the inside of each tomato and place in the ovenproof container, preferably pyrex.

Before grating the cheese, cut four thin slices to be kept on one side. Put the half-cooked potatoes around the tomatoes in the ovenproof container. Put a pinch of parsley, some grated cheese and half a teaspoon of olive oil into each tomato. Purée the pulp of the tomatoes. Season and add the parsley and the rest of the olive oil. Mix well and pour this over the potatoes. Bake in a moderately hot oven, 375°F, for 35 minutes. Remove and place a slice of the cheese in each tomato. Break the eggs and carefully pour one into each tomato. Season the eggs and add the rye crispbread crumbs. Finally, with a spoon, pour some of the liquid from the ovenproof container onto the potatoes and onto each egg. Place back in the oven and bake for a further 20-30 minutes.

Boil the rice in salted water. When ready, add the butter and a pinch of freshly ground black pepper. Serve 2 tomatoes on each plate and surround with the potatoes and rice. Dress the rice with the remaining juice and sprinkle grated cheese over the top.

TOMATOES STUFFED WITH MAYONNAISE
Domates Gemistes me Mayoneza

(Serves 4 as a side dish or starter)   *Gluten and Dairy-free*

8 small tomatoes
Sea salt and freshly ground black pepper
½ cup diced cucumber
1 medium-sized zucchini, boiled and diced
1 medium-sized potato, boiled and diced
Mayonnaise (page 43)
8 black olives
⅓ cup chopped parsley

Select small and very firm tomatoes. Cut a slice from the top and scrape out the pulp. Season the empty tomatoes with the salt and pepper, turn them upside-down and allow them to drain for about 1 hour. In a bowl, mix the diced cucumber, zucchini, potato and a little of the tomato flesh (having first removed the seeds). Season and add 1 or 2 tablespoons of the mayonnaise. Stuff the tomatoes with this mixture. Finish with a teaspoon of mayonnaise on top of each tomato. Decorate with a black olive in the middle surrounded by the freshly chopped parsley. (If parsley is not available, chopped watercress can be used.) When ready, refrigerate and serve cold.

Note: Ideally, this dish is used as a starter on a warm summer's day.

MIXED GRILLED VEGETABLES
Lahanika sti Shara

(Serves 1 as a side dish)

1 large tomato
1 large clove of garlic, crushed
1 spoon parsley, finely chopped
1 tablespoon polyunsaturated margarine
Pinch of oregano
Sea salt and freshly ground black pepper
2 large mushrooms
1 small onion, cut in half

Cut the tomato in half. Gently empty the pulp with a spoon into a bowl. Cut the tomato flesh into small pieces. Add the crushed garlic, parsley, half of the margarine, the oregano and a little salt and pepper. Mix well and refill the empty tomato halves with the mixture.

Wash the mushrooms and onion well, sprinkle with salt and pepper and add a little of the remaining margarine. Place these and the tomato under the broiler until the tomatoes are slightly brown. Serve hot.

PIES

Pies are traditionally made with very fine pastry called "fyllo", which is as thin as rice paper and made with very fine white flour. To make this as a wholefood is impossible since brown wholewheat flour cannot be reduced to the thinness of cigarette paper. The taste though, and the nourishment are found in the pie contents which, in the following recipes, are described in the traditional way. I have only changed the dishes by describing them as being made with wholewheat flour rather than the more easily prepared, ready-made fyllo.

When fyllo is used, several layers are placed on the bottom of the ovenproof container, each one being brushed with a little butter or margarine, using a pastry brush. The mixture is then put in, followed by more buttered layers of fyllo before the dish is baked in the oven. Ready-made fyllo can be bought in gourmet food shops; however, for wholefood cooking, the short crust pastry recipe (below) should be used.

SHORT CRUST PASTRY

2 cups wholewheat flour
Pinch of salt
4 tablespoons nut butter (from health food stores)
1-2 tablespoons butter or polyunsaturated margarine
Cold water to mix

Sieve the flour and salt together and rub the fat into the flour until the mixture looks like breadcrumbs, then add enough cold water to make a stiff dough (about ½ cup of cold water). Roll out with a floured rolling pin (or floured bottle if no rolling pin is available) to about ¼ inch thick.

The above quantities will make 2 layers of short crust pastry for an 8-inch diameter container (this would serve 4 portions as a main course). Greater quantities could be useful, as all the following pie recipes freeze well.

SPINACH PIE
Spanakopita

1 pound spinach
2 tablespoons polyunsaturated margarine or butter
½ small onion, chopped
2 scallions, chopped
2 cloves of garlic, chopped
⅓ cup chopped dill
⅓ cup chopped parsley
Sea salt and freshly ground black pepper
2 eggs
8 ounces white cheese (féta or cottage cheese)
⅓ cup milk
Short crust pastry (page 85)

Wash the spinach well and cut into small pieces. Put the margarine into a frying pan together with the onion, scallions, garlic, dill and parsley and sauté until they begin to soften. Then add the spinach, salt and pepper and allow to cook uncovered until all the liquid produced by the spinach has evaporated. Remove from the heat and allow to cool.

In another bowl, beat the eggs. Add a little salt and pepper and when well beaten, add the cheese. If féta is used, crumble the cheese. If cottage cheese is used, first place on paper towels to remove excess liquid before adding the cheese to the beaten eggs. Add the milk, mix well and then add to the spinach. Mix thoroughly and test for seasoning.

Line a buttered pie plate (about 2 inches deep) with a layer of the short crust pastry and then empty all the spinach mixture into it. Level this and cover with the remaining layer of pastry. Score the surface to mark the portions. This facilitates serving when cooked. Place in a medium to hot oven at 375°F until the pastry looks brown (about 30-40 minutes). Serve hot or at room temperature.

LEEK PIE
Prasopita

(Serves 4 as a main meal)

3-4 medium-sized leeks
⅓ cup polyunsaturated margarine or butter
2 eggs
1 cup cottage cheese or féta, crumbled
Sea salt and freshly ground black pepper
2 tablespoons powdered rye crispbread
Short crust pastry (page 85)

Wash and chop the leeks coarsely. In a frying pan, place the margarine and the leeks. Sauté over low heat with no cover until all the liquid has evaporated.

In the meantime, beat the eggs, add the cheese (if féta is used, crumble, if cottage cheese, then place it for a while on paper towels to remove surplus moisture). Add the egg-cheese mixture to the leeks, together with some salt and pepper and the powdered rye crispbread.

Line a buttered 8-inch pie plate with the short crust pastry. Empty the leek mixture into it and cover with the remaining pastry. Mark the surface with a knife to facilitate cutting into sections when serving, and bake in a medium to hot oven at 375°F. Remove when the surface is golden brown and serve hot.

CHEESE PIE
Tyropita

(Serves 9-12 as a main course)

Short crust pastry (page 85)
1¼ pound féta cheese, crumbled
1 cup parsley, finely chopped, and/or dill
Béchamel Sauce

For the bechamel sauce:
3⅓ tablespoons butter
7 tablespoons wholewheat pastry flour
3 cups milk
Sea salt and freshly ground black pepper
6 eggs

Prepare the short crust pastry for an ovenproof pie dish with dimensions 12 in. x 10 in. x 2 in. For this, approximately four times the quantities given on page 85 will be required.

In a large bowl, crumble the cheese. In the meantime, melt the butter in a frying pan and add the flour. Stirring constantly, add the milk a little at a time; add some salt and pepper (if the sauce is too thick add a little more milk). Allow to cool and add this to the cheese together with the herbs. Beat the eggs lightly and combine them with the other ingredients. Line the pie dish with pastry and then empty all the cheese-béchamel-egg mixture into the pie dish and level out. Cover with the remaining pastry. Mark the surface with a sharp knife to facilitate cutting into portions when serving. Place in a medium to hot oven at 375°F. Remove when the surface is golden brown and serve warm or cold. This pie also freezes well.

FOODS WITH OLIVE OIL
Lathera Fagita

This type of food is widely used in Greece and particularly during the spring and summer. Such dishes can be used as appetizers or as main courses. If used as a main course, then it should be accompanied by fresh wholewheat bread, féta cheese and a small tomato-cucumber salad.

The use of garlic in many of these dishes enhances the ability of the body to digest the oil. Serve hot or cold.

STEWED ZUCCHINI
Kolokythia Lathera

(Serves 3-4 as a side dish)

1 large onion, finely chopped
¾ cup olive oil
¾ cup canned tomatoes
½ cup finely chopped parsley
5 cloves of garlic
Sea salt and freshly ground black pepper
3 pounds medium-sized zucchini

Place the onion and oil in a saucepan. Heat and stir until the onion is slightly discolored. Add the tomatoes, parsley, garlic, salt, pepper and a cup of warm water. Allow to simmer until the sauce slightly thickens and then add the zucchini which, in the meantime, have been washed and cut into 3-4 large pieces each. Simmer until all the water has evaporated and serve hot or cold. This dish freezes well.

CAULIFLOWER STEW
Kounoupidi Stifado

This very popular Greek side dish is cooked in tomatoes and spices.

(Serves 4-6 as a side dish)   *Gluten and Dairy-free*

1 large onion, chopped
4 cloves of garlic, coarsely chopped
¾ cup olive oil
1 pound canned tomatoes
Sea salt and freshly ground black pepper
4 bay leaves
⅔ teaspoon rosemary
10 very small onions, whole
1 large or 2 medium-sized cauliflowers
3 tablespoons wine vinegar

Place the chopped onion and garlic with the olive oil in a saucepan (preferably non-stick), and cook, stirring constantly, until the onion is lightly browned. Add the tomatoes with their juice to the onions, together with salt and pepper, the bay leaves (bruised for extra flavor) and the rosemary. Add a cup of warm water and simmer for 20 minutes. Add the small whole onions, stir and simmer for a further 15 minutes. Then add the cauliflower which should, in the meantime, have been washed, detached from its leaves and cut into large pieces. Add another ½ cup of warm water, stir gently and allow to simmer until the water has evaporated. Add the wine vinegar, stir gently and simmer for a further 3-4 minutes on a gentle heat. Remove from the heat. The result should be a slightly undercooked cauliflower in a thick tomato and onion sauce.

Note: Serve hot or at room temperature. Remove the bay leaves before serving.

CORFU ONIONS WITH TOMATOES
Kremydia Stifado

(Serves 3-4 as a side dish) *Gluten and Dairy-free*

1 large Spanish onion, chopped
½ cup olive oil
8 ounces canned tomatoes
4 bay leaves
½ teaspoon paprika
3 cloves of garlic, sliced
Sea salt and freshly ground black pepper
16-20 small onions, whole
2 tablespoons wine or cider vinegar

Place the chopped onion in a non-stick saucepan with the olive and cook until the onion becomes slightly brown. Add the tomatoes (cut into small segments), the bay leaves (bruised), paprika, garlic, salt, pepper and half a cup of warm water. Allow the mixture to simmer for 20 minutes, stirring occasionally. Then add the whole onions. Cover and simmer gently until all the water evaporates, leaving the onions in a thick sauce. Five minutes before removing from the heat, add the vinegar. Serve warm or at room temperature.

OVEN-BAKED EGGPLANT WITH HERBS
Melitzanes Fournou

(Serves 4 as a side dish)   *Gluten and Dairy-free*

½ cup olive oil
1 large onion, chopped
4 cloves of garlic, chopped
⅓ cup white wine
1 pound canned tomatoes
¾ cup parsley, finely chopped
1-2 bay leaves, fresh or dried
Sea salt and freshly ground black pepper
1 tablespoon raw cane sugar
2 large eggplants

Place the olive oil in a large non-stick saucepan or a deep frying pan. Add the onion and garlic. Stir constantly over medium heat until the onion is slightly golden. Add the wine and stir for a few more minutes. Then add the tomatoes, parsley, bay leaves, salt, pepper and sugar. Add a cup of hot water, cover and simmer over medium heat until all the water evaporates. The sauce should be thick and tasty.

In the meantime, cut the eggplants lengthwise (4-5 thick slices from each). Place the slices in a bowl, sprinkle with salt, cover with water and set aside for 30 minutes. Wash the eggplants under a running tap and dry them with a paper towel. Fry the slices (preferably in olive oil, or any seed oil) until they are golden brown. Place a layer of eggplant in a pyrex container followed by a layer of the sauce and then another layer of eggplant and finally the remaining sauce. Bake in a medium oven, 350°F for 30 minutes.

Note: The judicious use of wholewheat bread to sop up any remains of the sauce is suggested in order to waste as little as possible.

EGGPLANT WITH OLIVE OIL
Melitzanes me Voutyro

Gluten and Dairy-free

1 large eggplant
½ cup olive oil or 4 tablespoonsful polyunsaturated
   margarine
5 cloves of garlic, chopped
1 cup canned tomatoes
½ cup parsley, cnopped
Sea salt and freshly ground black pepper

Cut the eggplant into cubes and put them in a saucepan with cold water and sea salt for 30 minutes to draw out the bitter juices.

In a non-stick saucepan, place the oil or margarine, garlic and eggplant, which should have been thoroughly rinsed and patted with paper towels. Heat and stir constantly for 5 minutes and then add the tomatoes and their juice, the parsley, sea salt, pepper and a cupful of hot water. Simmer until all the water has evaporated and serve warm.

Note: This side dish is ideally served with Skordalia (page 18).

LIMA BEAN STEW
Yigantes Yiahni

(Serves several as a side dish)　*Gluten and Dairy-free*

1 pound lima beans
1½ cups olive oil
2 onions, chopped
½ cup parsley, chopped
2 carrots, chopped
Sea salt and freshly ground black pepper
Pinch of paprika

Soak the beans overnight. Drain and cover with fresh water in a saucepan with a little salt and simmer for 10 minutes. Drain the water and add the olive oil, onion, parsley, carrots, the pepper and a little more salt. Sauté until the onions are soft and golden. Cover with water and allow to cook over low heat until all the liquid has evaporated. Sprinkle with paprika.

ROASTED LIMA BEANS
Yigantes Plaki

This is a traditional, tasty, nourishing dish and carries with it a very Greek flavor.

(Serves 4-6 as a main course or several as a side dish)
Gluten and Dairy-free

1 pound lima beans
½ cup olive oil
½ cup parsley, chopped
1 pound canned tomatoes
6 cloves of garlic, halved lengthwise
2 celery stalks including green leaves, chopped
1½ onions, chopped
2 carrots, chopped
1 teaspoon paprika
Sea salt and freshly ground black pepper

Soak the beans overnight and then, after washing them well, place in boiling water and cook for 30 minutes. At this stage, change the water and continue to cook the beans for another 30 minutes in the new water. (This method effectively destroys enzymes which can produce flatulence and distention.) Place the beans in a pyrex or metal casserole (2-3 inch deep), together with all the other ingredients. Mix well, and cover the mixture with water. Place foil over the container and place in the oven at 425°F for 1 hour. Remove the foil and continue to cook at this heat until all the water has evaporated and the beans are tender, with a degree of browning or crispness to those on the surface. The timing can vary with different qualities of beans and hardness of the water.

BEAN STEW
Fassolakia Yiahni

(Serves 2 as main course, several as a side dish)
Gluten and Dairy-free

1 pound string beans
1½ medium-sized onions, chopped
½ cup olive oil
1 pound canned tomatoes
3 medium-sized potatoes, each cut into 3 or 4 pieces
2 teaspoons chopped parsley
Sea salt and freshly ground black pepper
1 teaspoon raw cane sugar

Trim the beans. Place the chopped onions in a saucepan with the oil and cook until *soft* (*not* until golden or burned). Add the tomatoes and bring to the boil. After 10 minutes add the beans, potatoes, parsley, salt, pepper, sugar and a cup of water. Cover and simmer until all the liquid has evaporated. Serve this dish with wholewheat bread, low-fat cheese and black olives.

Note: Leeks can be used instead of beans in a similar manner except for the use of parsley, which should be omitted; brown rice (which has been pre-boiled) can be used in place of potatoes.

BAKED VEGETABLE STEW
Lahanika Yiahni

(Serves several as a side dish)   *Gluten and Dairy-free*

4 ounces mushrooms
½ pound zucchini
1 eggplant
1 green pepper
2 small potatoes
½ pound string beans
3 large tomatoes, sliced
2 onions, chopped
1 cup parsley, chopped
1 tablespoon raw cane sugar
½ cup olive oil
4 cloves of garlic, chopped
Sea salt and freshly ground black pepper

Wash and chop all the vegetables. Place them in an ovenproof container and add the parsley, sugar, oil, garlic, salt, pepper and a cup of hot water. This should be sufficient liquid as the ingredients add a quantity themselves; however, if the stew is drying out, add a little more water. Bake in a moderate oven at 350°F for 1½ to 2 hours.

Note: Ideally, serve this dish with Skordalia (page 18), lima beans, olives and wholewheat bread.

POTATO CROQUETTES
Kroketes Patates

(Serves several as a side dish)

3 pounds potatoes
4 eggs
¼ cup finely chopped parsley
1 onion, finely chopped
Sea salt and freshly ground black pepper
1 cup grated hard cheese
Wholewheat pastry flour
Vegetable oil for frying (preferably olive oil)

Scrub the potatoes and boil them in their skins in salted water. When soft, peel and mash them while still hot. Make a purée mixture by adding 1 egg and 3 yolks (well beaten), parsley, onion, salt, pepper and cheese and blend thoroughly.

Allow the potatoes to cool and then prepare the croquettes by hand, shaping them into balls. Roll these in the flour before dipping them into the beaten egg white and then again into the flour. When ready, place them on paper towels. Serve hot or cold.

Note: These croquettes can be made without first dipping them into the egg white. When the croquette is ready, simply roll it in a little flour and fry. Powdered rye crispbreads can be used instead of the flour.

SPINACH CROQUETTES
Kroketes Spanaki

(Serves several as a side dish)

2 pounds spinach
1 onion, very finely chopped
1⅓ tablespoons polyunsaturated margarine
1½ cups grated hard cheese
3 eggs
Sea salt and freshly ground black pepper
1¼ cups wholewheat breadcrumbs
1½ cups powdered rye crispbread

Wash the spinach well and steam it until soft. Place in a colander and drain before shredding it into small pieces. Place the shredded spinach in a mixing bowl and add the chopped onion, melted margarine, cheese, 1 egg and 2 egg yolks, sea salt, pepper and the breadcrumbs.

Mix all these ingredients thoroughly. Place the crispbread powder on a plate. Beat the 2 egg whites with 2 teaspoons of water. With the hands, shape 2 heaping tablespoons of the spinach mixture into balls or croquettes and then roll these in the rye powder before dipping in the white of the egg, and again in the rye powder. Fry the croquettes in oil or margarine until all sides look crispy. Serve hot for crispness, or cold for extra flavor.

Note: This may be used as a side dish and can accompany any meal. It can also be used as a mezze, in which case make each croquette much smaller. If whole rye crispbreads are not available, plain wholewheat flour can be used instead.

ZUCCHINI CROQUETTES
Keftedes me Kolokithia

(Serves several as a side dish)

2½ pounds small zucchini
1 cup powdered rye crispbread
1 cup grated hard cheese
3 eggs
1 medium-sized onion, very finely chopped
½ cup parsley, finely chopped
Sea salt and freshly ground black pepper
1⅓ tablespoons polyunsaturated margarine

For frying:
Wholewheat pastry flour
Oil (preferably olive oil)
Sea salt and freshly ground black pepper

Wash and boil the zucchini in salted water. When soft, remove, place in a colander and allow them to drain well. Place them in a mixing bowl and mash with a fork before adding all the other ingredients. Mix well. The result should have a thick consistency; if not, add more crispbread crumbs or wholewheat flour.

Form the mixture into croquettes by hand. Roll these in seasoned flour and fry until golden. Serve hot or cold.

CHICKPEA CROQUETTES
Revithia Kroketes

(Serves several as a side dish)   *Dairy-free*

1¾ cups chickpeas (soaked in water for 1½ days)
1 cup wholewheat pastry flour
1 large onion, finely chopped or grated
1½ cups parsley, finely chopped
1 cup wholewheat bread (soaked and squeezed out)
3 scallions
Sea salt and freshly ground black pepper
Olive oil for frying

Soak the chickpeas in water for 1½ days, remembering to change the water 2-3 times. Rinse well, trying to get rid of the skins of the peas. Place in a saucepan with water and boil for 1 hour. Drain and mash them into a creamy texture. Add 1⅓ tablespoons of the flour and the rest of the ingredients. Mix well and form into balls or croquettes. Dip these in the flour and fry them in pure olive oil until golden.

Note: Serve with Tjatjiki (page 20), lettuce and tomato salad, black olives and wholewheat bread.

9. Cooked Salads

Many vegetables are more nutritious when cooked than in their raw state. This is because cellulose, which binds some of the constituents, is broken down in the cooking process. Overcooking, especially if the fluid is not also ingested, is undersirable because of the loss of essential minerals. Steaming is an ideal method of cooking since it ensures the retention of these minerals and also produces lightly cooked, crisp and delicious vegetables. The use of cooked vegetables, served cold, individually or mixed, is perhaps a novel idea to some. In Greece it is common. The taste of cooked salads can be marvelous and the nutritive value high. My advice is always to slightly undercook rather than the opposite.

POTATO SALAD
Potatosalata

(Serves 4 as a side dish)

4 large potatoes
1 onion, sliced
16 black olives
Sea salt
½ cup olive oil
⅓ cup wine or cider vinegar
1 teaspoon oregano
Fresh parsley

Boil the potatoes in their skins. When cooked, peel them and place in a shallow dish. Allow them to cool and then cut into slices. Put sliced onions between the slices of potatoes. Add the olives and dress with salt, oil, vinegar and oregano. Garnish with the parsley and serve warm or cold as a side dish.

BEET SALAD
Batzaria Salata

(Serves 4 as a side dish)

2 large or 4 small beets
1 large onion, sliced or 4 cloves of garlic thinly sliced
½ cup olive oil
½ cup wine or cider vinegar
Sea salt
Fresh parsley

Peel and slice the cooked beets and place the overlapping slices around the sides of a shallow container. To each slice add either a slice of onion or a slice of garlic (not both). Dress with oil and vinegar and a little salt, and garnish with parsley. Serve warm or cold.

Note: Beets contain significant amounts of calcium, iron and phosphorus as well as vitamins A, C and some of the vital B vitamins. Their health-promoting qualities are many and they should be a major part of salad meals, grated raw or cooked, as above.

CAULIFLOWER SALAD
Kounoupidi

As a member of the cabbage family, cauliflower is rich in sulphur, calcium, iron and phosphorus. Known in healing circles as a blood purifier, it encourages detoxification. It is a useful vegetable, raw or cooked. The quantity of cauliflower depends on the number of people to be served. When buying a cauliflower, choose one which is firm and white. Its firmness will ensure crispness and its whiteness will ensure freshness.

For a dressing:

Olive oil
Lemon juice
Black pepper (touch)
Sea salt

Cut the cauliflower into quarters, wash well and place in a steamer. Steam for no longer than 8 minutes, to ensure that the crispness is not lost and the nutritive value is retained as far as possible.

Dressing:
Mix 2 parts oil to 1 part lemon, with a little pepper and sea salt, pour onto the cauliflower and serve hot or cold.

MIXED VEGETABLE SALAD
Lahanika Anamikta

Gluten and Dairy-free

This type of cooked salad provides a rich supply of essential minerals, vegetable fiber and vitamins. It should play a regular part in the balanced wholefood diet.

1 carrot, well washed and sliced
4 ounces string beans, trimmed
½ fennel, washed and cut into large pieces
1 globe artichoke (see instructions on preparation of artichokes, page 60) cut into 8 pieces
4 ounces peas
1 potato, cut into 6 pieces
1 celery stalk, sliced and with strings removed
1 small beet, undercooked and diced
10 black olives
1 small Spanish onion

For the dressing:
Olive oil
Wine or cider vinegar
Oregano
Sea salt

Place the first six vegetables in the steamer. Steam for 10 minutes and then add the celery and steam for another 5 minutes. Empty all the ingredients into a serving dish. Add the diced beet, the olives and the raw onion. Add the dressing with 2 parts oil, 1 part vinegar, the oregano and salt. Mix well, but gently.

DANDELIONS AND FENNEL
Prikalida ke Marathro

Dandelions grow almost everywhere. In some countries the dandelion is considered a weed. In Greece, it is cultivated and sold in the markets. This delicious and most edible plant contains many minerals and it has a deserved reputation as a cleanser of the liver. Seeds are available in the market and a corner of any garden could be put aside for their cultivation.

Pick the desired quantity and wash them well. Put water and a little sea salt in a saucepan and bring to the boil. Add the dandelions and fennel (which should have been cut into 8 pieces). Cook the vegetables until tender (approx. 15 minutes). Serve hot or cold and dress with lemon juice and olive oil. Finely chopped garlic also complements this dish.

DANDELION JUICE

The water in which the dandelions have been cooked is very good to drink. It contains the essence and has a high mineral content. This is an excellent natural diuretic and liver stimulant. In a cup containing the dandelion water add the juice of half a lemon and a tablespoon of olive oil. Drink hot or cold, at any time of the day, or before going to bed. The juice of zucchini, zucchini tops and turnip tops, can be used in the same way.

The content of dandelion leaves includes a very high vitamin A and C concentration and some of the B vitamins, as well as high iron, potassium and calcium levels. It has been used widely in treating rheumatic conditions, anemia, digestive complaints, diabetes and kidney ailments.

TURNIP TOPS
Goggilia

This plant, which grows easily in any garden, is highly nutritious. It contains a very high concentration of potassium and calcium as well as vitamins A, C, E and K in good quantities. This vegetable is very suitable for young and old as a health-enhancing part of a wholefood diet.

Pick as many tops as are required. Steam and dress with a mixture of olive oil, lemon juice and sea salt. Serve warm or cold as a side dish.

ZUCCHINI TOPS
Kolokithokorfades

Greeks, especially those who don't live in big cities, look forward to the end of the zucchini season when they will find, in the market, zucchini tops! These are very rich in minerals and enzymes and aid liver function. It would, of course, be ideal to grow one's own zucchini as this ensures that there has been no spraying.

Zucchini tops are the young tender leaves of the zucchini plant, its very heart. These are only picked when the plant stops producing any more zucchini. Pick the desired quantity, wash well, and steam to the desired tenderness (only a few minutes). Serve warm or cold and dress with olive oil, a little sea salt and lemon juice or wine vinegar.

Note: This vegetable is traditionally served with Skordalia (page 18).

BEET TOPS
Batzaria

Not many non-Greeks know that beet tops are not only edible and very tasty but extremely nourishing. They can either be picked from the garden when young and tender, or bought with uncooked roots. Any yellow leaves should be discarded. Wash well and add the beet tops to a saucepan of boiling salted water an inch deep. Cook until tender (but do not overcook – approximately 10 minutes).

For a dressing:
Olive oil and vinegar are ideal. Serve with Skordalia (page 18).

COOKED GREEN SALADS
Prasines Vrastes Salates

Fresh beans or zucchini or endive or spinach and carrots
may be used in a cooked salad. The vegetables should be
cooked as follows in order to ensure little loss of food
value and retention of flavor.

Place the vegetables in a steamer and cook until they
begin to become tender (test with a fork from time to
time). Serve with a dressing made of lemon juice or wine
vinegar, olive oil (2 parts oil to 1 part vinegar or lemon),
and sea salt. Any other oil could be used, if preferred.
Oregano may be added to the dressing when zucchini and
carrots are used. Crushed garlic may be added for any
vegetable of the cabbage family and zucchini. Decorate
with black olives. Serve as a side dish, hot or cold.

LIMA BEAN SALAD
Yigantes Salata

(Serves several as a side dish)   *Gluten and Dairy-free*

¾ pound lima beans
2 tablespoons minced parsley
6 scallions, chopped
10 black olives
¾ cup olive oil
¼ cup lemon juice
Sea salt and freshly ground black pepper
Watercress, chopped

Soak the beans overnight. Wash them well and boil for 15
minutes. Change the water and allow them to cook until
tender. Five minutes before removing from the heat, add
a little sea salt. Drain, allow to cool, place in a bowl and
add all the ingredients except the watercress. Cover and
when completely cool mix gently. Add the watercress
before serving.

Note: Oregano may be used instead of parsley and wine
vinegar instead of lemon juice, if preferred.

STUFFED ARTICHOKES
Agginares Gemistes me Hortarika

Gluten and Dairy-free
This dish can be served as a starter or side dish. It is an ideal accompaniment for any other vegetables and for any of the recipes in this book.

Artichokes
Carrots
Peas

For the dressing:
Mix thoroughly ¾ cup of olive oil, ¼ cup of lemon juice, sea salt, black pepper, very finely chopped parsley and very finely chopped scallion.

Choose very tender artichokes. Cut off the stalk and remove the choke using a sharp knife. The outer leaves are left intact as, in a young artichoke, these will be edible. Boil the artichokes with the carrots and peas in salted water until tender. Remove from the heat and allow to cool.

  Mix the dressing. Stuff the artichokes with 4-5 slices of carrot and 2 teaspoons of peas and then pour on 2-3 tablespoons of the dressing. Serve warm or cold.

ZUCCHINI FLOWERS
Kolokytholoulouda

The flowers of the zucchini or summer squash plant are a delicacy. They can be eaten raw in a salad or, if stuffing them (page 79) is too much trouble, then they can be steamed. After washing carefully (they are very delicate), steam them for no more than 1½ minutes. When cooked, dress with olive oil, lemon juice and sea salt and serve, ideally with Skordalia (page 18).

10. Cakes and Desserts

STRAWBERRIES WITH ORANGE JUICE AND BRANDY
Fraoles me Himo Portokali ke Koniac

Quantities should be adapted as required, but for, let us say, 1 pound of strawberries, this dessert should be prepared as follows:

1 pound strawberries
¼ cup brandy
½ cup fresh orange juice
⅓ raw cane sugar (optional)

Wash the strawberries in cold water. Mix the brandy and orange juice together. Place a layer of strawberries in a bowl, then sprinkle with a little raw cane sugar and pour a few drops of the juice-brandy mixture over the top. Carefully, so as not to bruise the fruit, lift and mix the ingredients. Continue in the same way, adding the fruit, sugar and juice until they are all used up and well mixed. Refrigerate for 2 hours before serving. Serve in open champagne glasses or glass bowls.

NEW YEAR'S DAY CAKE
Vassilopita

1 cupful polyunsaturated margarine
1 cup dark brown sugar
5 eggs
3 teaspoons baking powder
½ wine glass Grand Marnier or plain brandy
Rinds of 2 oranges and 2 lemons
¾ cup peeled and ground almonds
¾ cup currants and raisins, mixed
½ cup milk
Juice of ½ orange
Sesame seeds
2½ cups wholewheat pastry flour

Place the margarine and the sugar in a mixing bowl. Mix well to a smooth consistency. Add the yolks of the eggs. When well blended, add the baking powder, diluted in the brandy first, finely grated lemon and orange rinds, ground almonds, the raisins and the milk. The contents should be mixed constantly.

In the meantime, beat the whites of the eggs to form frothy peaks. Add to the basic mixture a little of the egg and orange juice until all the ingredients are used. Place in a buttered cake pan, sprinkle with sesame seeds and bake in a hot oven at 425°F for 50 minutes. Allow to cool before removing from the pan.

Note: More and/or different nuts may be used, such as walnuts. The number of the new year is usually written on the surface of the cake with sesame seeds or split almonds, prior to cooking. Traditionally, a golden coin (sovereign) was hidden in the Vassilopita, and, of course, the lucky finder kept this as a souvenir.

YOGURT CAKE
Keik me Yiaourti

1½ cups raw cane sugar
1 cup butter or polyunsaturated margarine
6 ounces plain goat's yogurt
5 eggs
3 cups wholewheat pastry flour
2 teaspoons baking powder
3 tablespoons grated lemon and/or orange rind

In a mixing bowl, place the sugar and butter and blend until smooth. Add the yogurt and mix well. Beat the egg yolks and add them to the mixture. In the meantime, beat the egg whites well. Add to the mixture a little of the flour, baking powder, a little of the lemon rind and a little of the egg white. Continue mixing and repeat until all the ingredients are used.

Empty the mixture into a large oiled loaf pan and place in a medium to hot oven at 375°F for approximately 1 hour. Allow to cool before removing from the tin.

Note: To check if the cake is done (this applies to any cake) stick a knife into it. If the knife comes out dry, the cake is ready. If it comes out with small crumbs of cake on it, it needs further cooking.

Variation: Peeled and grated almonds and/or walnuts (½-⅓ cup) may be added to the basic cake mixture, if liked.

EXOTIC FRUIT SALAD
Exotiki Froutosalata

The following fruit salad is a memorable end to a meal. Use any of the following fruits that are available.

Guavas
Chinese gooseberries
Pineapple
Lychees
Bananas
Passion Fruit
Papaya
Mangos
Juice of tangerines or grapes

According to the required quantity, chop up the above fruits into a serving bowl. Empty the pulp of the passion fruit, and pour on the juice of the tangerines or grapes. Mix gently and refrigerate for 1-2 hours. Serve on its own.

FRUIT SALAD
Froutosalata

This salad can be made at any time of the year and it is delicious and nourishing. Quantities should be according to requirements.

Wash the fruit well. Peel peaches, bananas, pears and apples, remove the seeds from melon, grapes and cherries and cut everything into small pieces. Place in serving bowl and add a little raw cane sugar, if desired. Squeeze the juice of a lemon over the fruit (this is to slow down the oxidation process which discolors fruit). Mix well but gently. Add a small quantity of brandy to the salad with some fresh walnuts. Mix, cover, and refrigerate for 2-3 hours before serving. Serve with natural yogurt or soy milk as a dressing, if liked.

11. Children's Recipes

A combination of legumes and cereals offers a balance that contains all the essential amino acids (the building blocks of protein); for example, lentils and brown rice, or beans and millet. To provide a variety of minerals and vitamins and to obtain variations in flavor, vegetables in season are widely used in these recipes. The resultant mixture contains complete vegetable protein, vitamins A, B_1, B_3 (niacin), folic acid, potassium, calcium, phosphorus, iron, etc., as well as the necessary vegetable fiber which guarantees healthy bowel function.

The nutritional values of some of the ingredients mentioned in these recipes are as follows:

Millet
9 per cent protein, 4 per cent fat, 70 per cent carbohydrate.
Rich in: potassium, magnesium, iron, phosphorus.

Lentils
25.7 per cent protein, 1.9 per cent fat, 53 per cent carbohydrate.
Rich in: potassium, sodium, calcium, iron, phosphorus.

Chickpeas
13 per cent protein, 1.6 per cent fat, 50 per cent carbohydrate.
Rich in: potassium, magnesium, calcium, phosphorus.

Brown Rice
8 per cent protein, 8 per cent fat, 70 per cent carbohydrate.
Rich in: potassium, magnesium, phosphorus.

Lima beans
7 per cent protein, 1 per cent fat, 18 per cent carbohydrate.
Rich in: minerals and B vitamins.

The recipes below are suitable for any child from nine
months or so onwards. Depending upon the child's
ability to chew, the thickness of the mixtures should be
varied. For a young baby, a food processor provides the
ideal texture of food. The cereal and legume dishes as
described below can, for an older child, be prepared as a
loaf. The lentil and rice or lentil and millet dish with the
addition of some milled nuts and wholewheat breadcrumbs
can be placed in a tin and baked into a loaf. Where seeds
and nuts are required, they should always be prepared in a
processor.

Some ideas for a day's menu for a child of 18 months to 3 years:

Breakfast: Fresh juice of 1-2 oranges
               Nut, Seed, Fruit, Yogurt and Honey Delight
               (page 121)
               Alternate days, 1 boiled egg
               Glass of milk (soy)

Lunch: Spinach, Rice and Chick-Pea dish (page 120)
            Grated raw carrot
            Grated raw beet
            1 piece of fresh fruit
            Glass of pure fruit juice, soy milk, or water

Evening: Egg and Potato dish (page 122), with salad
             or steamed vegetables or Nut, Seed, Fruit,
             Yogurt and Honey Delight (page 121)

Before sleep: Glass of warm soy milk with molasses or a
             little honey

RICE, LENTILS AND VEGETABLES
Ryzi-Fakes ke Horta

(Serves 3) *Gluten and Dairy-free*

½ cup lentils
½ cup brown rice
2 carrots
1 tomato
1 celery stalk ⎬ **chopped**
2 mushrooms
1 clove of garlic, crushed
2 teaspoons olive oil
1 cube clear vegetable bouillon (optional)

Soak the lentils overnight, rinse well and place in a saucepan with 2 cups of water. Cook over medium heat until the lentils soften and then add all other ingredients and cover with water. Simmer until all the water has evaporated. Place the contents in a blender and reduce to a creamy texture. Brown rice may, depending upon its type or on the quality of water, require extra cooking and it is advisable to cook it on its own for approximately 20 minutes before adding it to the mixture.

LENTILS, MILLET AND VEGETABLES
Fakes – Kehri ke Lahanika

(Serves 3-4)   *Dairy-free*

½ cup lentils
½ cup millet
2 carrots
1 zucchini   chopped
½ onion
1 tomato
1 small potato, scrubbed and chopped (most of its
  value lies just under the skin)
2 tablespoons olive oil
⅓ teaspoon oregano
Sea salt

Prepare the lentils as in the recipe for Rice, Lentils and Vegetables (page 117), then add all the other ingredients and simmer until the water has evaporated. Blend to a consistency suitable for the child (i.e. creamy before teeth are present and more "lumpy" when chewing is possible).

CHICKPEAS, MILLET AND VEGETABLES
Revithia – Kehri ke Lahanika

(Serves 3-4 – according to the age of the child)
Dairy-free

¾ cup chickpeas
½ cup millet
2 tablespoons olive oil
⅓ teaspoon rosemary
1 tomato ⎱ chopped
2 carrots ⎰
1 zucchini or 2 fresh asparagus or 1 artichoke
Sea salt

I find that chickpeas require much more soaking and cooking than lentils. Soak these overnight and cook over medium heat until tender, then add the other ingredients and follow the same procedure as for previous recipes.

LIMA BEANS AND MILLET WITH VEGETABLES
Fassolia Yigantes me Lahanika

(Serves 3)   *Dairy-free*

¾ cup lima beans
½ cup millet
2 leeks
1 medium or large tomato
1 onion ⎱ chopped
2 carrots ⎰
1 celery stalk
1⅓ tablespoons olive oil
Sea salt

Soak the beans overnight. Simmer for 45 minutes. Add all the other ingredients and cover with water. Simmer until all the water has evaporated. Reduce to a creamy texture for very young children.

SPINACH, RICE, CHICKPEAS AND VEGETABLES

Spanaki – Ryzi – Revithia – Hortarika

(Serves up to 4 meals, according to the age of the child)
Gluten and Dairy-free

1 pound spinach
½ cup brown rice
¾ cup chickpeas
2 carrots
1 clove of garlic and/or 3 scallions
3 tablespoons parsley
1⅔ tablespoons olive oil
1 artichoke (optional)
Sea salt

Soak the chickpeas overnight. Change the water and simmer until tender. Add the rice and simmer 15 minutes before adding all the other ingredients. Cover with water and prepare as for previous recipes.

NUT, SEED, FRUIT, YOGURT AND HONEY DELIGHT
Karydia me Frouta ke Yiaourti

Gluten-free

The following makes one large helping. A six-month-old child would be satisfied with half this quantity as a main course.

1 walnut
4 almonds
1 teaspoon sunflower seeds and/or pumpkin seeds

For an infant these must be reduced to powder in a food processor. For an older child they can be grated finely

½ a peach or nectarine or pear or apple
4 grapes
¼ avocado
½ to 1 banana
2 teaspoons pure honey
3-4 ounces goat's milk yogurt

The seeds and nuts are prepared first in a processor and then the fruit is added to reduce the contents to a creamy purée. Place in a bowl, add the yogurt and honey and mix well with a spoon.

This is a nutritious and delicious mixture containing all the value of complete protein as well as vitamin C, B, and minerals such as iron and calcium. It is a complete meal for a baby and a dessert for an older child.

EGGS WITH POTATOES
Avga me Patatas Poure

(Serves 2-3)   *Gluten-free*

2 pounds potatoes
1 cup cow's or goat's or soy milk
1½ cups grated hard cheese
6 eggs
2⅔ tablespoons polyunsaturated margarine
Sea salt and freshly ground black pepper

Cook the potatoes and mash them with the milk and margarine. Oil the sides of a 10 inch baking dish and sprinkle some of the grated cheese on the bottom. Add the mashed potato and make six holes, into which the eggs should be broken whole. Season and sprinkle the remaining grated cheese on top and after putting a little melted margarine over each egg, bake in a hot oven at 425°F for 10 minutes.

Note: This dish could be complemented with grated raw beet, grated carrot, a sliced tomato and watercress or steamed vegetables such as carrots, peas, cauliflower, mushrooms, etc., dressed with a little sea salt, olive oil and lemon juice.

12. Balancing the Diet

Among the many Greek sayings is one that translates: "A healthy mind in a healthy body". A healthy and strong body can be built with the help of a balanced diet, and variety is important, not just for the sake of providing interesting meals.

My suggestion is that once you have become accustomed to the recipes in this book (especially those that will freeze well), then make them again in larger quantities and keep them in the freezer. This will enable you to stock up on a number of meals, which will conveniently bring a variety of wholefood goodness to the table.

While initially the preparation of the variety of foods suggested in the week's menu that follows will entail a great deal of cooking, the use of the freezer to store the surplus will mean many weeks of reduced labor. I find it so, and with a little thought and planning the freezer can be kept well stocked.

The general pattern of eating should be such that 50 per cent or more of the diet comprises raw foods such as salad, fruit, seeds, nuts and cereals. Breakfast should be a fruit, seed, nut and cereal meal. One of the main meals should be a salad-based meal with wholewheat bread or potato salad. The other main meal should contain protein and vegetables. Desserts should consist of fresh or dried fruit. Fruit and seeds (e.g. sunflower) make handy snacks.

Drinks should be taken between meals and consist of either fresh fruit juice or spring water.

Sunday

Lunch
Mixed Salad
Tjatjiki (Yogurt and
Cucumber Dip)
Chick-Pea Croquettes
Fried Artichokes
Choice of fruit

Dinner
Artichoke Moussaka
Mixed Grilled Vegetables
Skordalia (Garlic Potato)
Choice of fruit

Monday

Lunch
Peasant Salad
Potato Salad
Féta or cottage cheese
Wholewheat bread
Choice of fruit

Dinner
Macaroni Pie
Roasted Lima Beans
Choice of steamed vegetables
Choice of fruit

Tuesday

Lunch
Salad Lettuce with Eggs
Tjatjiki (Yogurt and
Cucumber Dip)
Sliced tomatoes
Wholewheat bread
Cottage cheese
Choice of fruit

Dinner
Millet Pie
Skordalia (Garlic Potato)
Beet Salad
Choice of steamed vegetables
Choice of fruit

Wednesday

Lunch
Cucumber Salad
Hummus
Wholewheat bread
Rice with Golden Raisins
Nuts
Fruit

Dinner
Artichokes Vinaigrette
Wholewheat bread
Choice of cheeses
Choice of fruit
Yogurt and honey

Thursday

Lunch
Mixed Salad
Lima Bean Salad
Rice with Golden Raisins
Wholewheat bread
Choice of fruit

Dinner
Moussaka with Eggplant
Skordalia (Garlic Potato)
Chickpea Croquettes
Choice of steamed vegetables
Choice of fruit

Friday

Lunch
Fresh salad
Eggplant Dip
Wholewheat bread
Potato Salad

Dinner
Lentil Soup
Wholewheat toast
Choice of cheeses
Choice of fruit

Saturday

Lunch
Fresh mixed salad
Potato Croquettes
Tjatjiki (Yogurt and
Cucumber Dip)
Wholewheat bread
Choice of fruit

Dinner
Stuffed Tomatoes with Eggs
Brown rice
Lima beans
Skordalia (Garlic Potato)
Steamed vegetables
Choice of fruit

Breakfast throughout the week may comprise of one of the following cominations:

1. Overnight soak the following in water: 2 to 4 teaspoons each of oat flakes, sesame seeds, linseed, pumpkin seeds and 2 or 3 ounces dried fruit (cut into pieces). In the morning, add 2 to 4 teaspoons of sunflower seeds, wheat germ, unprocessed bran (optional) and walnuts or almonds. Add a grated apple or a sliced banana or some grapes. Natural (live) yogurt may also be eaten with this dish.

2. Fresh walnuts and/or almonds and honey, yogurt and fresh fruit, with wholewheat breat or toast and a yeast spread (such as Marmite, etc.); a sugarless jam can be added, if still hungry.

Index

BEAR
ENCOUNTERS
Tales From the Wild

Jim Nelson

Lone Pine Publishing

The Publisher: Lone Pine Publishing
10145 – 81 Avenue   1808 B Street NW, Suite 140
Edmonton, AB T6E 1W9 Canada   Auburn, WA, USA 98001

Website: www.lonepinepublishing.com

Library and Archives Canada Cataloguing in Publication

Nelson, Jim, 1949-
    Bear encounters / Jim Nelson.

    ISBN-13: 978-1-55105-534-3
    ISBN-10: 1-55105-534-1

    1. Bears--Fiction. I. Title.

QL795.B4N44 2005   C813'.6   C2005-904477-2

Editorial Director & Project Editor: Nancy Foulds
Illustrations Coordinator: Carol Woo
Production Manager: Gene Longson
Book Design & Layout: Trina Koscielnuk, Heather Markham
Cover Design: Gerry Dotto

Track illustration by Ian Sheldon; bear illustrations by Gary Ross.

We acknowledge the financial support of the Government of Canada
through the Book Publishing Industry Development Program (BPIDP) for
our publishing activities.

PC: P5

Dedication:
Til Torbjørn

Acknowledgements

The majority of these stories feature events I have had a personal connection with. One is based on a collection of news reports, and the remainder I have appropriated from the mouths of those directly involved.

From there I have "fictionalized" some characters and timelines—it would just be irrelevant (and boring) to detail, for instance, the mundane circumstances that brought me to the scene of Alberta artist Bob Guest's spectacular encounter. However, though some of the people and timelines may be fictions, I have tried to depict the bear essentials pretty much as they happened.

Contents

Revenge:
An Introduction

Why a bear book in the 21st century?

Because there still exists that state of grace once known
as "Creation." The concept eventually came into disrepute
and had to be replaced by the term "Nature." Nature itself
has most recently been upgraded to "The Environment"—
that is, the environment occupied by whatever birds, fishes
and other animals are still believed to be on the loose.

Creation belonged to the Creator, and Nature to Natural
Science. The Environment seems to fall under the auspices
of ad-hoc advocates known generally as environmentalists.

Through time immemorial, Creation stood as a mystery,
omnipotent in its power and grandeur. The Environment,
on the other hand, limps along as a charity like a disfigured

beggar at the gates of our consumer society. The Environment, it seems, is not doing well. Its air is now indexed to indicate the level of poisons it may contain on any given day. Wise consumers now prefer to take their water from a bottle—only a madman would drink directly from a free-flowing stream. The sun itself, once believed to be the source of all life, is now known to cause cancer.

Logically enough, the remaining wildlife, that is, those creatures that cannot avail themselves of the protective services and wisdom of city life, are suffering the consequences.

Save the whales? Despite the most charitable, almost saintly, efforts of government and science, even species that once clogged the oceans in numbers beyond number, like the Atlantic codfish, now seem poised to go the way of the Dodo bird along with the fisher-folk the cod supported.

Our forests are now "managed," largely by corporations. We hear of the "improvements" these companies have made to the original design of this boreal treasure trove. Through clearcutting, wide-scale use of herbicides and the introduction of a monoculture of "genetically superior" varieties of trees, these companies have been able to turn hopelessly inefficient old-growth forests into "models of multi-use sustainability."

And yet species like our local mountain caribou refuse to cooperate. Indeed, it seems that wildlife in general just doesn't get that their problems have been solved. Outside of a few scavenger species like crows, magpies and coyotes, the wildlife population seems hell-bent on reducing their numbers to levels that some fear may result in impractically small gene pools.

Why don't these creatures wake up and get in on the affluence of the consumer lifestyle exploding all around them? When did they stop practising the well-known wisdom of Evolution which made them the survivors of the ages?

It's pathetic!

Or, could it be that they know something we don't know?

As a person who has been accused of being an environmentalist, I must confess that I've never really understood what that is. As one who has, on occasion, been lauded for upholding the environment as a worthy cause, I must admit that I've never actually been able to see it as a cause at all. After all, my old hound dog seems wholly dedicated to sleeping in the sun, drinking the water and breathing the air around him. Should any one of these luxuries ever be denied him, he would set up a verbal protest that would be the envy of the most vociferous defenders of these amenities. But would that make him an environmentalist?

While I'm at it, I might as well reveal that I harbour a festering resentment on behalf of some of these more reactionary species. When I hear, for instance, that our mountain caribou, which numbered in the thousands within living memory, have now been reduced to "fewer than 200," I get angry. I find myself wishing that these animals were equipped with the power to stand up for their right to survive.

Even species that are equipped with the means to turn terrorist don't generally seem inclined to do so—with the odd exception.

When Alexander Mackenzie traversed the north country to become the first white man to reach the Pacific Ocean by land, he kept a journal. In it he reports sighting an "ursus horribilis." Even through the abbreviated language of Mackenzie's notations, one gets a sense of the fear and awe this creature inspired in the man. Mackenzie, obviously, was not alone. First Nations people gave the animal the kind of respect usually accorded a deity. Trappers and guides I have known speak of grizzly bears in the same tones they would use describing floods, fire and other forces of nature not to be trifled with. Only a fool would antagonize, or, God forbid, injure one of these monsters on its home ground.

An injured grizzly, it is said, is one of the few animals on earth that will systematically hunt down and kill the man who has assaulted it. But the majority of us know that this sort of talk is merely the stuff of legends, quaint myths manufactured late at night around the campfire. Although very few of us actually share the turf of our daily lives with these antiquated beasts, we know that they are nothing, more or less, than what used to be referred to as "dumb animals." To romanticize them into "lords of the wild" or "man hunters" would just be silly. Of course one wouldn't seek out a grizzly and poke it in the eye with a stick just to test the theory. That would be like playing catch with a wasp's nest.

But the bear's reaction, just like the wasp's, would be nothing more than that: a reaction. To think that a bear could actually hold a grudge, to think that it could single out the cause of its insult and swear a vendetta—like some

sort of ursine gangster—would be to assign the animal intellectual powers it simply does not possess.

Or so one would think...

Not long ago, my wife Lynne came home with a story that could cause one to question these assumptions. Lynne had been travelling by bus. The man sitting next to her, she learned, had been working in the foothills of the Rocky Mountains. Without going into the exact details, he informed her that his work—probably some sort of geological survey—involved travelling the alpine regions on foot alone. The man impressed upon her the beauty of that landscape, and noted that he enjoyed his job. He even referred to his days spent hiking through these wild lands as a "paid holiday."

The normal cadence of conversation between strangers on a bus or plane usually involves this sort of "How far are you going? Where are you coming from" exchange, then lapses into silence as one or the other of the seat-mates opts for a nap or a book. But this man seemed to want to talk. More to the point, he seemed to have the need to divest himself of something that he could not stop thinking about, something that seemed to amaze and amuse him, something that demanded to be shared.

"Every day out there is different," he said. "That's one of the great things about it."

Lynne commented that she could easily imagine that to be the case.

"You wouldn't believe it," the man enthused, replaying in his mind the images he referred to. "Mountain goats, caribou—I saw a cougar take down a sheep once..."

"Really..." Lynne said. "Do you take a gun with you?"

"No," said the man. "That cougar didn't even know I was there—I was up on the ridge opposite. Just happened to catch sight of him before he let loose." The fellow seemed to dismiss the episode as old news.

"We get flown in by helicopter," he said, launching into his story, "out of camp like—well not right out of camp— the camp's down at the river. A chopper couldn't land there, so there's a landing place and fuel dump in a big clearing a mile or so out of camp. Anyway, so we drive up there in the morning, and they fly me out to the program, drop me off and pick me up at the end of the day." At this point the fellow was shaking his head. "The pilot we got right now is a real idiot. I mean, usually they're pretty good, really, most of them are great, but this guy…"

As Lynne passed on the description the man had given, I had no trouble imagining the pilot—I may even have flown with him! Because the man was right; most people in this profession seem well trained and highly disciplined, so the exceptions stand out. I won't forget a ride I once had up a wild river canyon. Skimming the water at a ground speed probably somewhere between 60 and 100 miles per hour, dipsy-doodling through the winding curves of the valley—with Led Zeppelin blasting at full volume on the headsets—we suddenly rounded a bend to find ourselves coming head to head with an unscheduled island. Unable to decide which of the channels, left or right, seemed best, the pilot chose to go over the obstacle. The rails of the helicopter topped the spruce trees at the head of the island, which seemed to provide the pilot with a shot of adrenalin to go with whatever else he was on.

When the ride was over, I vowed never to leave the ground with this individual again.

The man on the bus had little choice but to carry on flying with the pilot assigned to him, although he did point out that he had had words with the guy concerning gratuitous aerial acrobatics.

The day of the incident had started out normally. The weather had been favourable for flying, and they had taken the usual half- to three-quarter-hour flight out over the steep canyons, alpine meadows and saddle-backed ridges of stone. The weather had been a little hotter than the man liked, but other than that it had been one more day spent enjoying his surroundings. The pilot had arrived on time for the rendezvous, "for a change," the man pointed out, and they had just gained cruising altitude and were headed home when they came over a large alpine basin.

There, ambling along through the shrubs and flowers, obviously minding its own business, was the biggest bear the man, or his pilot, had ever seen. The pilot instantly decided that they had to go back for "a closer look." Upon their return, the grizzly, which had taken no notice of them on their original fly-past, now stood up to sniff out the nature of this noisy intruder.

"Let's buzz him!" the pilot had shouted, and before his passenger could voice an opinion one way or the other, the helicopter swooped into a dive and cruised over the silver-tipped giant, "like maybe a hundred feet above him," the man on the bus said, "… the first time."

When the bear surprised them by not ducking and running for cover, the pilot took it as a challenge and immediately

banked and went in for another pass. The bear was enraged. Its jaws were wide, as it let out what must have been a terrible roar, inaudible to the men over the sound of the chopper as they cruised by, "this time maybe only 20 or 30 feet above him," said the narrator.

The animal actually lunged in their direction, swiping the air as if daring its attacker to come within swatting distance.

"Whoa! He wants to fight!" the pilot yelled, banking again.

"Are you crazy!" the man on the bus remembered yelling back. "Leave it alone and get us out of here!"

But the pilot didn't. Instead, he began hovering lower and lower over the raging bruin, laughing at the animal's fury, taunting it to greater and greater efforts.

"I thought, any minute that grizzly's gonna get a piece of this thing." The man was reliving the experience as he spoke. "If he'd caught one of those rails—and we were damned near low enough for him to get ahold of one…" The fellow paused, mentally reviewing the unspeakable consequences he'd imagined.

"Anyway, I finally yelled at him that if he didn't get us out of there right now, I'd lay a complaint with his boss, and he finally quit." The man said he'd had trouble sleeping that night. The next morning, the pilot was bragging of his exploits over breakfast with their co-workers. His passenger was not supportive. "I told that idiot that it was all right for him, he didn't have to get out of the chopper. But I had to go back down there and spend the day wondering if I was going to bump into a pissed-off grizzly!"

The pilot had laughed off the suggestion, saying that the bear would be "long gone by now." The argument had continued on the drive from camp to the helicopter, until the helicopter—or what was left of it—came into view. The thing was demolished: tail rotor ripped off, tail shredded, bubble smashed, one door hanging from its lower hinge, seats and instrument panel vandalized beyond repair.

The claw and teeth marks left no doubt as to the identity of the vandal responsible. The return flight from where the pilot had left off teasing the bear had taken 20 minutes or more. That meant that overnight, the grizzly had probably traversed a distance of 40 or 50 miles to exact its revenge. Given the terrain, it could not have tracked the helicopter visually to its landing place, raising the question of how it had been able to even locate its foe.

The pilot had lapsed into a state of shock, apparently unable to believe his eyes. The man on the bus, according to his own admission, had "laughed his head off."

I haven't asked, but I doubt the grizzly's behaviour can be easily explained by modern science. I've noted that the conclusions made by individuals given to radio collaring, tranquilizing and counting animals like *Ursus horribilis* tend to be gross generalizations masquerading as absolutes. They infer that what they have observed one bear doing, all bears must do. The idea that bears, like humans, might be individuals exhibiting different or even opposite behaviour patterns is, I suppose, difficult to document in an academic paper on the subject.

Walking through a meadow one day, I noticed a doe mule deer emerging from the thick aspens surrounding us. I guessed that the wind, or lack of it, must have been in my

favour. I wondered why she hadn't seen me, and expected that when she did she would spook and bound back into the surrounding cover. But she didn't. As I continued walking, realizing that our paths would converge about mid-meadow, she stopped and calmly sat down, literally. I'd never seen any hoofed animal voluntarily sit in this position: front legs straight, hindquarters resting on her tail. As I kept walking, she regarded me in a lazy, more or less friendly manner, and actually gave a sort of yawn as I passed by.

I have no idea why she did this, and I'm not at all sure that there is an answer to that question, other than she did it because she wanted to.

Similarly, I doubt there is much point in asking why the grizzly decided to go to all the trouble of tracking down and demolishing the helicopter, except to say that the helicopter had obviously annoyed it. But I don't think we can write this reaction up as a behavioural observation. The next grizzly might not care a fig for helicopters; the next might melt into a heap on the spot and require weeks of counselling before daring to enter that meadow again.

I've given up keeping track of numbers in general, but recently I was informed that the grizzly population in Alberta has plummeted. Grizzly bears are now firmly established among those species that enjoy "threatened" status. I didn't find that hard to believe, given what I've seen happening to the forests they live in—never mind the fact that our government continues to license annual grizzly hunts.

We do seem bent on eradicating all of Creation in favour of some murky, unidentified—bogus—alternative.

As tragic—perhaps catastrophic— as this is, the important thing to keep sight of is that the mystery of Creation in all its original power and grandeur does still exist. It has to; we're a part of it. Nothing reminds me of this fact more than bumping into a bear on its home ground.

Baby
Bear

It was that time of year when northerners cling to the summer sun. Only a month earlier, some may have been heard to actually complain about the unaccustomed heat. But this late in August, the days were getting shorter. Talk of the weather turned to speculations of "an early fall," chilling the hearts of golfers and gardeners and those given to the idea of scorching their winter-whitened hide a toasty brown.

Madge Smythe, *Ms. Smythe* to the students of the neighbourhood elementary school where she worked as a librarian, fell into the latter category. She had spent most of her summer creating a water feature in her backyard. The landscaping contractor had done the heavy work: installing the pump, erecting the slate waterfall, excavating

the pond and so on. But Madge had done the surrounding flagstone patio herself. She had also run a three-foot margin of flagstones between the lawn and the six-foot-high fence enclosing the yard.

Clay flowerpots sporting geraniums of alternating white, pink and red marched around this stone margin in three-foot increments (exactly).

Finally, after days and weeks of toil, the yard was orderly. The water feature hummed quietly to itself, obediently spurting its trickle of water over the mini-mountain of mortar and slate.

Madge, lathered in sunscreen, reclined in a full-length lawn chair next to the pond, contemplating the question of fish. Goldfish, she was told, were dirty. A filter would take care of that, but the filter itself would obviously have to be cleaned. *Water-lilies*, Madge had thought, *would be a suitable alternative.* She had invested in a pair of these only the week before. The plants were supposed to be mature and as such had been expected to bloom within days. They hadn't. Rather, they had taken on a slightly jaundiced hue, which led Madge to question the fluoride and chlorine content of her water. Goldfish, she was told, could survive anything.

Refilling her glass from the pitcher of homemade lemonade she had prepared herself, Madge resolved to give the lilies a few more days. She sipped the lemonade, which she decided might be a little too sweet, then lay back to gain maximum exposure to the sun, which she thought might be a little too hot. She reached for the sunscreen and reread its label, satisfying herself that she was good for several degrees over the present temperature.

She lay back, once again arranging her limbs, tilting her head in such a way as to offer the sun complete access, and was about to let out a contented sigh when they started up again.

Her neighbour owned a pair of Afghan hounds that were given to bouts of semi-hysterical barking. They were the only blemish on an otherwise idyllic location. Madge had the corner lot; there was no alley. The street outside her fence was travelled by local traffic only. Parallel to that was a train track that saw only one train a day—or rather, night—a fixture she had soon gotten used to. On the other side of the tracks was the back end of a shopping mall to which Madge could walk for her basic needs. The dogs were the only intrusion into her much sought-after privacy.

At the moment, they seemed even more agitated than usual. Worse, they seemed fixed on Madge herself. *Are they doing it on purpose?* she wondered. Through the narrow gaps between the boards, she could make out their tawny forms as they gambolled from one end of their yard to the other. One actually stood up against the fence, sniffing and whining while the other dashed witlessly back along its length, barking its head off.

On rare occasions, the neighbour would stick his head out a window and shout at them to "quiet down!"—thereby adding to the uproar. The dogs themselves seemed oblivious to his commands. The neighbour had done absolutely nothing with his yard. Its dimensions were exactly the same as Madge's, as was its fence. (The developer had provided the fencing and laid sod throughout the development as per the contract.)

Mrs. Wolgemuth, who owned the next house down, found the noise as repugnant as Madge. Mrs. Wolgemuth was older than Madge and retired but still very capable. Like Madge, she valued her privacy and resented the noisy intrusion into the peaceful bower that she had made of her backyard. Mrs. Wolgemuth was an inveterate gardener who specialized in flowers. She had erected a small glass greenhouse in which she coaxed species of orchids to live at a latitude far beyond their normal range.

Madge and Mrs. Wolgemuth had discussed the dog problem. Mrs. Wolgemuth was firmly of the opinion that the city should do something about it. Madge did not like the idea of getting involved, but agreed that the problem needed to be dealt with.

The hound that had been standing against the fence now seemed to be attempting to leap over it. Only its head would appear as it rose and fell, but it seemed to be gaining altitude with each successive bound. Were these animals on the attack? This was the last straw!

Madge picked up her cell phone and dialed Mrs. Wolgemuth's number, which she had filed in the telephone. The phone rang several times. *Probably out in the yard,* Madge speculated. "Hi," she said, when Mrs. Wolgemuth came on the line. "It's Madge Smythe, from down the block? I hope I didn't take you away from something..."

"No, just out in the yard—it's a wonder I heard the phone over that racket!"

"Yes, they're getting worse, aren't they?"

"Of course they are!" said Mrs. Wolgemuth indignantly. "He's done absolutely nothing to control them!"

"It's really getting to be too much," Madge prompted.

"Getting to be!" Mrs. Wolgemuth huffed. "I don't know why we've put up with it for as long as we have!"

"What do you feel should be done?"

"Well, the city should get someone down here to put an end to it. I've been saying that for weeks now."

"Well," Madge said, "I suppose if you think that's best."

"Of course it is! What do we pay taxes for?"

"Who, exactly, would you talk to about something like this?"

"I don't care who I talk to," said Mrs. Wolgemuth indignantly. "I'd go to the mayor himself if I had to!"

"There must be someone in bylaw enforcement designated to handle these types of complaints. I'd look under the city listings for the bylaw division and the animal control division under that," said Madge thoughtfully.

"Exactly!" said Mrs.Wolgemuth.

"I don't have a phone book handy—I'm out in the yard—but if you like I could go in and look up the number for you," Madge suggested.

"Oh…" Mrs. Wolgemuth said, apparently taken somewhat aback by the offer. "No, no, I've got the phone book right here, Animal enforcement, you say?"

"Look under the city for 'Bylaw Enforcement,'" Madge corrected. "I would guess there would be a separate listing for the animal control division but if not, I'm sure anyone at city hall could assist you."

"Well, I should hope so!" said Mrs. Wolgemuth, sounding more than up to the task. Madge wished her luck and rang off. She reached down to where the variable speed dial for the waterfall was inset on the edge of the pond and turned it up as high as it would go. The sound of the trickling water

did not begin to compete with the barking of the hounds, but at least it could be heard amidst the din.

Once again, she lay back in the sun, content in the hope that uniformed officers were being dispatched to the rescue.

The screeching of tires skidding to a halt on the pavement next to her yard brought Madge bolt upright in her chaise. A car horn sounded a long, sustained, angry blast. Before Madge could rise to investigate, a huge, hairy black thing with a face like a gargoyle came barrelling over her fence onto the patio, where it stopped short, eyeing her with unmistakably evil intent.

She screamed! The thing screamed back, dwarfing the sound of her own utterance. Madge, quailing before the thing, rolled out of her chair and, hobbled by fear, crawled behind the chair where she cringed, unable to offer so much as a second scream.

For a moment, the thing seemed to consider going back the way it had come, but in the next instant let out a second horrifying screech and leapt across the patio to the water feature, which it perched on top of, as if its next leap would land it upon Madge herself! It did not take its eyes off the poor woman, even as it reached a hand—it had hands!—into the trickling stream of water. It brought the hand to its lips where it sipped from its cupped palm. A heightened outburst from the Afghan hounds behind it seemed to draw its attention from Madge. The hounds had reached a new level of hysteria, both of them now leaping brainlessly against the fence. One actually managed to catch the top of the boards with its front legs and haul itself, however awkwardly, over into Madge's yard—where it recommenced trying to bark the thing to death while

leaping in a frenzied circle around to Madge's side of the water feature.

Madge, sensing her chance and fuelled by the adrenalin now coursing through her veins, rose, lawn chair in hand. Without a thought as to the damage it might cause to the water feature or the plastic and aluminum chair itself, she raised it over her head and launched it at the thing. The beast saw it coming and leapt out of the way in the direction of the neighbour's fence. Madge, once she had begun throwing things, couldn't seem to stop. Two more lawn chairs, her glass of lemonade and the cell phone all landed on or about the beast before it opted for retreat.

It scaled the fence easily and disappeared into the neighbour's yard. The noise was now deafening as the thing tried to outscreech the hysterical hounds. Madge had a vague sense of the hound that had remained in its own yard hitting the fence. A pitiable yelping ensued.

"Gorilla…" the word came vaguely to Madge's lips as she stood gripping the lemonade pitcher ready to send it after the rest of the items she had peppered the thing with. She caught a glimpse of the animal as it climbed Mrs. Wolgemuth's fence, then leapt from there onto the roof of her greenhouse. The sound of glass shattering was added to the mix as it went through the roof. Madge began to feel weak.

"Gorilla?" she asked, as her legs began to shake. She needed to sit down.

Mrs. Wolgemuth had started with the main switchboard at city hall, was transferred to someone else and was in the process of reciting her address and the details of her complaint to a third person in the chain when she was interrupted by the sound of glass breaking.

"What in the world…" she said, turning to a kitchen window that looked out into the backyard. The sight of a gaping hole in the roof of her beloved greenhouse galvanized her into action.

"One of them has just jumped through the roof of my greenhouse!" she said, by way of a summation to the complaint, and crashed the phone into its cradle. She charged into the yard, broom in hand, on a beeline for the greenhouse. Broom raised, she threw open the greenhouse door, prepared to inflict the maximum penalty for the dog's errant behaviour.

The volume of the verbal counterattack pre-empted her swing. Such was the power and nature of the screeching coming from this coal black—not tawny brown—creature, that for a second or two Mrs. Wolgemuth simply froze.

The greenhouse door seemed to slam shut of its own accord as Mrs. Wolgemuth stared blankly through its panes at the demon that had fallen from the sky into her orchids. "Excuse me, ma'am," said a voice behind her. Mrs. Wolgemuth turned to find a pleasant-looking young man dressed in a white shirt and jeans standing behind her.

"It's…not a dog," she said with a weak gesture toward the greenhouse.

"We know…" the man said, gently moving her out of the way of the door.

"You'll need this," said a second man. He passed a glove to the man in white, who nodded, draped the silver chains he was holding over his left arm and slipped the glove (actually a gauntlet lined with lead) onto his right hand. He then pulled the door of the greenhouse open a crack and looked in. Satisfied by what he saw, he slipped through the door and closed it behind him.

"Perhaps we should step over here, out of the way," the second man said quietly and guided Mrs. Wolgemuth away from the entrance. In something of a daze, she took note of the second man's appearance. He was completely bald; his complexion was swarthy. He wore a gold ring in his left ear, a scarlet shirt and white slacks. Questions began to reel through the elderly woman's mind, but they were drowned out by the screeching that emanated from inside the greenhouse.

"Down!" The man in the greenhouse sounded stern but not panicked, or even worried. "Reggie, down!" He was interrupted by another screech. "Reggie…down." There was the sound of a brief scuffle. "Reggie, come!"

The door opened and the man came out, leading the creature on a chain fastened around its neck. It started to lunge away but was checked firmly by the sturdy chain.

"Reggie!" the man said, lifting his gloved hand in a gesture the animal seemed to interpret as a warning. The man led the way toward the gate, the animal following almost contritely.

"I believe this will cover the cost of the damage," said the bald man, depositing an American 100-dollar bill in Mrs. Wolgemuth's hand. Her hand closed on the bill while her eyes followed the creature through her yard.

"Its name is Reggie...?" she asked absently.

"Reginald, actually," the bald man said, striding to the gate, which he held open for Reginald and his keeper. When they had passed through, the bald man followed, closed the gate carefully behind himself, then added, "Please accept our most sincere apologies." With that, he gave a curt bow and was gone.

Once again, the questions began to rise in Mrs. Wolgemuth's mind—none of which could be answered by the two uniformed bylaw officers who arrived about a half-hour later. The officers seemed bewildered by the whole story, as confirmed by a still-shaken Madge Smythe. However, they did agree to leave a warning concerning the noise complaint in the neighbour's mailbox. He was, apparently, not at home.

Once they had Reginald safely inside the motorhome, Jules and Eddie (the bald one) lost no time in exiting the neighbourhood. "How did he get loose?" Eddie asked from the driver's seat.

"I didn't take the time to figure it out," Jules answered. "He might have pried up the floor of the cage."

"Tie him in," Eddie said.

"Yeah," Jules agreed. "I'll padlock the chain."

The motorhome lumbered slowly through the busy parking lot and finally to the rear of the shopping mall where they had parked their small caravan next to the train tracks. A pretty young woman carrying a toddler approached the driver's window as they pulled in. It was Eddie's wife, Markie.

"You got him?" she asked.

Eddie nodded. "We're packing up," he said. She gave an answering nod, waited for Jules and Reginald to exit the motorhome, then climbed in with her young son, who they usually called "Baby Eddie."

There really wasn't much to pack up. They had only just arrived. The shopping mall parking lot had looked like a good location to set up their tent and offer their one-ring circus to the public, possibly for a three- or four-day run. They had opened the side doors on the tractor-trailer unit to vent the thing. It kept cool in transit, but could get pretty stuffy for the bears when they stopped.

Eddie had gone into the mall in search of the manager's office, leaving Jules to water the animals. Markie had begun fixing lunch in the motorhome. By the time Jules had made it around to Reggie's cage, it was empty. Horrified, Jules had shouted the news to Markie, then rushed into the mall looking for Eddie, who he had found in the mall office patiently waiting for the manager to return from lunch. Reggie was a full-grown male chimpanzee who had distinguished himself by attaining "rogue" status in his previous career. As such he had been available at a very affordable price.

Jules had believed he could work with the animal, a daunting prospect for any trainer. Reggie's biceps were the size of a man's thigh. His teeth were capable of inflicting lethal damage. After working with the animal most of the present season, Jules—and Eddie—had concluded that Reginald was a hopeless psychotic. The best Jules could now hope for, in Eddie's opinion, was to wait until they made it to their winter home and find a greater sucker than Jules had been. They spent the "off-season" in Florida, as many circus and carnie people did.

Jules' worst fear, and Eddie's, was the scenario that had just taken place. There was no conceivable limit to the havoc the chimp could wreak, loose in suburbia. So far today they had been lucky. If they could now get out of this town ahead of whatever lawsuits might be pending, Jules would consider himself very lucky indeed.

"Did you water him?" Eddie asked.

"I'd like to drown him," said Jules, "but yeah, he's got water."

Markie joined them and passed Jules a bag of sand-wiches.

"I'll follow you," Eddie said, "just in case." The motorhome usually took the lead scouting the route for the more cumbersome tractor-trailer unit. Jules nodded and climbed into the cab.

The trailer was brightly decorated with graphics typical of a circus wagon. If they could get it out of town without being pulled over, they were probably in the clear. They threaded their way slowly into the traffic. *It was too bad we couldn't have worked this town,* Eddie thought. *It's a busy place; the weather was perfect; we would probably have*

done well. They crossed a service road and turned onto the main thoroughfare headed south out of the city.

"How did you find him?" Markie asked, passing Eddie a sandwich.

"Just followed the screams and the barking dogs," he said, and smiled.

"Lucky," she said.

"So far…" Eddie agreed, glancing in his rearview mirror.

"So, he didn't get into too much trouble then?" Markie was almost afraid to ask.

"Not as far as we know," Eddie shrugged. "He did manage to jump through the roof of a greenhouse."

"Really…" Markie grimaced.

"Made him easy to catch." Eddie could find the positive side of almost anything.

Out on the open highway the traffic thinned considerably. Eddie pulled into the lead, giving Jules a thumbs-up as he went by. These northern Canadian highways offered the traveller a peace unparalleled by the more populated U.S. interstates. Hundreds of miles of lone highways stretched through wilderness without a single billboard or gas station to mar the scenery. The distances between stops added to the overhead, but some things were worth the extra price.

Baby Eddie began fussing, and Markie took him into the back to settle him for a nap. Eddie was breathing easier with every mile they put behind them. Even in the best of times, they had an arm's-length relationship with what Eddie referred to as "Townies." They depended on Townies for their livelihood, but never really felt at one with them.

Eddie had been born on the road somewhere in Eastern Europe. His parents had been Romany gypsies; his first language (of several) Romanes. He had been raised in the old circus traditions. Everyone did "everything." Typically, a child would start out almost as a prop, popping out of an impossibly small suitcase in the clown act, topping an impossibly high human pyramid, or some variation on the theme. Methodically, one would slowly find his "act" while sharing the endless labours that went with life on the road.

Eddie, a natural gymnast, had eventually become a flyer working some of the best rings from Paris to Moscow. But his family had never specialized in trapeze. For generations they had distinguished themselves as animal trainers. Bears, in particular, had been their stock and trade. Eddie had returned to bear training when his age moved him out of the spotlight above the centre ring. Eventually, he had come to America where he and his bears had risen to the top of their field. In the off-season they found work in film and television and nightclubs. In the summer they toured with a Big Top as a centre-ring attraction receiving wide acclaim...until Chicago.

Eddie was not one to dwell on the past. What was done was done, but...Chicago meant more than the end of a successful act. Eddie's bears, just as his father's bears had been and his father's before him, were more than assets. They were not regarded as livestock. After all, they lived and worked together daily, depending on each other for their livelihood. The contentment and sense of well-being one naturally sought for oneself could not be realized at the expense of the suffering of the animals, any more than it

could be realized at the expense of any other echelon of the family.

And when the bears suffered, as they had suffered in Chicago…

Times were changing. Eddie had tried to imagine the well-meaning, if misguided, nature of those persons responsible—after all, they called themselves "animal rights activists." Their fight was supposedly the fight against animal cruelty in all forms. They could not have imagined the pain the bears went through, having ingested the particular brand of poison identified in the baits left in the animals' cages. It seemed to tear their guts apart, resulting in as slow and painful a death as it was possible to imagine. Eddie, when it became clear that they could not be saved from this agony, had shortened it by going down the line with a final goodbye and a bullet to the brain of each of his six beloved bruins.

Why?

He had finally accepted that he would never understand the answer to that question, and moved on. But the experience had left him…empty. He had somehow not been able to find the desire to start over in the life he'd known. For a while he'd actually become a Townie. He had not found it particularly difficult, making his living selling cars in a mid-sized city in Florida. It kept him, as he often said, "in silk shirts and fine wines." But eventually he had grown restless, and drifted back to Europe and then to Kenya where he had signed on as a wrangler with an American movie company. There, on the first day of shooting, he had met Jules.

The scene was an African village, supposedly under attack by lions. The entire village was enclosed by a fence located out of the view of the cameras. The lions were to be let in to this enclosure and the resulting action was to be captured from several camera locations shooting simultaneously.

Eddie and Jules had been presented with long sticks and were instructed to "guard the camera-men." They were also admonished not to "hurt the lions"—some of which, it seemed, were of the trained, or "tamed," variety and others of which were definitely not. It made for interesting times.

Kenya was also where he had met Markie. Her father owned a large ranching/safari operation that had been, for a time, the headquarters of the film company. The rest, as they say, was history.

Back in America, Eddie and his new bride and Jules had put together their one-ring circus and hit the shopping mall circuit. Eddie had first found Edith, a young sun bear. She was gentle in nature but possessed a quick mind. Willing and affectionate, Edith had probably done more than anyone else to bring Eddie back into the spirit of the business. Boris, an older, gelded male black bear, had been in the business for some time and was set in his ways. Still, he was an honest performer who carried his share of the load and asked no more than a fair share of the spoils. Although animal acts were out of favour with some segments of society, the Big Top was still alive. Two or three companies continued to fill seats on the "A" circuit, albeit under steady flack from self-appointed animal rights police. Eddie often wondered if any of these people had

ever had personal contact with "wild" animals—other than in movies like the one he and Jules had helped make. If they did, Eddie couldn't imagine what it might be.

At any rate, these current trends had resulted in a decline in the value of captive-bred performers like Edith and Boris. It had helped set them in a price range he could afford, so he really couldn't complain.

The two bears, while a good start, did not comprise a unit he could pitch the Big Top on, however. But he had the germ of an idea he thought might make the grade: "Goldilocks and the Three Bears." (Ironically, these current trends resulted in a swing in public tastes to even more anthropomorphized presentations.)

It was no good doing the whip and the chair thing—where the illusion was that a man or woman tames the voracious lions or the all-powerful behemoth of any type. These days, people wanted their animal entertainers to "act" as in the case of the movie of a few years back which had featured bears in the leading roles. While Eddie had admired the training displayed in the antics of the stars of this film, the preposterous nature of the story he had found revoltingly stupid—the only way a wild boar grizzly would take in a stray cub would be as lunch! Nevertheless, if that's what the public wanted, after all, it was their dime.

Eddie and Jules had toyed with the notion of casting Reggie as Baby Bear, but Reggie was a psycho. If their audiences had any idea of what was really going on when Reggie and Jules stepped into the ring, they would either be giving Jules a standing ovation, or running for the exits. (They worked with a caged ring.)

For several miles Eddie had been patiently following a semi-trailer transport unit. The motorhome would gain on it on the uphill grades. The transport would then run on ahead on the downhill side. They were on a fairly even stretch, the transport about a quarter-mile ahead, when its brake lights flickered on, and then off, as if the driver had thought of stopping but had changed his mind. Instinctively, Eddie took his foot off the accelerator, coasting until he could ascertain the reason for the driver's hesitation. Something rolled off to the right—a tire? Whatever it was continued over the shoulder of the road and out of sight in the ditch. Eddie continued to coast, waiting to see what other debris might materialize in the transport's wake. Nothing did, but as he drew near the place where he'd seen the article roll off the road, he suddenly began to brake, and turned on the right signal light, informing Jules in the tractor-trailer unit behind him that they were making an unscheduled stop.

By the time Jules eased the truck to a standstill behind the motorhome, Eddie was standing in the ditch, diagnosing the injuries a black bear had sustained in its collision with the semi. Jules came up to stand beside Eddie, and Markie watched from the open entrance to the motorhome.

"Its back is broken," Eddie said, grimly watching as the poor animal writhed in agony, tearing at the ground with its front paws.

"What happened?" Jules asked.

"Truck hit it," Eddie said. "It'll have to be put down." He took a deep breath, then turned to Markie. "The gun..." Markie disappeared into the motorhome. A car went by on

the far side of the highway. The circus vehicles blocked its view of the scene in the ditch.

"If we get caught…" Jules started to say.

Eddie gave a shrug. "What else can we do?" he asked, taking the pistol and box of shells from Markie.

Jules nodded and moved up onto the shoulder of the highway to act as lookout. Eddie moved into position a few yards from the broken bear. He put a bullet in the chamber of the gun and glanced at Jules, who gave him an all-clear sign. Then, looking down at the bear, he said "Sorry," and pulled the trigger. The animal stiffened, arched its neck, and rolled onto its side. A series of involuntary shudders signified to Eddie that the bullet had done its work.

"We better move it out of sight of the highway," he said to Jules, and passed Markie the pistol and ammunition. Jules and Eddie each took a hind leg and dragged the animal on its back toward the trees lining the far side of the ditch. The bear was heavy, but the men made it into the trees, disappearing from view just as a line of cars appeared up the highway. The cars passed without slowing down.

"We'd better get going," said Jules. "If the highway patrol should happen by—I mean, I wouldn't count on them believing our explanation for the bullet hole."

But Eddie wasn't listening. He was staring down at the dead bear with renewed fascination. "Look," he said, crouching beside the body and reaching out to part the black hair surrounding a milk-swollen teat. Clearly the bear had been a nursing mother. Eddie rose, scanning the surrounding trees like a hound sniffing the wind. "The cub won't be far," he said. "She probably sent it up a tree before coming out into the open."

"Did you see which side she came from?" Jules asked.

Eddie shook his head and started for the truck. There, he opened a hatch near the front of the trailer and pulled out "the stick"—a stout aluminum pole with a loop of cable protruding from one end, and a hand grip and cable tightener on the other. He passed it to Jules. "You take the other side of the road," he said, and reached back into the hatch for a coil of rope. "If you get lucky, give Markie a holler," he added, and turned to Markie. "If you hear a holler out of either of us honk the horn once. If the highway patrol or anybody else pulls up, honk twice."

Markie nodded; Jules set off across the highway.

"Just tell the patrolman we're stretching our legs," Eddie said over his shoulder as he set off through the ditch. At the dead bear he paused. "Wish us luck," he said quietly. Left on its own, the cub would starve, if it didn't fall prey to predators first.

He moved among the trees, listening, picking places to set his feet so as to avoid snapping a twig or rustling through the undergrowth. Every five or six paces he stopped to scan the treetops. Somewhere in the distance a bluejay was sounding off—a squirrel seemed to answer. *Are they talking about me?* Eddie wondered.

Ten or 15 minutes later he began to question whether he had come too far. He listened for the sound of traffic on the highway, trying to imagine where the mother bear would have gotten nervous and sent the cub safely up a tree. It would probably be out of sight of the highway, he decided, but not out of earshot. He listened to see if he could still make out the sounds of the traffic. He couldn't; but maybe there was no traffic. Still, this was probably too far.

He turned around and surveyed the ground he had just travelled. To his left the land fell away slightly, the trees growing thicker the lower it went. To his right the trees thinned out as the land rose.

He decided he would work the lower ground first. Keeping an eye on the treetops, so as to avoid missing a swath, he walked to his left a dozen paces then turned back toward the highway. He was sweating. He would need to remember exactly where he started this second swath to avoid covering the same ground twice. Looking around for a distinctive landmark, he glanced up, and there was the cub, staring down at him out of a poplar tree not 20 feet away!

For a moment they stared at each other—Eddie trying to calm the inner excitement he felt, and the cub apparently content to take in what it seemed to regard as a novel spectacle. Eddie decided against hollering for Jules. For several minutes, he did nothing but slowly and methodically take inventory of the situation, while letting the cub get used to his presence.

The tree itself was straight as a pole. Its trunk was bare of limbs up to about the 15-foot mark. The cub was draped over a limb at the third whorl of branches up from there, which put it a few spindly branches from the top. The tree would be nothing to climb, but then what? Eddie wished he had thought of the lead glove—maybe he should holler for Jules.

But the cub was so calm. If Eddie could get the rope on it without spooking it out of the tree, he might save himself a long chase.

Keeping one eye on the orphan, Eddie moved a few paces closer to the tree. The cub's eyes widened warily. It glanced up the tree as if assuring itself it still had room to move, but stayed where it was. Eddie looked away, waiting for the cub to relax—hopefully to the point of boredom.

The sound of a vehicle passing on the highway drifted through the trees. The cub twitched its ears and looked toward the sound. Eddie moved again, this time stopping within an arm's reach of the tree. The cub shifted to look directly down the trunk at Eddie, but did not retreat.

Eddie waited. When he judged that once again the cub had started to lose interest, he reached out and touched the tree. Watching the orphan's reaction, he then gave the tree a gentle shove. The cub moved to hug the trunk but stopped short of climbing higher. It looked down over its shoulder as if annoyed.

Leaving his hand on the tree, Eddie surveyed the branches. He would need to commandeer one when he was finally within reach of his prize. He checked the loop in the rope, then put an arm through the coil and draped it over his shoulder.

It was time: keeping his eyes fixed on the cub, Eddie slowly reached up and wrapped himself around the tree, like a python with limbs. He began in slow, undulating movements, to pull himself up the trunk.

The cub dug its claws into the white poplar bark and looked down, nervously monitoring the man's ascent. Eddie didn't stop until he had his feet on the first branch. There he waited in a crouch. The orphan lifted its head and let out a series of plaintive calls for help to its dead mother. Eddie slowly rose to a standing position on the limb. He

was still out of reach, but too close for the little bear's comfort. It hiked itself a body-length or two farther up the narrowing tree trunk.

Eddie now reached for a nearby branch, which he broke off, then stripped of its leaves and twigs. He then pulled himself up onto the next limb. The cub started to move higher but seemed to distrust the thin stem, which its tree trunk was becoming. Its wails were now tinged with terror. Bracing himself against the trunk, Eddie removed the coil of rope from his shoulder, widened the loop, and hooked it on the end of his stick. Picking the moment, he reached the stick upwards and set the loop gently over the bear's head. It hung loosely around its neck to about the middle of its back. *So far, so good,* Eddie thought. He turned toward the tree, placing himself directly below the little bear, and was reaching out once more with his stick when he was met with a thin, hot stream of piddle.

He lowered his head, cursing under his breath as the last trickle splashed off his bald head. He wiped his face and pate on his sleeve and looked up, sympathetically, at the terrified orphan. With the stick in his right hand, the rope in his left, he reached the stick up to "tickle" the orphan in the ribs. The move had its desired effect.

As the bear lashed out with its right paw, thereby reaching its arm through the loop, Eddie jerked the loop closed. But as the rope tightened under its armpit, the bear spun around to face the constricting threat and spun itself out of the tree! Eddie's reflex was to drop the stick in favour of the tree trunk, while tightening his grip on the rope. Unfortunately the cub's fall took it to the far side of the limb above. When the slack came out of the rope, the cub

was swinging wildly in the air at a height even with Eddie's knees. Before Eddie could let out some rope, the cub had swung into him! It clutched at his legs as it would a branch, but finding these limbs to be alive, instinctively bit into them. Eddie kicked it away but not before it had sunk its sharp little teeth deep enough into a calf to come away with a noticeable chunk of muscle. Gritting his teeth, Eddie let out enough rope to leave the cub swinging harmlessly in mid-air.

For a moment, Eddie braced himself against the tree to inventory the pain and the extent of the damage. He decided it felt worse than it was. The bear, bawling and snarling, swung slowly back and forth below.

"Jules!" Eddie hollered. "JULES!" he hollered again, louder, and was gratified to hear the answering blast on the horn. Minutes later, he called again, and then again, to give Jules his bearings.

When the man found them, Eddie was sitting on the lower limb of the tree, the cub tethered at ground level, tight enough to prevent it from getting at the rope. Jules took note of Eddie's bloodied leg and the dangling bear.

"Loop him tail-first around the armpits," Eddie said.

Jules immediately bent to the task. When it was completed, Eddie dropped his end of the rope down to Jules, then gingerly lowered himself to the ground. "He's a beauty," Jules said admiringly.

Eddie nodded, smiling down at the orphan. "We'll have to bag him to get him to the truck," he said wearily.

Jules nodded, passed Eddie the stick, and hurried off to the truck to get a sack. Eddie sat down and pulled up his pant leg to better view the damage. It would need a stitch

or two—he'd have to get to that, and a shower, as soon as they could get squared away.

The little bear squirmed against its constraints, then gave up and looked at Eddie, wide-eyed with fear, helpless in its bonds. It would take him a while to settle into his new life. *He and Baby Eddie would grow up together,* Eddie thought.

They could all use a few days off, camping along one of these northern rivers or creeks. Boris and Edith definitely needed some free time—they'd been cooped up far too much lately.

Funny, how sometimes a day could start out threatening to rain down on you with all the trouble of the world, only to end up showering you with gifts—and bear piss. Eddie really needed to get to that shower.

The Patience
of Job

Thomas and Leif were back in the bush, this time to set
up a base camp. Summer was passing fast. It would not be
long before the leaves would turn and the annual migration northward of "mighty hunters" would begin.

On a whim, they decided to take a little side trip. They'd
heard Job Jameson was setting up camp over on Bald
Mountain Creek. Jameson often guided with them but
always had a few hunters of his own, regulars mostly, who
came back year after year. Job's was a one-man operation.
He guided, packed, skidded, skinned and did the cooking
all without the help, or interference, of a single partner or
hired hand.

As Thomas and Leif rode down onto the flats along the creek, Leif had his first intuitive twinge that something was wrong. As they crossed the wide meadows just downstream of Jameson's camp, they were both alarmed by the sight of Jameson's horses grazing unattended. One dragged a tether rope along beside itself. A couple of others trailed halter shanks, but none of them were hobbled or tethered as they should have been. Thomas noticed the smoke first—not a lot of smoke, but not the smoke of a cooking fire either. The riders came through the draw at the edge of the meadow and emerged from the willows and alders to receive their first view of what had been Job's camp. The smoke came from the smouldering remains of his large wall tent. Its charred ridge pole leaned at a rakish angle above the rubble that had once been the comfortable interior of the tent. Bottles, cans, rifle shells, clothing and rolls of toilet paper lay strewn over the entire site. As he rode through the rubble, Leif noted in amazement that certain types of debris had actually found its way into the trees surrounding the once-pleasant campsite.

Jameson himself sat on a stump in front of the now-defunct tent. The campfire in front of him had long been wanting wood and was now just another wisp of smoke joining the haze rising from the remains of the tent.

Job did not rise to greet the approaching riders in his characteristically positive manner, but continued to stare into space as if they weren't there. Even when they pulled up directly in front of him, he did nothing to acknowledge their presence but only stared.

Leif noted the open bottle of whiskey the man was holding in his hands. That in itself was odd, for although

the man was known to have a great fondness for "the drink," he usually abstained when "in camp."

"Anybody home?" Leif asked the man on the stump.

Job slowly lifted his head to peer at his two visitors through thick eyeglasses, which were something of a trademark with him. Leif noted that one of the lenses, as thick as the bottom of a beer glass, was cracked.

"Bear…" Jameson said dazedly, "grizzly bear…"

With that he drifted back into his meditative trance, pausing on the way to take a pull on the whiskey he held in his hand.

Leif and Thomas dismounted and immediately set about stabilizing things in the camp. When they had tended to the horses and located the coffee pot and coffee among the ruins, they joined Job beside the rekindled fire.

Somewhere into his third cup of hot black coffee, the poor man seemed sufficiently composed to begin dredging up a more detailed explanation for the sorry state of their surroundings.

It seems that Job had been suffering the visits of an unusually troublesome bear. It had started with the man's very first trip in with supplies. Job had cached a wagonload of provisions and went for the next load only to find the first ripped to shreds when he got back. He'd gathered up the mess, salvaged what he could, and gone for a third and final wagonload. Again the stash of goods and gear had been trashed by the time he returned.

Again Job cleared up, saving everything he could, and set about building his camp. Tents, an altar fire, even camp furniture began to appear as the chainsaw howled and the sweat rolled off Job's forehead.

He did not give the bear another thought. Job generally got along well with bears and had a particularly soft spot in his heart for the "Griz." He considered the losses suffered to be part of the cost of doing business out here. Did he pay anything for the moose he marketed?

But when he returned from a little scouting trip to find everything ripped to pieces—again—he decided to take matters in hand.

This attack had been the bear's first daytime invasion. Both times previously the bruin had come in during the night. It was an older bear, a male—maybe it was sick or injured? Job set his size 11 gumboot down in a track. There were inches to spare both front and back.

Big bear, he had pondered. Job had no electric lights to flick on the next time the bear dropped in. He didn't even have a flashlight. The sky was overcast; there would be no moon. He decided that he would have to let the bear come to him.

That night he mixed up a bowl of molasses, sardines and strawberry jam guaranteed (he hoped) to drive a hungry bear mad, and placed the temptation just outside his open tent flaps. Even in the dark, he reasoned, and once he heard the slurp and smack of the bear licking up the special dish, he'd open fire through the tent flaps. At that range and with a bear "big as a barn," he couldn't miss—even if he couldn't see anything.

The more he thought about it, the more he became convinced of his plan. Sometime after dark he rolled and smoked his last cigarette and settled in. He knew it would be a long wait, probably most of the night, but that was all just part of the game. He did decide that he might as well

be comfortable and lay back on his folding cot with his 30.30 cradled across his chest. There was a slight chill in the air but Job decided against the wool blanket. He didn't want to get too comfy in case he should fall asleep.

It must have been a good three hours later he became vaguely aware of a smell, a rotten smell, a putrid smell…and a sound, like someone snoring in bed beside him…or above him? With a sudden start, Job became terrifyingly aware that what he was smelling was the fetid breath of the very animal he lay in wait for. The bear was in the tent sniffing over Job as if he were the main course set to follow the appetizer he'd just finished.

Automatically, almost out of reflex, Job cocked, not the rifle, but his right fist. He let fly with all his might, successfully planting one on the end of the big bear's nose and sending it pell-mell back the way it came.

It brought the tent down on Job just as he was remembering the gun he held in his hands. By the time he found his way out from under the heavy canvas, all was silent in the pitch black of the night.

He was furious with himself for falling asleep and vowed that it would not happen again. He guessed that his haymaker had given the giant an awful scare, but would not serve as a deterrent to its returning to scrounge for delicacies like the molasses and fish.

The following night, just before dark, he mixed up a similar batch, this time simmering it on the fire for a couple of hours before turning in. The smell wafted through the camp and oozed along the creek bed. *He'll be here,* Job promised himself. This time he sat up in a chair. He wished for the light of the kerosene lantern but knew there would

be nothing to see as long as its light informed the bear of his vigil.

An hour ticked by…and another. A sound so faint he thought at first he'd imagined it came to the hunter's ear. He stiffened in his camp chair. A moment later, he heard the horses spook and knew. "He's here…" he muttered. Several minutes later he heard supplies tumbling out of the wagon box and cursed the messy marauder.

"Go for the gloop, damn you," he said under his breath.

A while later, it seemed like hours, he heard the rattle of the doubletree falling to the ground. *He's after the oats,* Job thought. The bear was slowly working its way closer. Job guessed it just wanted to be sure that there was no punch in the nose waiting for it when it moved in to claim the delectable delight its nose told it waited for it in front of the tent.

Job waited. He was a hunter who knew the art of waiting. He knew the moment would come soon enough when everything would happen very fast again, and he waited some more.

Now he could hear the wheezing breath of the animal just outside the canvas! The sound brought back the memory of the smell of that breath and Job curled his top lip.

He waited…he could actually hear the bear's fur brushing along the side of the tent. It grunted, and smacked its lips.

Why the hell didn't it go for the bait so that Job could get a bullet into it? The alarming realization suddenly hit Jameson that the bear was actually attempting to enter the tent again, this time by crawling under the side—but where exactly? Job's cigarette lighter was five inches from his left

hand in his left shirt pocket. He moved as one defusing a bomb, avoiding even the slightest sound as he finally felt the lighter in his hand. Holding it aloft, he butted the rifle against his right shoulder and aimed it in the general direction of the sounds the bear had made last.

Silent seconds pounded by...

The light came on with a single flick, and Job stared at the side of the tent. There was a large round bulge near the ground pressing in hard on the tent. It had to be the bear's head!

Job aimed and fired; he couldn't miss. The retort and the orange flash of the rifle were followed by a "KABOOM" of deafening volume and an orange flash of awesome proportions. Indeed, the fireball seemed to engulf the entire tent—actually, the entire campsite.

It was also accompanied by a certain impact that rocketed Job off his perch and into the far wall of the tent.

It turned out that the bulge was not the bear's head, as Job had guessed, but a 25-pound propane bottle that he had stored outside the tent for safety reasons—and which he had obviously plugged dead centre!

"Why the hell would that bear be playing with a damned propane bottle like that?" Job asked his two friends.

Neither Leif nor Thomas could hazard a guess, but they were both pretty sure that Job would not be bothered any further by that particular bear.

Out on
a Limb

Mags waited high above the forest floor like a hunter in a tree stand, except that he was not the hunter but the hunted. His only weapon was his increment hammer—a tool with a steel ball and hollow spike at its end, used for extracting core samples from trees.

Leaning against the trunk of his tree, he shifted the hammer into his left hand so he could wipe his sweaty right palm on his jeans. Looking down through the branches, imagining the route his attacker would take, he wished for an axe instead of the stubby hammer.

He lifted his head, held his breath and listened… Nothing. If Nixon—his partner—was being eaten alive, he was doing it quietly.

It was all Nixon's fault, anyway. Normally they would have been back in camp three or four hours ago. It was almost dusk; in an hour or so it would be dark.

Nix was one of those people who believed that anything was possible if one had enough paper and pencil lead to work it out. For several nights prior, he had sat up poring over maps and aerial photographs devising a route that would make it possible to compress two days' work into one—thereby winning a day off to visit a remote waterfall. Magnuson had not argued.

The two men were partners on a crew of timber cruisers. Quite simply, the work involved tramping through miles of virgin timber doing spot checks on the density, age and condition of the timber. The compass man (Mags) would take the lead, dragging a 100-metre survey chain (a band of thin steel not unlike a measuring tape). The second man would wait, calling out "Chain!" when the 100 metres was reached, then catch up and the chainman would go again. Every half-kilometre, they would stop to count the trees visible through a prism from the centre point of a plot. Soil samples, core samples and a variety of other notations would be logged by the forester (Nixon) at each of these plots. It was a simple job, and a pleasant one.

They were working in the foothills of the Rocky Mountains. Bears had not been a problem—with the exception of a young black bear that had become something of a nuisance.

The men lived in two tin camp trailers parked side by side with a board sidewalk running lengthwise between them. Camp rules dictated that all garbage must be secured

in a pickup truck that had a metal canopy on the box specifically for that purpose. But someone had gotten lazy and "temporarily" stuffed a bag or two under the cook trailer.

"Something" had broken into the bags and scattered the contents half the length of the trailer. An argument ensued over who had stored the garbage there in the first place, and who, therefore, should have to crawl under the trailer and clean up the mess. The argument went on without a resolution until one night Nixon, scampering down the dark sidewalk between the trailers in his stocking feet, fell headlong over the young bear. The bear, apparently alarmed by the sound of Nixon's approach, had backed out from under the trailer directly into the man's path.

Alerted by Nixon's screams, one of the men had stuck his head out a window in time to see the poor animal—he guessed a two-year-old—make good its escape.

It had taken some time to assure Nix that he had sustained nothing more than a somewhat prolonged bout of hysteria, despite having prostrated himself on a live bear. The bear was never seen again.

Mags' legs were starting to cramp up. The narrow limb he was standing on did not offer much in the way of opportunities to vary his stance. He thought of easing himself into a sitting position on the limb, but the idea of dangling his legs in the direction of those terrible teeth dissuaded him. He looked upwards but the limbs above seemed too spindly to support his weight.

Higher yet, the crown of the surrounding old-growth timber was starting to glow in the rays of the dying sun.

Most of the trees were branchless up to about the 20-metre mark. That was how Mags had come to choose the stunted, deformed specimen he now took refuge in. Mags was built a little on the hefty side, and although he was in pretty good shape, there was no way he could climb the telephone-pole-like tree that Nixon had chosen.

Why was this happening? Bears, even grizzly bears, do not roam the country looking to feed on unsuspecting timber cruisers! Hiking through the bush day after day, Mags had long since lost any residual fear that such may be the case. It was a rare day when he failed to sight wild animals of some kind: moose, elk, beaver, a pair of pine martens frolicking along beside him like monkeys. One day he'd even caught a fleeting glimpse of a lynx. Having gotten in the habit of scrutinizing the ground for tracks, he'd come to realize that the area was also home to wolves and cougar as well as bears. Eventually, it had dawned on him that they saw him much more frequently than he saw them. Coming back on his own tracks at the end of a day, he'd realized that he and Nixon had been followed to work that morning by a pair of wolves—and then there was the grizzly...

Earlier, in the spring, the partners had cruised the right-of-way that fallers and bulldozer crews were scheduled to clear in the preparation of the main haul road. Day after day, Mags had noticed the tracks of what at first he took to be a very large black bear. By the time he realized that it had to be a grizzly, he was already comfortable with the idea of the animal's presence and constantly on the lookout for a glimpse of it. The area was not far from camp, and one evening he'd gone out on his own to

stake out an area where the tracks appeared most often. He'd been rewarded by a prolonged view of this magnificent silver-tip as it grazed its way over a hillside. Indeed, at one point, the viewing had almost turned into a visit as, sensing his presence, the bruin had stood upon its hind legs and squinted into the clump of deadfall Mags had chosen for a blind. Thrilled, if slightly spooked, by the encounter, Mags had then retreated to the security of the camp.

A week or two after that, the bulldozers were nearing the grizzly's territory. When one of the catskinners dropped by for coffee, Mags had told him about seeing the bear. The man had thanked him for the "warning." Two days later, the bear made the mistake of walking out of the bush onto a cutline and the catskinner shot it without even getting off his seat on the Caterpillar. The guy had then roared up to the cruiser camp in his pickup to brag about his kill and invite the men back to take a look at the thing. Three or four of them, including Mags, followed him back to where the bear lay. They gathered around the crumpled form, marvelling at its size and the length of its claws. The shooting was highly illegal, and the catskinner set to work immediately gouging a shallow pit in the cutline. He then bulldozed the carcass into this makeshift grave and covered it over without even salvaging the silver-tipped hide. Mags, sickened by what he viewed as a senseless atrocity, wanted to report it, but was told not to "make waves."

Mags had to sit down. The cramp in his right leg was threatening to turn into a full-blown charley horse, the consequences of which were not pleasant to think about.

He took a long, careful look around, and then eased himself as quietly as he could onto the limb. A small branch below offered a convenient, if somewhat tentative, footrest.

How long had he been up this tree? It seemed like hours since he'd seen the last of Nixon and the bear, but it was probably no more than 45 minutes. The sun had dropped beyond the horizon and the light was growing dim on the forest floor. A shiver went up Mags' spine at the thought of running into the bear in the dark, but it was obvious that sooner or later he was going to have to risk it. He'd been awake since 4:00 AM, and although sleep was the last thing on his mind at the moment, it wasn't hard to imagine himself dozing off eventually and falling out of the tree.

"Damn it…" he muttered, "what's the matter with this bear anyway?" They'd been down to the last plot of Nixon's compressed two-day program. It had gone well, especially this last leg through these high pines. The open forest floor made for easy hiking. The only dense bush was the intermittent runners of alders wandering through the pines. Mags had just come up against one of these when he heard Nixon call out "Chain!" He had selected a sample tree, drawn his increment hammer from his belt, and was down on one knee when Nixon arrived. He was about to let fly with the hammer when he was distracted by a rustling sound and the snap of a twig close by. He'd looked up to see the brown muzzle of a very large black bear emerge from the alders. "Look at the bea…" he'd started to say, but in that same instant it had become all too obvious that the bear had been looking for them!

With one brief "Woof!" it had launched out of the alders leaving no doubt in the men's minds that it was there on business. The next thing they knew they were running shoulder-to-shoulder in an impromptu steeplechase over fallen logs and through the shrubbery. Mags recalled, with a shudder, the sound of the animal's breath escaping in great huffs as it lunged after them. Mags would pass Nixon and Nixon would pass Mags, expecting any second to feel those awful jaws closing on the back of a leg! And then it was gone. The men had kept on running for several minutes without hearing the sounds of the bear in pursuit. Stolen glances behind confirmed that it had vanished like a hallucination. Gasping for breath, the men stared back in wide-eyed terror.

"What is with that bear?" Nixon had demanded, outraged at the blatant injustice of the attack. "Maybe it was bedded down in the alders, and we scared it?" Mags had guessed. "We scared it?" Nix countered. "It didn't look scared to me!" Mags had conceded the point, but as the two of them replayed the scene, they agreed that their approach had been relatively quiet. Perhaps they had walked in on the animal while it slumbered. They'd left the survey chain and other paraphernalia—including the clipboard with two days' work recorded on it—in the plot. They had to go back.

Taking empty pop cans and whatever other noisemakers they could find from the pockets of their cruise-vests, they had let off a great hullabaloo and started the march back. Whether they had now overdone the noise, or whether the bear just happened to be extra diabolical, Mags could not decide. The fact was that their counterattack had

only lasted about three paces before the bear popped up out of nowhere and the chase was on again!

This time, their terror was complete. Whereas their first retreat had been a reflex action fuelled by adrenalin, with no clear thoughts except to outrun those jaws, now their brains had been engaged on the subject as well as their legs. For one thing, it had dawned on both of them that a man cannot outrun an able-bodied bear. According to the experts, it was supposed to be a very bad idea to attempt to do so. Bears, the theory went, were only encouraged in their attack when a prospective victim turned tail and ran. Obviously their brains had been too busy to properly analyse the situation as they sprinted through the pine trees, but the mental picture they now had of their predicament was horrific! It was like running through a nightmare, desperately wishing to wake up before finding out how it would end. Panic fuelled their flight as they ran like they had never run before. And then, once again, they experienced the illusion—which they did not believe—of having outrun the animal. One moment it had been huffing along only a leap or two behind them; the next moment it had disappeared. The men stared into the forest, straining to hear over the sound of their own breathing. The snap of a twig or the flutter of a leaf would have set them off again, but all was still on the forest floor.

"Maybe it's got a kill back there in the alders?" Mags whispered.

"Then why doesn't it go back to it?" Nixon spat the words out in his own rasping whisper in between breaths.

"Maybe it has," Mags offered.

"No…" Nix sounded bitter. "It's out there."

There was a blowdown nearby, a giant birch tree pushed over in its old age by the wind. One or the other of them had gotten the idea that they should climb up onto it for a better view. There they had stood back-to-back a metre and a half off the ground, waiting to see what would happen next; nothing did. Minutes ticked by, each second of which weighed more than the last. They began speculating on where the bear might come from next. They even began imagining that they could put up a defence—Mags resolved that if it came to it, he would score as many blows as he could to the animal's head with the spike of the hammer he still held in his hand.

"Do you know," he'd said, looking around at the surrounding pines, "I don't think I could climb one of these even if I…"

"WOOF!" The bear popped up again less than a stone's throw away. Mags launched himself off the birch and hit the ground running while Nixon leapt, monkey-like, at one of the pines. Seconds later Mags spied his tree and clambered up through its branches without looking back. When he did, he could see Nixon, who had somehow managed to pull himself three or four body-lengths up the big pine. He held himself there in a desperate body press, arms wrapped as far around as he could reach, knees squeezing, face crushed into the bark. Below him sat the bear on its great rolling haunch, tongue lolling out of the side of its open mouth. It made a sort of mewing sound as it eyed its prey.

Noise! It occurred to Mags that a shout from him might be enough to draw the bear off—but he looked down

through the branches and decided that if he could climb this tree, so could the bear. In the greatest moment of cowardice he'd ever experienced, he'd gripped his hammer and remained silent. Nixon had begun to slip; then, whimpering, he had jacked himself back up. But it had been obvious to all, including the bear, that Nix would not be able to maintain his grip forever. When he started to slip again, the bear actually licked its lips. With fingers, face and knees leaving tracks in the rough bark, Nixon had slowly given in to gravity. About halfway down, he'd pushed himself away from the tree, letting himself go in a standing position. The bear, to Mags' inestimable joy and amazement, had jumped out of Nixon's way. When Nix hit the ground it was with spring-loaded heels as he bounded off in great leaps. The bear had then fallen in behind him at what seemed, by comparison, a leisurely canter.

That had been the last Mags had seen or heard of either of them.

It was time, Mags decided, to give up his roost. It was almost dark. He imagined the bear contentedly dining on what might be left of Nixon, then tried to put the image out of his mind. He slowly and methodically scanned his surroundings, straining his senses for any sign of movement in the gathering gloom. Somewhere high above him a nighthawk began its monotonous beeping, punctuated by the occasional silence and the thrumming sound given off by its wings as it pulled up out of a power dive.

Carefully Mags lowered himself onto the next limb. He tested the limb by degrees before committing his full weight to it. It seemed to hold. For a while he was at a loss,

attempting to identify the next foothold. The next limbs within reach were either dead or mere spindly stems.

He threw an arm around the broad tree trunk, preparing to view the side opposite the one he was standing on, and felt the yawning split in the wood. A dim recollection of a fork came back to him from his scramble up the tree. Lightning or some other deforming influence had long ago made two trees out of one, about two-thirds of the way up from its base. His next foothold would have to be the crotch where the two were still one. Craning around the trunk, he thought he could see where it was, but it was going to be a reach. How he had ever been able to make it up here was more than he could imagine, but what goes up…

Mags holstered his increment hammer in his belt and had begun to ease himself downward when he was suddenly electrified by a sound from below! His first impulse was to reverse directions and somehow regain the limb above. His second was to reach for his hammer. The result was that he was left dangling for a terror-stricken moment in uncertainty—as silently as he could. Near panic, he swung his left leg around the tree trunk. The toe of his boot seemed to find something solid under it. He kicked the boot into a firmer stance on the crotch while letting go of the limb to hug the tree trunk. Heart pounding, he drew his hammer prepared to do battle…with the surrounding silence.

He had not imagined the sound, of that he was certain. It was a sort of bawling sound, like something a sick calf might make—or a dying Nixon?

Mags was suddenly angry. He was ready to fight—ready to get it over with, whatever "it" might be.

When the sound came again, it set the hair on the back of his neck on end. He twisted his body in the direction the demonic wail had come from, and squinted into the shadows. Something was moving on the forest floor; something blacker than any shadow. It was moving slowly but steadily in Mags' direction. He gripped the steel handle of his increment hammer and waited. He could see it more clearly now, but it seemed small; much too small to be a…but it was a bear! A miniature one. Mags watched in wide-eyed wonder as the toddler came to within spitting distance of his tree. He held his breath as it sat down to scratch an ear with a hind foot. It sniffed the air curiously, then let out another of its plaintive calls. Getting no answer, it finally decided to move on, and Mags began breathing again.

So that was it! he thought, relief washing over him in waves. Somehow the old sow had become separated from her cub, and she'd been keeping tabs on him and Nixon until she could find it. He watched the roly-poly bundle of black until it faded into the dark. The moon came out. The cub had disappeared in an easterly direction—Nixon and the mother bear to the south. Mags left his tree and began a slow march in a wide westerly arc south. Eventually, he began calling Nixon's name in hoarse whispers. About the time he was ready to give up, he heard an answering call: "Up here!"

Perched in the crown of a spindly pine as it swayed gently to and fro, Nixon was not easy to talk down. Nor was it easy retracing their steps in the moonlight to where they had left their tools and clipboard. It helped that they now understood why the concerned mother had a problem with

them being there. It terrified them to think that she might still be looking for the cub. They didn't breathe easy again until they made it back to the sanctuary of their pickup truck. Even the next day, hiking in to the waterfall on their much-deserved day off, Mags couldn't help imagining bears waiting in ambush at every bend in the trail.

Diary of a "Towerman"

He was there again, sitting calmly in the middle of the clearing, watching her. She pretended not to notice, and continued splitting wood. He seemed to be waiting for something; waiting for her to wander too far from the safety of the cabin; waiting for her to put down the axe and turn her back on him...what did he want?

The wood was dry and split easily. There was something satisfying, almost pleasurable, about driving an axe through a round of pine, splitting it in two, in one whack! Stooping to pick up one of the halves, she stole a glance in his direction. No change. She brought the axe down hard, too hard, sending the quarter-rounds flying and burying the blade of the axe head in the chopping block.

Maybe she should report him. How long had he been hanging around? A week? Ten days? He wasn't there every day—it had to be at least two weeks since she'd first seen him wander through the clearing.

She'd intended on keeping a daily journal, a record of her solitary summer in the tower. She had imagined logging her "journey into self," mapping her thoughts as evidence of the dawning awareness she'd experience with the passing of each day and night alone. It would be a defence against the inevitable loneliness, as well as a unique record of the challenges that came with the job: The Diary of a Towerman.

"Towerman"—there had been long entries in the journal on the subject of "de-genderfying" such terms. She resented that the government, and whoever it was who made an issue of these things, seemed to feel that they were doing it on her behalf. It implied that she, and others like her, were actually doing what they were doing to attain some sort of equality with men—Tower-Woman, Mail-Woman, Super-Woman!

Roberta had never felt that she needed to attain equality with anyone. She recognized that there were women who were subjected to inequality, confined to lives bound by "lesser-than" status culturally, economically, even politically, but so were men! Equality was something one had to possess within oneself. If it didn't exist there, it could not be achieved by stamping a label on the outer shell.

The entries in the journal had dwindled to the mundane: "Rained again today—all day." "May take a hike later—still wet." "Guys made it in with the groceries—said road is really bad." "Hasn't rained for a few days now—fire hazard still extremely low." Eventually she had put the journal away. It

was simply too depressing chronicling the nothingness that dominated her days.

Roberta picked up the stove wood scattered around the chopping block, cradling the load in the crook of her arm, and headed for the cabin. The cabin, painted the same dreary off-white colour inside and out, was typical government issue, in Roberta's opinion. It lacked soul. The essentials were laid out counter-clockwise, as if dictated from a list: countertop and cupboards, one window, curtain in the partition (marking the entrance to the cave-like bedroom), wood stove and wood-box, row of coat hooks running the length of the wall, back to the doorway.

Roberta deposited her load in the wood-box and, brushing herself off, crossed the room to look out the window. He was gone—or at least had moved out of view. It would be out of character for him to come much closer to the cabin. Up until now, he seemed to have confined himself to the clearing. Roberta had made a point of circling the cabin in search of tracks, in case he happened to be coming closer under cover of night (she had imagined him sneaking up to look in the window), but had found no evidence that such might be the case.

She had a gun, her father's old Lee Enfield .303 rifle, leaning against a back corner of the closet. Her father had insisted. "You just never know," he'd said, and also insisted on paying for the weapon to be registered in her name, which was a legal requirement. Technically she was not quite legal yet, in the eyes of her superiors, as she did not have the special firearms certificate required if one were to handle firearms in the course of one's duty with the department. So she kept the old thing out of sight in the closet in case the

brass should happen by, on one of their rare excursions out of the office. It was hard to imagine what kind of hullabaloo would be raised if she should actually use the thing.

Roberta had worked as a tree-planter to help put herself through college. For three summers she had tramped over all kinds of terrain kicking seedlings into the ground for a nickel apiece, or sometimes more if she hired on with the right contractor. It had been tough work but she had enjoyed living in the bush. Not a day went by when she didn't see some kind of wildlife, including bears.

Her father had insisted on sending the old rifle along then too, even though it hadn't yet been registered. She'd left it in the tent—it was simply too heavy to pack. Some of the other planters carried pepper spray or wore "bearbells," but Roberta never had. The bears, she found, went about their business and left others to go about theirs, as long as you didn't stumble onto one with cubs, or onto a kill. The point was that if you kept your wits about you, observing what was going on around you, you should not need a gun to co-exist with bears.

The department didn't see it quite like that. They tended to categorize bears into exceptions dubbed "problem bears." A young grizzly had once wandered into a camping area where she and some friends were staying. They had seen nothing alarming in the creature's behaviour, as it sniffed them out and casually moved on. They had been quite thrilled to get pictures of it, from a distance. But some other campers had freaked out and reported the bear's presence to the park ranger, who had shot it! It was not a "problem bear." It probably wouldn't have become a problem bear—unless someone had started feeding it, or

wounded it or left food and garbage laying around for it to start feeding itself.

The "problem ranger," who looked to be about Roberta's age and who probably had even less experience with bears than her, seemed to suffer from some sort of hero-complex. He'd even posed for pictures with the carcass, much to the delight of the fools who had reported seeing the animal in the campsite. What was the matter with these people? Most tourists who travelled or camped in the back country did so with the express hope of actually seeing a bear.

But the bear in the clearing was not playing by the rules. He'd been hanging around too long. He'd been exhibiting behaviour that...well, just didn't make sense. Why sit out there in plain view less than 100 metres from the cabin, watching her as if...as if what? That was the question: What did this bear want?

If Roberta could figure out the answer to that question, she would know whether or not to report it to the guys.

In the meantime, she couldn't even discuss it with them. She could just imagine their response. Whatever she said about the bear would sound like she was scared of it. They'd either tease her—"don't let the bears get you!"—or leap to her rescue and do away with it. So far the animal had done nothing wrong—it was just a feeling Roberta had—maybe she was scared—so what?

It was time to climb the tower and report in. She reached down and removed the stick of kindling with which she'd propped the window open that morning—on warm days the cabin grew stuffy. She slid the window closed and latched it, feeling a little silly about doing so—but this bear...

There were a variety of firetowers in this part of the country, and Roberta had drawn her least favourite. Some were perched high in the mountains. She'd visited one located at such an altitude that no tower was required. The cupola was mounted on the roof of the cabin and accessed by a ladder fixed to an inside wall.

Bald Mountain Tower was aptly named except that it wasn't on a mountain at all, but on a scruffy ridge in the foothills—which was almost bald. Its decadent stand of poplars had suffered extensive blowdowns in what must have been hurricane-force winds. The cabin and tower had been constructed on the edge of the resulting clearing, which was now littered with windfall, rotting logs and scrub-brush.

Roberta liked the long climb up the metal ladder to the trap door of the cupola. The view, while it didn't offer the spectacular mountain-scape she'd dreamed of, was still impressive. She could see for miles in every direction—which was the purpose of a forestry tower. Thus far, the season had not provided much danger of forest fires. Nevertheless, she dutifully scanned the hills unfolding in all directions and went through the routine conversation on the radio. She learned that her supply truck was scheduled to arrive sometime the following morning—which, though she hated to admit it, was welcome news. To actually sit across the table conversing with someone, anyone, was a luxury she'd begun craving.

It would probably be Bill, which would be a disappointment. Bill called her "Bert," which was either supposed to be some kind of compliment or funny—Roberta couldn't decide. Bill would have all sorts of departmental gossip to share concerning the latest postings, hirings, firings, back-stabbings

and rumours of cutbacks, none of which interested Roberta in the least. Bill was all right, but she yearned for conversation on something other than forestry.

Roberta found herself scrutinizing the ground below for signs of the bear. When he'd first wandered into the clearing, she'd been quite happy to see him—it was the first bear she'd sighted since her arrival. Deer were common visitors on Bald Mountain; a cow and calf moose wandered into view occasionally. As far as black bears go, this was a big one, certainly the biggest Roberta had ever seen. It was his size that led her to believe he was a male, as she watched him picking his way through the clearing, ripping open rotting logs and digging up anthills. She'd assumed she'd seen the last of him when, finally, he waddled out of sight over the southern brow of the ridge.

So, three or four days later, she'd been quite surprised to find he was back—quite unsettled to discover him sitting in the clearing staring at the cabin. She'd laughed it off, the first time. Two days later, when it happened again, she'd yelled at him, waving her arms in the air, mocking him—until he had shown no sign of fear, and doubt had crept into Roberta's mind concerning the big bear's intentions.

Still, he'd done nothing more threatening than ignore her—which was threatening enough, especially when he'd persisted in fearlessly repeating his visits. Lunchtime came, but Roberta didn't feel like firing up the wood stove just to cook something. She made do with tea and rye-crisp, boiling the water for the tea on her little primus stove. Neither did she feel like cooking supper. Setting out the molasses to go with the rye-crisp and waiting for the water to boil, Roberta began questioning herself on the subject of appetite.

When was the last time she'd actually gone all out and fixed herself a hot meal? She couldn't remember. Could this be a sign of depression?

Roberta had been warned that the solitary life wasn't for everyone. It was said that the real work of being a towerman, or a lighthouse keeper, was living with oneself. But she'd decided that she was all right with herself, or all right enough to put up with her own company for the summer. The rains had gotten her down—as they would anyone. True, she had given up on her journal, and her reading had dwindled, but...

The job was probably taking its toll, she decided, and resolved that she would have to take evasive action. Bill would be here in the morning with a fresh grocery order and all the delicacies that went with it. Tomorrow would be a feast day— maybe she would start by fixing Bill a lunch to remember! There was always some fresh meat included in the order, which had to be used right away since she had no refrigeration. Steak and potatoes? Spaghetti and meatballs? Well, she didn't need to plan the menu in advance. She would simply spin off of whatever came with the order. It would be fun. She began thinking of food in general, some of her favourite examples of her mom's cooking: Yorkshire pudding, scalloped potatoes, Hungarian goulash. Since she had moved out on her own, Roberta had moved in her own culinary directions, not eating nearly as much meat as her parents. Corn fritters, lentil soup, an endless variety of salads—salads were one thing she missed out here—a garden! The idea brought a smile as she considered it. A spot out back of the woodpile would be perfect. It was still early enough in the summer to put in a little salad garden: some radishes, lettuce, parsley.

She thought of trying to track Bill down on the radio to get him to pick up the seeds for her, and maybe a few plants. But there was no point; Bill would probably already be on the road, staying overnight at one of the other towers en route. Tomorrow would be soon enough to place the order. He'd bring it out the following week, and in the meantime she could get to work with the shovel preparing the plot.

It was getting dark, which at this time of year meant it must be quite late. Roberta didn't feel sleepy, but neither did she feel like lighting the lantern to read or to fix another pot of tea. She pushed through the curtains into the stale, blind dark that was the bedroom. (The partition had been put in as an afterthought, too late to provide the bedroom with a window.) Roberta found it claustrophobic. She lay on her back, staring into the absolute dark and imagining her little salad garden, and eventually drifted into dreamless sleep.

She awoke with a start, to the sound of...glass breaking? The window in the other room was being smashed to pieces! A wheezing snort, or grunt—the bear! The bear was breaking into the cabin through the window!

Roberta had rolled out of bed and was crouched on the floor fighting panic with every breath. She needed to get out—escape the cabin—make for the tower...but the escape route led through the other room. Was the bear now inside the cabin? More glass breaking; the grunts were escalating to a roar—which reverberated through Roberta's entire being, wilting her plan of attack...counterattack...was she actually under attack?

The gun! She pawed through the coats and jeans and shirts and finally had the rifle in her hands. The bullets?

She'd brought at least three bullets with her—they were in the front pocket of her pack, which she started rifling through while remembering: the junk drawer. She'd taken the bullets from the pack and tossed them into the…third drawer from the door—basically, in the middle of the room with the roaring bear in it. Each new utterance from the bear brought a reflex response from Roberta to scream, though the only sounds she actually allowed to escape were involuntary whimpers, as she peered from the dark bedroom through a slit in the curtain.

There was a little more light in the other room, enough for her to see that the bear was still at the window. She fought an impulse to simply bolt through the room to the door. Light…she had a flashlight somewhere on the floor, next to her bed—there! Would the light alert the bear to her hiding place? It would blind the bear to all but itself, she decided, and snapped it on, peeking through the slit in the curtain. The bear, as it lunged forward clawing at anything within reach, or pulled back bulging against the surrounding window frame, was stuck! Could that be?

Quailing before the volume of the now-continuous roaring, Roberta studied the spectacle filling the shaky circle of light. The bear took no notice of the light as it flailed away, forward, then back—it really was stuck! For now…

"Oh, god…" Roberta whimpered, shifting the light to the junk drawer only half a room away from the enraged burglar!

She knew she was going to go for it before she'd truly even considered the question. "Oh, god…" she repeated as she stepped through the curtain, keeping the flashlight on the bear as it bucked and roared trying to tear itself free. She

flashed the light on the drawer and yanked it open—wrong drawer. She clawed at the next, spilling the light into it as she tore the top layer of junk out onto the floor. There! There was a bullet, and a second; she jabbed around for the third which she knew had to be there—right at the back! Juggling the flashlight, rifle and shells, she started to insert the first bullet and dropped it. It spun off into the dark to clatter into the junk on the floor. Concentrating on the mechanics of the task, she willed her shaking hands to insert the next bullet into the slot, successfully, and then the next...

The bear had taken no notice of her as she moved into the room. It leaned forward, as she turned the light back in the direction of the window. It then seemed to lunge skyward, more like some great sea lion than the four-legged predator it was.

Roberta fired. She jacked the other shell into the chamber and pulled the trigger again. Again the flare and retort slammed into her senses like a massive electric shock. The bear slumped forward in the shaking light of the flashlight, and was still...a kill shot.

"If you ever do have to shoot a bear," her father always said, "don't even think of handling it, or turning your back on it till you're sure it is dead."

She aimed the light at the floor, picked the bullet out of the junk...she was shaking too hard now to get the bullet to stay still. She forced her hand against the gun, making her fingers perform the task. She aimed carefully at the centre of the big head. The bullet accomplished its purpose. The bear was dead.

Roberta's legs were refusing to support her weight. She sank slowly to a sitting position, leaning on the butt of the

gun, holding the light on the blood and black hide, as if the light was all that was keeping the thing there. The bear was dead…its head had twisted almost sideways as the animal slumped forward. Roberta could see its face, frozen in an anguished mask, its grizzled muzzle…its teeth—the rows of teeth, one upper and one lower, were almost nonexistent. Some were broken off, some were rotted out all together. So that was it! An old bear, gone in the teeth; no longer able to fend for itself properly, the seductive scents of Roberta's larder had proven too much to resist.

For a long time Roberta sat on the floor before the old bear, replaying the whole thing through in her mind. Suddenly she felt cold, chilled right through to the core. She rose, shivering, and returned to her bed where she wrapped herself in a blanket and stared into the dark…

She'd killed a bear.

The sun had been up for a while by the time she awoke. She felt stiff, like she had overdone it pushing weights in the gym. She pushed through the curtain. The bear lay draped over the windowsill in a grotesque heap. A pool of blood had congealed into a black scum on the floor in front of the window. It had apparently cut itself coming through the window; the wall was streaked with blood where the furry arms had flailed in the terrible attempts to free itself. Roberta was numb. She realized that she needed to eat something, but she also realized that that would be out of the question until this, this mess, was cleaned up.

Moving closer, she began studying the position of the carcass. It was well and truly stuck. It looked as though the poor old thing had reached through with its front legs and head, and once through had set its shoulders and forelegs in such a way that they simply did not fit back through the opening. As to hauling the rest of its bulk on into the cabin, Roberta could see that that had been out of the question. The bear's paunch could never have been compressed to the size of the opening.

But how to remove the body? Roberta lifted a bloody front leg and pried it upwards and across the body, attempting to tuck the elbow in enough to get it past the window frame. But it was hopeless. The head was heavy, too heavy to lift even if she had been successful in forcing a leg through. Roberta looked at the sleeves and front of her sweatshirt, now smeared with blood—it probably wouldn't come out—and knew what she had to do. To remove the bear from the window, she'd have to chop it in half.

It wasn't such a big deal, really. She'd helped her dad gut, skin and quarter deer. This was no different, really, and it had to be done. She went out to the chopping block, lingering in the fresh air and morning sunshine, before returning with the axe. She'd have to sever the spine just back of the shoulders, which would probably take no more than three or four good whacks…which would leave the hide. She'd need her good knife; the guts would probably spill into the cabin…

She couldn't do it.

She was just at the point of admitting this to herself when she heard the truck. Usually she would have heard it

labouring up the hill, but this morning she was distracted. The truck was already pulling up outside.

Roberta let the axe slip to rest on the floor, leaned against the counter and waited.

"Hey, Bert…?" Bill was probably gazing up to see if she was in the tower.

"In here…" she called back.

"How ya doin', to…day…?" Bill's expression, as he surveyed the bloodied young woman and the axe she had obviously just killed a bear with, was one Roberta would cherish.

"Well actually, Billy, I could use a little help chopping this bear in half!" With that, Roberta began to laugh. She laughed at "Billy," at the blood, at the poor old bear, and she laughed at the fact that she was laughing.

Chopping the bear in half proved not to be necessary as, with Bill's help, she was able to compress the left leg into the body far enough to force it back through the window. After that it was a simple, if messy, task pushing the head, and finally the right leg back through the window. The blood was harder to get rid of, but when that had been accomplished, Roberta insisted on making lunch—the biggest, fattest, spiciest, leafiest salad Bill had ever seen. For once he did not recite all the latest Forestry squabbles, but seemed content with replays of Roberta shooting the bear.

She made him write down the order for seeds and bedding plants, which had grown to include some flowers—why not?

That night, she sat up late by the light of the lantern entering the story of the break-in in her journal.

Ghosts

A colder, more lonesome and frozen place to spend eternity could not exist on the face of the earth. The graves themselves gave new meaning to the phrase "as cold as the grave," for the bodies they contained lay beneath the permafrost. It was not difficult to imagine men dying here. Indeed, considering the dark months when the snows and dagger-like winds of winter enveloped the landscape, it would be difficult to imagine men surviving here. This island in the High Arctic might as well be on another planet. Without the umbilical cord of modern technology that sustained them, Paul knew that he and his employers would themselves become prime candidates for eternal residency.

And yet, there was a time when another race of men had called this land home. There was a people who had

known the secret life of this place—where it hid its food, where it offered shelter, when it was willing to share its comforts. These people had also known that this land was unforgiving in its judgement of the vain and foolish. They had known and respected the death-dealing nature of their land just as they had revered its willingness to support life. Descendants of this race still dwelt in remote pockets of this vast territory, but knowledge of many of its life-giving secrets had been lost.

Elias Angatkot was the only member of this party of men now huddled over these forsaken graves who had descended from the ancient peoples. Paul was the only other member of the party who was not directly connected to some related department of anthropology, medicine or history in one or the other of participating universities.

The men who lay beneath the permafrost had not been members of the northern race either—although they had been among the first foreigners to penetrate this mysterious and foreboding space. Unravelling the enigma of their deaths and the fate of the rest of their party was the subject of the dig now in progress.

Paul was a freelance cinematographer whose job was to record on film every minute aspect of the exhumation and autopsy. The work had been tedious. One of Paul's first tasks was to establish the location exactly as it had appeared before being discovered. These pictures would not only portray the dwelling place of these abandoned souls, but would also help in its restoration. It was a condition of the permit the scientists had received that they would replace the human remains and the rocks that covered them in the exact order that they had found them. The object agreed

upon was to leave no evidence that anyone had ever disturbed this vault of human misery.

While it was true that the hours seemed to pass quickly, the same could not be said for the days. Perhaps it was the absence of true night. This far north, the sun didn't really set so much as tease the horizon. The result was an intermittent period of relative twilight signifying the passing of another mark on the calendar.

Paul was not complaining. The business he was in tended to be slow in winter, and the preceding winter had been even slower than usual. He was grateful for the work, and despite the glamour commonly associated with film, he was used to the tedious reality of his chosen profession. This particular contract offered an element of intrigue that went well beyond many that he encountered.

He had recently spent a similar number of days on an oil pipeline shooting "intelligent pigs." A pig, in pipeline jargon, was a brush of sorts that resembled a metallic hedgehog. An intelligent pig was one loaded with electronic sensors to record certain aspects of the interior of the pipe as it brushed its way through the line. There are limits to the number of angles any shooter could find to flatter a greasy crud-encrusted pig no matter how intelligent the creature is reputed to be.

However tedious the hours spent filming yet another layer of rocks, as they were carefully stripped off the grave and painstakingly numbered, the promise of the visuals waiting to be revealed held Paul's professional interest.

Perhaps it was the isolation he found disturbing. The seemingly infinite nothingness surrounding them did little to relieve the intimate familiarity of the tents they worked

and lived in. Hour after hour, day after day as they moved in and out of each other's way, a certain degree of mutual contempt for each other's existence should be expected. Maybe he just needed a little privacy.

It was evening. Having logged and filed the results of the day's work, Paul was technically on his own time. He did not feel sleepy. A stiff breeze blowing out of the west had temporarily tamed the clouds of mosquitos that usually plagued their days. Donning his parka and gloves, Paul slipped away from camp and headed out over the tundra facing the breeze. The undulating landscape was ribbed here and there by craggy ridges of solid rock. The stony tundra floor was embroidered by flowers riotous in their colours. Lichens and mosses decorated the stones in colours only slightly subdued by the brilliance of the flowers. Looking back, Paul saw that the camp was lost from view, swallowed up in the undulations of the land. It was satisfying to think that he was alone. Would they be alarmed to find him missing? Maybe he should have told someone he was going.

But going where? A stroll out onto the tundra could hardly be construed as a leave of absence. It was technically impossible to absent oneself from the only habitation to exist for hundreds of miles. In any case, he certainly had a right to a few moments alone...except that he did not feel alone.

He walked on, no longer facing directly into the wind. Instead, he angled off to his right, following a faint path that led up onto a nearby crag. There he sat down upon a giant boulder. Now even the sound of the camp generator was lost to him, erased by the persistent wind.

No single landmark stood out from the rest. In 360 degrees there was no single feature to fix one's eye upon: no river, no mountain, no obvious trail. East, west, south—it was all virtually directionless, except for the wind—and the sun hanging in the north at this time of the day, or rather night. A shiver went down Paul's spine at the thought of being lost out here…alone out here. And yet, once again he did not feel that he was alone. On the contrary, he had the sensation that he was being watched—which was stupid because he could see for miles in every direction and nobody was out there. Nothing moved over the trackless tundra laid out before him. No sound interrupted the moaning of the steady wind and yet…

Paul shrugged off the unwelcome feeling. He fixed his mind, as he was in the habit of doing at this time of day, on his home. He missed his wife and young son. They were used to being away from each other for intermittent periods of time, sacrificed to the demands of his work. But somehow this was different. Somehow this place, devoid of everything he and his family had ever shared, intensified the loneliness…

"You should not be out here alone."

Spinning toward the sound of the voice, Paul found Elias Angatkot standing next to the boulder. "You scared the life out of me!"

"Sorry," Elias said.

"Why shouldn't I be out here?"

"It's not safe," Elias said, gazing out over the tundra.

Paul was about to ask why not, but instead asked Elias if he'd been watching him.

"No," Elias said. "I saw when you left—but I came out just now to check where you were gone."

"What do you mean, it's not safe?" Paul demanded.

"It's just not," Elias shrugged. Elias, who looked to be in his mid-50s, had been introduced as a guide/consultant. He carried a rifle slung over one shoulder—more for effect than any utilitarian purpose, in Paul's view.

"Bears?" Paul asked.

"Maybe," said Elias.

"What else could be out here?"

"Lots of stuff," Elias said, and began rolling himself a cigarette.

"Stuff like what?"

Elias gave a low whistle before lighting the cigarette. A moment later, his dog Nanuk wandered into view on the tundra below them. Nanuk, a large dog by any standards, was one-quarter wolf according to Elias. The animal was moulting. Woolly chunks of fur littered the camp. The dog mostly kept to itself, shunning whatever attentions the staff offered it. Even with Elias, Nanuk showed no obvious signs of overt doggy affection, although it did seem to obey without question its master's subtle commands. The men watched the dog, now trotting toward them.

"Spirits…" Elias said.

Paul had forgotten his question. "Spirits?"

"Everything out here has a spirit, even the rocks and the wind—but there are other spirits too…and the Pinailat."

"Which are?" Paul prompted.

Elias went on to describe the giants of the old legends. "But they're not as dangerous as the little people—if you

see the little people you must not look at them or they will lead you to your death."

"Really," Paul said. "What happened to the pot of gold at the end of the rainbow?"

"Different little people."

Paul almost laughed, but Elias didn't seem to be joking. "So, have you actually seen these little people?"

"Obviously not," said Elias. "I'm still alive—but my cousin saw them once."

"And he's dead, I take it?"

"No. When he saw that they were there he covered up his eyes and refused to go with them; he knew what to do, do you see?"

"Right." Again Paul felt that it would be impolite to laugh.

They started back. Nanuk trotted on ahead.

"He's a good bear dog," Elias volunteered. "Nanuk means 'bear.' It's not really his name, it's just what he is—a nanuk dog."

"I see," said Paul.

"It's like me," Elias went on. "My name is not really Angatkot. Angatkot means medicine man—you would say shaman or witch."

"So you're a medicine man?"

"No, my father was; he was well known for it. So I got known as 'Elias that Medicine Man's son'—Elias Angatkot."

"You weren't interested in taking it up?"

Elias shook his head. "It's something that is given to you, but then you go through tests of hunger and cold and things like that—but he told me many things about the spirits and medicines."

Elias fell silent as they neared camp. Paul thanked him for the chat and they parted. As he drifted off to sleep, Paul pondered the eerie feeling he'd had out on the tundra. He dreamt of leprechauns.

Excitement had been building in the camp. The deeper the grave grew, the more excited everyone got. By the time the rough-hewn wood of the coffin lid came into view, some people were almost giddy. The coffin was not rectangular but angled in the old-fashioned box-ended dia-mond shape. As the moment drew near when the lid was to be removed, the entire population of the camp gathered around the open grave—except Elias, Paul noted, as he panned the eager faces with his camera.

One by one the nails, resembling horseshoe nails, were extracted from the ancient wood. The wood itself did not look its age. From what Paul had gathered from the ongo-ing discussions around him, this coffin had been in the ground for over 150 years. He would have imagined that it would have disintegrated to nothing but a mere residue collapsed around its skeletal contents. But encased as it was in the permafrost, the opposite was true. The wood, though aged, still held its integral strength. What would the body, or presumably the skeleton, look like?

The answer, as the lid finally lifted free, was not immedi-ately forthcoming. The interior of the coffin was solid ice. According to the commentary from the assembled personnel,

that was not unexpected. A methodology to deal with this jacket of ice surrounding the remains was already in place. Kettles containing water were set to boil. When the first steaming kettle was brought forth the eager faces again rimmed the grave. As the stream of hot water cleared the frosted surface of the ice, an audible gasp escaped the lips of the gallery. There, leering up at them from its tomb of ice, was a human face! Even through the ice the expression was all too plain. Pain, undiminished by a century and a half of "resting in peace" seemed to emanate from this tortured being like a muted scream.

The next in an innumerable number of kettles was brought on and the slow process of exhuming the man from the ice began. The water, or "soup" as the scientists referred to it, once it had cooled, was ladled off into buckets.

Paul, having recorded the process on film, took a lunch break while the slow but steady erosion took place. In the cook tent he took a seat next to Elias, who sat hunched over a cup of coffee. "You're missing the show," Paul said affably.

"Yes…" said Elias quietly.

"It's pretty amazing," Paul said, putting his lunch out on the table. "The guy looks like he was planted yesterday."

"Mmmm…" said Elias.

"You're not interested?"

"It's not right to disturb the dead," Elias said moodily.

"Not usually," Paul agreed thoughtfully. "But considering that the guy died 150 years ago, I doubt his family will object."

"It's not right." Elias was adamant.

Paul munched on his sandwich pondering the man's squeamishness. "It's not like they're doing it for kicks."

Elias did not respond.

"I mean, if they can find out how he died, or why he died here in particular—there's lots of things they can learn from this."

Elias looked unconvinced.

"Why not find out what they can?"

"They might find out it's not right to disturb the dead."

"I don't understand," said Paul. His tone seemed to dismiss Elias's reticence as mere superstition.

"Maybe this guy was taken by the little people," Elias said. He sounded reluctant to get into it, but resigned. "He might not have completed his journey into the spirit world."

"So…?" Paul prompted.

"If you disturb him, you might end up taking his place."

"And why is that?" Paul asked.

"The power of death could still be on him."

An idea crept unbidden into Paul's mind: little people, the power of death still on him. The scientists in camp had speculated that the men in the graves could have been taken by some unknown flu bug, or a smallpox outbreak, or diptheria or any number of infectious possibilities. Gloves and masks were to be distributed as the corpse emerged from the ice. What if Elias was talking about just such a possibility in the only terminology that would have been known to his father the medicine man? "Are you talking about a disease?"

"Maybe…" Elias said, shrugging, "but there's lots of ways to die."

The rest of the lunch break passed in thoughtful silence.

Camp life had become just that much more cramped with the arrival of the body, lifted carefully from the grave. Laid out on a makeshift operating table in one of the tents, the man did not look any less miserable than he had through the ice. The partial dehydration of his facial tissues accented the grimace of the death mask; his lips were drawn back as if to emit an audible expression of the anguish written in the taut lines of the face. He wore the short woolen jacket, cotton shirt and duck-canvas trousers indicative of the rank of "chief petty officer" according to the experts in attendance. His bony feet were bare—his boots and stockings probably having been salvaged for a surviving member of the party. Paul, as he made ready to record the man's portrait on film, had been seized by an absurd impulse to cover the poor fellow with a blanket. Every nuance of this being, from the expression on his face to his livid toes, seemed to cry out for warmth.

Strangely, Paul had not really been bothered by the gore of the evisceration. He'd filmed it all, from the analysis of the stomach contents to the extraction of tissue samples from the brain. Aside from the almost palpable pain the corpse seemed to emit in waves, it had only one characteristic that tended to get on Paul's nerves. Some unknown quirk of the elements had blackened the tip of the man's

nose. The eyes, only partially open, were also black. The result, especially when viewed from the foot of the table, was a face within a face. The round black nose flanked by the two elliptical caverns seemed to leap out at Paul visually. He would look up from his work to find this impish incarnation staring at him.

What he regarded at first as a mere curiosity had eventually become something of a minor aggravation. It was time, he decided, to get out of the morgue.

It was a nice day—windy but not cold. The past days had been busy, everyone absorbed in the various tasks related to the man whose clothing and vital organs now wandered around the camp. At each station the different academic disciplines gathered what information they could. New revelations were discovered, old theories confirmed or contradicted, as the facts of the case began to emerge. Paul, having filmed most parts of the process in action, was for the moment caught up with his shot list. He thought of checking with Elias, who would be at his post in the cook tent. But since Paul's purpose would be to dissuade the man from following him out of camp, rather than inviting him along, Paul decided that it would be simpler to just slip away.

Elias was still quite moody on the subject of grave-robbing. Paul had tried to get him to go and take a look at the chief petty officer, thinking it would help dispel the man's superstitious notions, but Elias had refused to consider the idea.

A flock of birds exploded out of the thatch of the tundra floor, as if out of the ground. They landed 100 yards on, only to disappear again into the thatch. As Paul continued

on, they would burst into view and disappear again, like a feathered wave.

Without really realizing it, Paul had been headed back to his boulder. His feet had found the faint path leading up onto the crag. He paused to look back in the direction of the camp, gratified that he could neither see nor hear any trace of it. He pushed back the hood of his parka to let the wind wash over his mind. It felt good to be out of the squalor of the camp, to fix his eyes on the infinity of earth and sky surrounding him and to think of nothing.

He had to admit that this land had a certain haunting beauty. If only there just wasn't so much of it—on the other hand, its immensity was obviously one of the keys to its grandeur. And as immense as it was, and as frightening as its endless expanse, there was also something fragile about it. As he wandered along the path, Paul began to speculate on the age of the pathetically stunted trees surrounding him. No more than mere shrubbery, he guessed that they had taken decades, perhaps centuries, to get as far as they had.

Something was wrong. Something was out of place. A sound, a voice fleeting in the wind. Had he imagined it? No, there it was again. A murmur, almost a moan…

The hair stood up on the back of Paul's neck. He almost bolted back in the direction of the camp but held his ground, listening. There! The sound seemed to be coming from some point ahead of him. He had not quite topped the crag. He moved forward as silently as he could, adrenalin pumping, eyes darting in one direction, then the next, as the shrubbery bobbed here and there in the wind.

Slowly, the top of the crag came into view, and with it Paul's boulder—and with that, Elias sitting atop the boulder!

His back was to Paul; he was looking skyward. As Paul watched, Elias let out one of the long murmured sentences that had caught Paul's ear, then lowered his eyes and lapsed into silence. It was as if he was praying. Paul smiled to himself: payback time! Moving as soundlessly as he could, trying not to snag a twig or dislodge a stone, Paul slowly edged up behind the man on the boulder.

"Hey there, Elias! Whaddaya up to?"

But the outburst did not have the desired effect—it seemed to have no effect at all. Elias, absorbed in his thoughts or meditations, simply continued to gaze out over the tundra. Several moments passed before he heaved a sigh and said, "You should not come out here alone."

Paul, miffed at having failed to startle the man and a little embarrassed at having attempted to do so, countered by asking Elias why it was all right for him to come out here alone.

"I didn't," Elias said. Assuming Elias was referring to his dog, which seemed to be absent, Paul asked where the animal was.

"I seen a bear track," said Elias, still gazing off into the distance. "He's checkin' it out."

"Where?"

"Out there."

Paul scanned the empty wasteland before them, but saw nothing. "Whaddaya mean, checking it out?"

"To see where the bear has went, and check where it will go."

"So you're just sitting here waiting for Nanuk to come back and tell you what the bear's plans are?" Paul said facetiously.

"Yes," Elias said.

"And how's he going to do that?"

"When I see what direction the dog comes from, I'll know if the bear was just passing by here or if it's checking out our camp."

"Aren't you afraid the bear will have the dog for lunch?"

"No, I'm afraid it will have you for lunch—if you keep coming out here."

Paul felt his temper rise. He felt like telling Elias to give it up. The man's ridiculously morbid outlook and folksy superstitions were getting annoying. Did he feel he needed to keep up this primitive wiseman act to justify his position in the camp? Why couldn't he do a primitive standup comic instead? But Paul said nothing. He knew it was silly to let the guy get to him like this—they weren't going to be cooped up here forever, even if it was starting to feel like it.

The verdict was in: 128 men had sailed from England in search of the fabled Northwest Passage, never to be heard from again. The expedition had not been put together on a shoestring. On the contrary, it had been one of the most highly funded projects of its kind. Records of the day showed that it had been provisioned with the most up-to-date equipment and supplies science had to offer. Here, it seemed, was the key to its downfall.

One of the innovations science had had to offer the ill-fated enterprise was a new process known as canning. The

hold of the ship had been crammed with more than enough canned meat to see its company through the Northwest Passage and back again. But science had not as yet caught up with the death-dealing properties of the lead used to seal the cans.

The autopsy had revealed lethal levels of this metal in the remains of the chief petty officer. That, in the opinion of the scientists in camp, could also account for a second mystery involving the behaviour of the members of the expedition who had carried on from the burial site. A lifeboat from their ship had been found far inland, laden with books and a variety of other items deemed to be as useless as the boat would have been in that location. The sanity of those responsible for this had already come into question. Insanity has been recognized as one of the symptoms of lead poisoning. Starvation was also cited as a contributing factor in the chief petty officer's death. Had the expedition members come to suspect the tainted nature of their canned meat, and decided to abandon it? Further examination of the pages of history showed that subsequent to the ship's departure, a scandal had erupted involving the true nature of "the meat." Political corruption had resulted in the contractor responsible for processing the meat "cutting corners." It was understood that a significant number of the cans contained nothing more than offal and barnyard waste.

Cause of death: exposure.

Contributing factors: lead poisoning and corporate greed.

At least, that would have been how Paul would have written up the consensus evolving around him. Scientists,

as a matter of principle, usually fail to agree on anything but the empirical evidence before them. Conclusions are commonly avoided, except for the conclusion that more information is needed. But their time had run out. Further study, including the exhumation of a second body, would have to be deferred. The scientists were breaking camp.

The chief petty officer had been returned to his coffin and the last of the rocks covering him were being carefully assembled above him. The camp was a flurry of filing, packing, departure schedules and all the last-minute details that crop up in such evacuations. Paul was to be among the last to leave so that he could shoot the site in its restored state. He had also been given an extra assignment in view of the preliminary findings of the project, that is, the role the lead-sealed cans had played in the story.

The men who had buried their shipmates out on the open tundra had actually camped in the lee of the wind along the base of a high ridge to the south. Their garbage dump, a litter of cans and broken bottles, was all that remained to mark the campsite.

Paul had not relished the extra work, as busy as he was preparing to head home, but it was obvious that the shots of the dump and close-ups of the cans would be a useful part of the overall picture.

Elias was assigned to accompany him because of the bear, which Elias had reported was still hanging around the camp. Paul doubted it. Nobody else had actually seen the animal, and Paul suspected the guide/consultant of making up the bear to secure his position on any future projects. But at least Elias could carry the tripod, and it couldn't do any

harm to have him along provided that he stayed out of the way and shut up.

It was a bit of a hike out to the dumpsite. Paul, laden with his camera, battery belts and other related paraphernalia, offered no opening for conversation. Elias, tripod slung over the shoulder opposite the one that carried his rifle, was also silent. Nanuk trotted on ahead, stopping to look back every now and then, as if to question the direction the hike was taking.

Paul surveyed the location. The dumpsite was on a little knoll at the head of what almost seemed like a valley. The ridge arched upwards from the floor of the tundra to end abruptly in an outcropping of tumbled-down cliffs at its southerly extreme. A snowdrift, or what remained of it, stretched along the base of the ridge.

An establishing shot began to assemble itself in Paul's mind: dump in the foreground, snow curving off toward the south framed on the one side by the face of the ridge.

With a change of angle he could then close in on a medium shot of the garbage. To show scale, he'd get Elias to reach a hand into a close-up and turn over one of the deteriorating cans.

A couple of tight close-ups of the lead-lined rims, maybe a macro pan of the rest of the debris, and he would be out of here. He took the tripod from Elias, thanking him for carrying it, and asked Elias to stay behind him.

When the gear was assembled, he put his eye up to the camera and began searching for the shot he'd pictured in his mind. It wasn't quite there. He picked up the tripod and moved back a few paces—Nanuk's ears were now visible in the bottom of the frame.

"Elias?"

Elias gave a low-pitched whistle. The dog whined but moved back to stand next to its master—where it whined again. Paul couldn't recall the animal having ever uttered a sound before this. He looked back into the camera. He liked the basic composition but didn't like the light. It was too bright, too high contrast. Paul got out his meter, took a reading, scowled and began pawing through his camera bag for the appropriate filter. The dog began whining again, and trotted past Paul into the middle of his shot, where it stopped to sniff the air. Paul gave Elias a look that showed his annoyance.

"We shouldn't be out here," Elias said, eyeing the dog.

"Elias, he's in the shot!" Paul's patience was at a low ebb.

Elias gave another whistle. Reluctantly, the dog returned to Elias, where it almost cowered at the man's feet.

Paul pulled the trigger on the first shot. Satisfied, he then moved the tripod and began focusing on the next.

Nanuk began to growl. His hackles rose as he crowded his master's legs. Paul was finding it difficult to concentrate. He gave Elias a look that he hoped communicated the fact.

Elias didn't seem to notice. Brow furrowed, he gazed without blinking in the direction of the ridge.

Paul looked into the camera, focusing his mind on his work. When he looked up, the dog was gone. *Good,* Paul thought. He moved the tripod into position above the tin cans, and began searching for a close-up. When he next looked up, Elias was gone!

Paul couldn't believe it. At the precise moment when the guy could have actually been of some use, he disappears!

Good riddance, Paul told himself. He could fix the trigger on the camera so that he could reach into the shot himself.

A flicker of movement on the periphery of Paul's vision caused him to look up. For several moments, his eyes wandered over the expanse before him, fixing on nothing. What had it been? A bird? Nanuk or his master wandering around the site? Paul was about to return his attention to the camera when it happened again. This time his eye was quick enough to identify the bear high atop the ridge, outlined against the sky.

Perfect! Paul thought. What better set dressing to show off an arctic location than a polar bear? In seconds, he had the animal in his lens.

It stood with its head raised, apparently sampling the air. It was enormous! Even at this distance, it filled the lens. Paul pulled the trigger, zooming back to a wide shot to tie the animal visually to the location. If he moved the camera back, he could actually show the dumpsite in the foreground with the bear posing above. But the bear suddenly decided to move. It began loping north along the ridge, looking down into the valley—looking directly at Paul, Paul realized, as he followed the animal's movements through his lens.

It occurred to him that he could possibly be in some danger. It was a sheer drop between the top of the ridge and the dump location, but if the animal was of a mind to, it could probably cover the considerable distance down off the sloping northern end of the ridge before Paul could make it back to camp.

Where was the guide/consultant? Where was the famous bear dog? *Obviously,* thought Paul, *they were afraid of bears.* Had Elias and Nanuk actually sensed the bear's

approach and beat a retreat back to camp—without telling Paul!? No, Elias wouldn't do that—would he?

The bear had stopped. It was now looking down off the ridge to the south of where Paul stood. Whatever had caught its attention, it now showed no further interest in Paul.

Two more close-ups of the cans and he'd be done.

The bear had turned and was headed south again, closer to the edge of the ridge, still interested in something on the tundra floor. Following the direction of its gaze, Paul scanned the area. Nothing moved. Nothing seemed out of place. A cold chill, accompanied by a wave of fear, almost panic, came over the cameraman. But why? There was nothing out there.

He looked back at the bear, still intent on whatever had caught its eye. Paul tried to shake off the panic attack— that's all it was, an attack of nerves, but…

Something moved! Paul's eyes shot back and forth along the mat of snow next to the ridge. Something was down there. Whatever it was had to be pretty small; there was no place for a large animal to hide against the ridge. He looked to the bear, then to the point it seemed fixed on, and saw something moving over the snow. It seemed to stop. Paul strained his eyes trying to make out a shape, but could see nothing but a round black dot like a lump of coal flanked by two smaller…eyes! It was the nose and eyes of a second bear! Using the snow for camouflage, it was stalking him!

As if sensing that it had been discovered, the animal now seemed to charge, its face careening along the mat of snow, quickly closing the distance between itself and

Paul—except that Paul was now running too. Flat out, over the tundra he flew, leaping over the shrubbery that snatched at his shins, springing headlong off the larger stones, faster than he'd ever moved in his life, faster than he could think…

Was that Elias who had gone by in a blur to his left? A stolen backwards glance confirmed that it was. Still running, Paul took a second look back for the bear, which had disappeared, or at least fallen behind. Was it actually possible to outrun a polar bear?

"Elias!" Paul shouted between breaths, "look out for the bear!"

Paul had stopped running, but was still dancing on the spot, expecting at any moment that they'd be overtaken by the bear.

"Elias!"

Elias was oblivious. He seemed to be in the midst of the prayer/meditation thing Paul had witnessed out at the boulder.

"Elias!" Paul shouted, gingerly moving toward the guide while nervously scanning the path of his retreat. "There's a bear behind you…"

Elias lowered his eyes, muttered a last incantation in his own language, then heaved a deep sigh and looked at Paul. "You forgot your camera," he said.

"You think this is a joke?" Paul cried, amazed at the man's stupidity.

"That bear is not hunting," said Elias, starting back toward the dumpsite.

"Maybe it's not hunting you, but it was definitely hunting me," Paul declared, following closely behind the man with the gun.

"He probably has killed an animal somewhere around here. He was just watching us."

"Not the bear on the ridge!" Paul exclaimed. "The other one, the one that chased me!"

"There is only one bear."

"Elias, I saw it. It chased me!"

"It wasn't a bear…"

"It wasn't a bear—then what was it?"

Elias didn't answer. As the dumpsite came into view, Paul found himself almost wishing the animal would pop up out of the thatch just to prove that he wasn't making it up. But nothing moved on the tundra floor.

"See…" said Elias, gazing upwards. The bear on the ridge was slowly ambling down the ridge to the south nearly out of sight.

"I sent the dog up there to watch him," Elias was looking at a point opposite them on the northern slope of the ridge. It took Paul a moment to locate Nanuk, sitting on his haunches, patiently watching after the bear.

"But…"

"Where did you see this bear that chased you?"

"It was right over here." Paul headed for the line of snow. "I couldn't see it at first, but the bear on the ridge was watching it. Then I saw it about there, and it started to run at me about here…"

Elias walked along the mat of snow carefully studying its melting surface.

"There's no tracks," he said, and looked at Paul.

"But I saw it!" Paul insisted.

"This is where that man died."

"What ma…" Paul stopped short, realizing that Elias was referring to the chief petty officer. "No," he said. "That's ridiculous." But even as he spoke the image of the face within a face forced itself into his mind. *Coincidence,* he told himself.

Elias had started back to the dumpsite where Paul's camera waited to finish the shoot.

Coincidence, nothing more, Paul repeated to himself, staring at the trackless snow. Had he ever mentioned the blackened nose and eyes to Elias? He was sure he hadn't. He hadn't mentioned it to anyone. Another chill went up his spine, although he was still sweating from the exertion of his sprint over the tundra.

"This guy's starting to get to me," he muttered, starting after Elias. Thank God he was heading back to the real world.

The
Bully

"You're a complete physical wreck," said the doctor, and recommended that Jerry be hospitalized immediately.

Of course, not all that could be blamed on the chicken.

If you wanted to get right down to it, and Jerry didn't, there is a definite balance between food and alcohol—not to mention exercise—which must be maintained if one is to keep up a modicum of natural resilience or "bounce-back-edness."

One look at Jerry as he drove in from his one-man assault on the Alaska Highway told Tim that Jerry was not maintaining that balance.

The car didn't look any better. It was coated inside and out with a layer of Alaska Highway, since several windows were missing from the four-door Plymouth sedan.

A light cotton rope protruded through one of the missing windows and under the semi-sprung hood—"the throttle," Jerry would explain with a wave of his hand, indicating that a longer explanation on the subject would come some other day.

Not that Tim's life could serve as a model of temperance, balance or control in all things. He and a handful of entertainers, writers and artists had rented a farm for the summer, boarded some cattle and bought a few horses.

The place had been dubbed "Rottingwood Acres," after the wide array of tumble-down buildings occupying the farmstead. Everyone who came there had thrown themselves into its many challenges and pursuits with undaunted courage and a curiosity for the "natural."

No one who witnessed the event will ever forget the epic battle between Lowell, artist and one-time farmboy, and a sprightly young heifer that "came fresh" not long after their arrival on the farm.

She had never had a rope on her, much less been milked. But, after a super-human effort on Lowell's part, and some rather extensive damage to the inside of the aging log barn, the man emerged, limping, with physical evidence of victory over the beast—a Coke bottle half-filled with a froth of warm, dirty cow's milk.

Fortunately for everyone concerned, no one in the group solely depended on the fruits of "the harvest" for their livelihood.

Even Bumfry (so named because he was a bum fry) had come to the farm via a short but illustrious career in show business. He was vain, an occupational hazard perhaps, but this vanity was mixed with a strong tendency to bully and

demean whoever he could intimidate. The cat and the dog frequently felt the wrath of his pointed beak. Small children who visited, unless armed with sticks, could find their lives at risk, or so the rooster liked them to believe.

All visitors, in fact, soon received a taste of a disposition as unsavoury as the sight of the semi-feathered fowl. His feathers, where he still had them, were a dirty shade of yellow-grey. His neck and tail, or rather the pink and pimply "pope's nose" where his tail ought to have been, had been plucked clean.

When he wasn't falling flat on his beak (one of his clubbed and gnarled feet having stepped on the other), he held his head, with its ragged comb flapping over one eye, aloft, with a dignity and aplomb enviable to thespians of much greater esteem.

In Jerry, the belligerently bullying chicken spied, if not a sympathetic understanding, at least a pushover.

As the man emerged from his dusty car on the day of his arrival, and everyone gathered round to greet their wayfaring comrade, the chicken sidled up unseen and delivered the first of a long series of blood-blistering pecks to the bony shins of the newcomer. Could he know that this was a man reputed to have an almost phobic aversion to hurting or maiming or—God forbid!—killing, anything?

"Just kick him, Jerry," Tim and several others advised him.

"Oh, I couldn't—shoo, shoo, go away!" was all he'd ever say.

While it was true that Tim and his friends were not seriously "farming," the same could not be said for their neighbours, landlords and friends, the Hutterites. These

gentle and long-suffering men of the land were deadly serious about it.

Their ripening barley surrounded "Rottingwood" on three sides. Unfortunately, its rotting and rusty barbed wire fences did not comprise a stiff enough deterrent to some of the more spry or determined cattle of a mind to partake of this lush and limitless greenery. One young fence-crawling troublemaker in particular had come to flaunt an almost total disregard for the rusty barbs and spindly posts delineating its legal feeding limits.

No sooner was she through the wire, usually taking a post down in her struggle, than the rest would join her, contentedly fanning out to see who could be the first to founder on the green barley.

A poke is a device made of willows, metal, rope, rawhide or whatever's handy, which, fitted to the neck of an animal, prevents it from "poking" its head and shoulders through a fence. Tim decided to make his, or rather hers, out of two-by-twos.

Cutting the culprit out of the herd had been no easy task. In a sprint at close quarters, she was almost as fast as Tim's horse. She was not averse to using her hind legs in a variety of ways and could leap like a deer, yet lacked very little in body weight to match the size of any full-grown cow. Like Lowell's milk cow, she seemed to know nothing of that state of barnyard grace known as "halter-broke."

Tim had chased her into the barn, dismounted and stepped inside, rope ready. She stared at him, a dull fire simmering in the depths of her usually docile eyes. As the rope descended around her head, she spun back on it, pulling it out of Tim's hands and nearly spinning herself off

her feet as she did so. She nosed her way into a large box stall in the back of the barn and waited.

Tim also waited. The trouble was that there were two ways out of that box stall. Whichever way he went in left her a clean leap to a getaway down the centre alley of the barn (trailing his 40-dollar lariat).

He thought of digging out the ancient door that years before had sagged on its hinges into the mud of the corral, but he was certain he wouldn't be able to budge it even if he did dig it free.

"Ya need a hand?"

It was Jerry. Tim lost no time in gratefully assuring him that he did.

"Just stand there; I'm going around this way. If she comes round that way, turn her back."

"Turn her back?" asked Jerry.

"Yeah, just watch her, and if she moves toward the door, just wave your arms and yell—she should turn back."

"What if she doesn't?" Jerry queried further.

"Then just grab the rope as she goes by," said Tim as he moved off into the dark barn.

With any luck, he'd catch her off guard, get a hand on the rope and a wrap on a post before she knew what was happening.

"Ouch!" said Jerry. The heifer's head popped up out of the manger just in time to see Tim reaching for the rope.

"Shoo," said Jerry politely, "shoo!" Bumfry had followed him into the barn. Jerry looked up in time to see the heifer thundering out of the dark, straight down the alley. Bumfry jumped one way and Jerry went the other as the heifer charged past. Jerry, much to Tim's amazement, reappeared in the

heifer's wake and clasped both hands onto the trailing rope. In an instant, he was skidding along the barn floor waterski-fashion and on out the barn door with Tim in pursuit.

Out in the corral, it was hard to say who was jumping higher—the heifer, taking long bucking leaps against the rope, or Jerry, taking eight-to-ten-foot strides with it.

When she got to the far side of the corral, she dove with practised accuracy between the upper and middle rails. The speed of her squeeze popped the top rail off. It soared on ahead as she bucked on into the near freedom of the pasture.

Jerry would not relinquish his grip on the rope as he took the second rail full in the chest; he should have. There was a sickeningly audible zzzzzzzzzzzztttttt as the lariat slithered through his ungloved hands. Tim was at his side in time to "take a wrap" with the remaining two feet of rope.

"Are you all right?" Tim asked. Jerry was white as a sheet, staring into his blood-stained palms.

"That chicken, the rope, I…" he said, as if waking from a bad dream.

"You don't look so good," said Tim. "Maybe you better go up to the house and lie down."

A violent jerk on the rope from the heifer bucking at its opposite extremity seemed to snap Jerry back into consciousness. "No," he said with admirable resolve. "I said I'd give you a hand."

"I think I can handle it from here," Tim said.

"I may be weak, but I'm tough," said Jerry, and looked squarely at Tim.

"Well," said Tim, his tone betraying a begrudging compliance mixed with admiration, "at least go up to the house

and get some gloves." That, Jerry would do gladly. *A trifle unsteadily,* thought Tim as he watched Jerry go.

Bumfry stepped out from between two old ramshackle granaries as Jerry passed. The chicken arched its head and surveyed the scene proudly.

Tim decided to let the heifer "cool out" as he gathered up the nails, hammer and boards for the poke. By the time he got back, Jerry was already making his way across the corral to join him.

"I couldn't find any gloves," Jerry said with a shrug, in answer to Tim's look at his hands. Instead he had pulled on a long pair of grey work socks. They hung two or three inches beyond the end of his fingers.

"Maybe…" Tim paused. "Maybe it would be best if you just went out and chased her in on the rope; I'll take up the slack."

Jerry looked at the cow looking back at him, that dull flame still present in the recesses of her cavernous eyes. "Chase her in?" he said. His throat seemed to be drying out.

"Yeah, just go out behind her and wave your arms, and when she comes closer to the post I'll take up the slack."

"The arm-waving part didn't work out so well last time," Jerry confessed. "Maybe it would be better if you did the chasing and I took up the slack."

"Suit yourself," Tim said as he held out the stub end of the rope to Jerry's woolen hand.

"Just pull on this?" Jerry said enthusiastically, already bracing himself.

"Yeah, but wait for some slack," Tim said quietly as he moved smoothly over the rail and in a wide arc into the pasture on the opposite side of the cow, which watched him

suspiciously as he went. *Slow and easy,* thought Tim as he moved in on her, hoping she might move toward the fence. And she did, a couple of inquisitive, experimental steps. The rope went slack. "Okay, Jerry, gently, don't scare her, pull it in."

"Get away," said Jerry sharply. "Get out of here!"

Bumfry was back!

"Jerry?" said Tim, his impatience showing as the cow took yet another couple of steps. The coils of rope slid down the post.

For some reason, Jerry seemed to think the system would not work down there, and with his free hand—as free as a hand can be inside a sock—he attempted to pull the slack coils back up the post. He couldn't get a grip. He looped them instead over his free arm. They tangled, and he attempted to straighten them with the hand that held the rope's end. The cow was watching him in wonder. Tim was watching the cow.

"Jerry?" he asked, quietly but intently.

"Get away!" Jerry snapped, presumably to the menacing chicken.

The rope was now draped over his arm, and he seemed to be trying for a coil about the neck. "Not you," he said politely to the cow, which still stared at him spellbound. A slight movement from Tim trying to see around the cow, to discern what the holdup was, broke the spell. The cow started to move. "Just a minute," Jerry said, as she lifted her head.

With one last puzzled glance in Jerry's direction, she launched into the air. She seemed to just soar higher and higher until she came to the end of her rope. A shudder on impact rippled through her entire body from neck to tail-tip.

In the same instant, a sickening jolt hit Tim in the pit of his stomach as, glancing through the churning legs of the air-borne cow, he saw the rope tighten around the tangled cluster of post, arm and stocking-covered hands. (Thankfully, the neck was spared.)

Jerry and the post jointly became the anchor for the tortuous tether as the enraged animal thrashed and bucked against the rope's ever-tightening grip on her neck. Alternately, Tim tried hazing her toward the post and pulling some slack, but to no avail.

Jerry, squeezed and mangled, lashed tighter and tighter to the post with every terminated leap, seemed destined to destruction when finally she quit, apparently all out of wind, and Tim was able to pull enough slack to release his bedraggled friend.

Standing on his knees in the dust of the corral, dazed, beyond pain, his face nearly transparent, hands hanging limply at his side, their stockings wrenched and rope-worn but valiantly clinging to his wrists, Jerry seemed deep in thought.

"Jerry?…" said Tim, unsure what to say after that.

"I think," Jerry said weakly, "I'll go up to the house and lie down for a while."

When the poke was on the cow, Tim went in search of his valiant comrade. He found him to be the centre of a discussion on the general merits of modern medicine and emergency wards in particular. His colour had not improved, and Tim soon joined the side of the debate in favour of Jerry visiting a doctor. Jerry was the only person opposed to the idea. He assured everyone that it only hurt when he moved, a thing he was planning to do very little

of, or when he laughed, a thing he did with increasing spirit reviewing the day's events with Tim.

After a bit of supper and a good stiff drink or two, he felt well enough to continue on at the table pursuing a more serious endeavour.

Tim and Jerry had worked together on theatre projects in the past, and now they were working together on a new proposal. The selling features of the new idea, the salient facts to be assembled, lay spread over the table. Proposal-writing can be as absorbing as any other creative task.

Within an hour, Tim having been convinced that Jerry was up to it, they were firmly ensconced in its ponderous intricacies and a rather large bottle of wine.

At a juncture between a particularly picayune point of procedure and a sufficiently inspiring vision of the possible eventual hope, Tim decided to exercise the "farmer's prerogative."

He strode out through the screen door, down the wooden sidewalk, through the caragana hedge and off to the end of the driveway.

Jerry followed, eyes glued to an assortment of papers he held in both hands and mouth automatically reciting the corporate conundrum before them, as far as the end of the walk, which ended at the hedge since he was in his stocking feet.

It was a beautiful summer evening, if either of them had taken the time to notice, that special time of day when the setting sun sets everything aglow with that special kind of inner light…

"Ouch!" Jerry yelped. "That does it! That really does it!" he said, with a chilling venom in his voice. Tim had never

heard Jerry utter anything using those particular tones before.

With a wind-up rivalling that of any free kicker in World Cup soccer, with deadly aim and blatantly murderous intent, his arms flying akimbo to offset the right stockinged foot now flying directly at the chicken—which leapt neatly out of the way—with a scream of excruciating agony as the foot went on to smash toes-first into the ancient cement gatepost concealed by the hedge…

The screaming continued as Jerry clutched at his multiple multiple-fractures and hopped up and down on his good leg, which Bumfry felt obliged to perforate with one final shin-peck before Tim could collect himself and come to his aid.

At this point, Jerry was ready to reopen the discussion on the merits of doctoring. Subsequent x-rays revealed broken and fractured bones of various sizes and descriptions throughout most of his "weak but tough" anatomy.

No one was ever able to discover why Bumfry had it in for him, but luckily for the chicken Jerry was not someone who could bear a grudge.

Indeed, his lasting regret seemed to be that he had allowed himself to get so insanely riled that he would actually try to take the life of a close friend's "family pet."

On the Wire

He needed to smoke. It was that time anyway, even if he was running behind. He'd been behind schedule before he'd even gotten to work. Both check-stops, one out on the main road and one at the entrance to the village, had swarmed his old Vauxhall, sniffing and probing into its most private corners and crevices, as if the military had nothing better to do. Joel couldn't have raised their suspicions any higher if he'd been driving a tank.

The parking lot usually assigned to hotel employees was off limits now. He'd had to park some distance away in the designated alternative lot, and walk from there. He'd been stopped entering the grounds, and stopped once again entering the hotel. Here security personnel were not in uniform—

although their suits could easily have been army issue. Joel had shown them the security clearance documentation he'd been provided with, but had been searched entering the building anyway.

Joel was in the habit of arriving early for work. He liked to visit with the kitchen staff coming to the end of their workday. He usually put on a fresh pot of coffee in the staff room at the end of a hallway past the cold storage lockers. There he would thumb through whatever daily newspapers littered the table, sipping his coffee and bidding goodnight to the last of those going off shift. This room was always the first he cleaned. From there, he went on a general sweep of the wing, rolling up soiled mats, turning chairs up onto tables and accomplishing an inventory of the challenges peculiar to that particular night.

He then attacked the waste bins, the contents of which he'd been successful in convincing the kitchen personnel should be sorted. Dry paper and cardboard, he recycled. Cooking oil had its own container system. But why, the staff had wanted to know, should they separate stale-dated produce, breads and pastries from plate scrapings and other spoilage? It all went into the same dumpster!

"It just makes it easier to handle," Joel had argued, and the staff usually complied. Joel had started in the kitchen as a prep-cook/dishwasher. He had liked working with food, but had failed to develop the speed the work demanded. It just wasn't in his nature to hurry through something like the creation of a salad—or 50 salads, as was typically the case. Meanwhile, he had displayed a natural fastidiousness in dishwashing and general clean-up, which had eventually evolved into the position he now held. It

was, in many respects, perfect for him. He could work at his own pace, setting his own standard—which was high.

He usually worked non-stop through the first part of the night, marshalling everything back into its rightful place. The second half of his shift would then be purely physical: wiping down the stainless steel counters, ventilation hoods, etc., and ending up with mopping the floor. He liked seeing the shine come up on the steel, the gleam return to the white tiled floor. By the time the morning shift began arriving, he would have fresh coffee waiting for them. Once again he would linger, visiting in the staff room before drifting home.

He usually spent his lunch break outside. It began with the march of the garbage cans, bags and bins out to the dumpster. Setting aside the plastic tub he had salvaged for the purpose, he would stuff everything else into the dumpster and lock it down—the dumpster was bear-proof—then hose out the garbage cans and leave them to dry while he ate his lunch. He would take the tub, full of whatever goodies were on the menu that night, down to a little alcove in the trees opposite the loading dock. Having placed the tub in the alcove, he would then retreat to the dock.

Lunch always began with a smoke—not tobacco, which Joel considered poisonous, but cannabis, which he considered mildly medicinal. This part of the hotel complex was not one that was frequented by the public. Neither, at this time of night, was there any likelihood of deliveries or movement of hotel staff.

From his perch on the loading dock, Joel could keep a lookout over the staff parking lot, the access to the rear of the hotel and the alcove in the trees. The light from the

parking lot slanted through the shadows of the trees into the alcove, providing just enough illumination to identify a moving shadow. It was uncanny how often the shadow would appear before Joel had even finished his smoke. Joel sometimes wondered if it was watching, waiting out of sight in the dark for Joel to set down the tub. If it was, it always held back until Joel was seated on the dock.

Occasionally, when it had devoured the contents of the tub, well ahead of Joel still munching on his own lunch, it would come out into the light and look at Joel as if asking for seconds—or perhaps to offer a nod of thanks. Joel was never sure.

If it failed to appear during Joel's lunch hour, Joel would leave the tub for an extra hour or two, always retrieving it well ahead of the first staff arrivals.

If the food hadn't been touched by this time, Joel would dispose of it in the dumpster. Joel was acutely aware that what he was doing was against all the rules, perhaps even a few laws. It would not do to get caught. But where was the harm? He always selected the healthiest food available at the hotel—food that would otherwise be feeding some overstuffed landfill. And he liked the company. The hour spent in quiet meditation on the loading dock, watching the shadow moving in the alcove, had become something Joel looked forward to—and it was that hour now.

The filters on the hoods above the grills still needed to be cleaned, as did the big steel bowls and paddles of the pastry mixer—what else? How far behind was he, exactly, and what about the battalions of security people scouring the hotel and grounds for bombs, or bugs, or whatever it was they imagined might have been planted in the hotel? Would they still be on the prowl at this time of night?

Knowing that the checkpoints were to be put in place as part of the preparations to "secure the area," Joel had previously left himself a small stash. It was under one of the large flat rocks that bordered the driveway into the parking lot next to the alcove. Should he chance setting out the tub of treats? His friend was probably having its own trouble keeping on schedule and out of sight of the patrols.

The first thing to do was to see who was out there. If necessary, he could retrieve his stash and walk down to his car for a smoke. If nobody was around, he could always come back for the tub and have his lunch and his smoke on the dock as usual.

He was on the run. For the past 48 hours, the little black bear had been on the move continuously. The problem wasn't simply that crowds of people had descended on the area—he was used to the annual hordes of hikers, bikers, hotel guests and golfers. Somehow everything had changed.

Foraging along the creek, which usually provided dependable cover in the daylight hours, he'd been boxed in by three, maybe four, large groups of people on foot. He'd been sighted twice while fleeing the area. The forested flat-land, just down from the village, seemed to be teeming with activity as a new campground sprang up. The bear had retreated to higher ground only to find construction in progress on the slopes where he'd hoped to sniff out a mar-mot. Crews and heavy equipment had completely overtaken

this terrain, which was mainly open ground. The tantalizing smell of carrion rotting in the sun had brought him back toward the highway—a road-killed white tail buck—but the level of activity there had prevented him from investigating further. He'd been flushed out of the marshlands below the golf course by a pack of barking dogs, and their handlers shouting in chorus with the dogs. The world had gone mad.

Under cover of night, driven by hunger, the young bear had stolen into the grove of trees behind the hotel and staked out the alcove. He had seen the man he knew as his provider talking to another man behind the hotel, but nothing had been delivered to the alcove. The sweet aroma of fresh garbage had almost drawn him into the open, but his fear had been stronger than his hunger.

"We're doing this for the benefit of the bears and for the benefit of our own staff," said the environmental spokesperson for the government's security operation. He was defending the decision to radio-collar all the grizzlies in the area.

"The benefit of the bears!…" Joel scoffed. He was preparing a late afternoon breakfast for himself, his television on in the background tuned to the news channel.

"…But if patrolling police and military personnel are to be kept informed of the grizzlies' whereabouts," the announcer continued, "what about protesters?" Joel was

shaking his head in disgust. As long as he'd lived in the area, grizzly bears had never been a problem. Compared to black bears, they tended to be downright reclusive. The idea that they would now start feeding on police and soldiers—who were armed to the teeth anyway—was beyond Joel's imagining. Nor was it likely, in Joel's opinion, that a grizzly would be attracted by swarms of noisy placard-waving protesters.

"Special bear dogs have been brought in to help patrol the area," said the anchorman. "Reporter Suzy Fraser has the story." A young woman dressed in fashionable hiking attire came on the screen. Beside her, another young woman dressed in what looked like a flack jacket seemed on the verge of being drawn in two by a pair of husky-looking canines harnessed to their leashes. "So these dogs are actually bred exclusively for this kind of work, is that correct?" prompted the reporter.

"Yes, they are," said the woman, yanking back one, then the other of her charges.

"So, does that mean they're trained to actually track down and attack bears?" asked Suzy.

"No," said the handler. "Basically what they do is drive the bear off with their barking. When a bear has been located in a danger area, we bring the dogs in to move the bear along without having to actually harm the animal."

"Perhaps you could give us a bit of a demonstration," the reporter suggested.

"Sure…" said the woman, and moved out of the frame.

The reporter, turning to gaze dramatically into the camera, added, "We understand that a small black bear has been sighted near here earlier…" The camera now panned

to the dog handler as she moved into a marshy-looking area—supposedly following the tracks of the offending bruin. "Bark at the bear! Bark at the bear! Bark at the bear!" the woman began shouting, and the dogs complied—while lunging at the ends of their leashes with such force that a second attendant was obliged to step forward and relieve the woman of one of them.

If the dogs had any idea at all that they were directing their barks at a bear, or even a bear track, Joel could not tell it from the performance he was witnessing on the screen.

Suzy Fraser signed off and the studio announcer came back on to wrap up the segment with the news that "The total costs of security for the two-day conference are estimated to reach 11 million."

"Dollars?" Joel shouted at the screen. "For what?!"

How was it possible to blow 11 million dollars cordoning off one hotel in the mountains for two days!? Joel had never understood why the resort had been chosen for the meeting place of the eight world leaders anyway. If they needed that kind of protection, why didn't they just meet at an army base? Apparently the popularity of these leaders was such that it was assumed that a large coalition of citizen groups and individuals—and assassins—would be storming the gates to protest the leaders' world-saving policies.

But why bring the bears into it? Earlier the environmental spokesperson for the security operation had admitted that they did not anticipate that the leaders themselves would be in any direct danger of bear attacks. It was the army bivouacked in the surrounding area they were concerned about. Joel wondered if the army found these suggestions embarrassing. "They should…"

The more he learned of the situation, the more concerned he became for the little black bear. "I should never have started feeding them," he lamented, but it was too late now. He knew the young bear would come to the alcove, or try to. Maybe he'd even been there last night. Joel hadn't been able to put anything out. He'd no sooner started dumping the garbage than he was accosted by some goon checking out "the unsecured access to the hotel"—meaning the kitchen door, which Joel had left open between trips to the dumpster.

Joel had eventually decided the coast was clear enough to have his smoke and lunch on the loading dock, but he didn't want to risk going back inside for the tub. Tonight would be different. He imagined the little bear growing desperate and was struck by a second wave of guilt. He'd gotten in the habit of feeding him while he was still a cub in the company of his mother, a large cinnamon that Joel had called Blondi. They had begun showing up at the rear of the hotel about the time of night Joel took out his garbage. Blondi had made him nervous; head in the air, sniffing menacingly in his direction, while he tried to concentrate on his work.

Although she had never actually challenged him, he had never felt comfortable enough to take his eyes off her—even after the dumpster was securely locked and the garbage cans washed clean. He'd continued feeling nervous while lunching on the loading dock. He also felt guilty eating in front of the bears, while they feasted on nothing but the smell of the garbage—they were obviously hungry!

Joel had guessed that expanding development in the area was probably affecting their natural food supply. But

the idea of putting out the tub had come to him as a method of distracting the animals away from himself and the dumpster, rather than of satisfying their needs.

He'd taken the tub out to the alcove an hour or two before Blondi was expected—she was amazingly prompt. Having shown up that night at the usual time, she had found and licked up the tub of treats, then faded quietly into the shadows. It hadn't taken long for the practice to become a habit. Joel and the bears seemed to have achieved a confidence in each other's behaviour that had grown into an arm's-length understanding of friendship.

But somewhere in her travels, Blondi had made a nuisance of herself—or so the charges read. Joel heard that she had been shot with a tranquilizer gun and relocated—which could mean that she was dead. Many bears did not survive this type of eviction.

At any rate, the cub had escaped. He was old enough by then to be on his own—Blondi would probably have kicked him out soon anyway. It had taken about a week for the cub to show up at the hotel, and he and Joel had continued doing business as usual—until now.

It was after dark. Anticipating the time it would take to get through the check-stops, and adding an extra hour to that, Joel had arrived at work well in advance of his usual time. He had put the coffee on in the staff room, but then

departed from his normal routine by going directly to work collecting, sorting and bagging the garbage.

Many of the kitchen staff were still on duty—just as Joel had hoped they would be. Two or three of them had commented on his advanced start to his night's work, calling him an "eager beaver" or asking outright why he was there so early. He'd responded that delays with security had put him so far behind the past couple of nights that he needed to catch up.

"Tell me about it!" Pam Withers had said, and went on to list her own complaints saying that she "couldn't turn around" without being asked who she was and what she was doing there. Pam had brought a tray of day-old bread deemed ripe for disposal, which Joel had relieved her of.

It was whole-grain, still in the bags—nothing wrong with it. With a razor knife Joel had sliced each of the bags open, quickly dumping the bread into a double-bagged garbage bag he'd kept to the side. The bag was already bulging with the remains of a pork roast, sandwich meats, a variety of wilted vegetable produce and a dozen cherry tarts. Joel lifted the bag, testing its weight, and decided that it would have to do. The bag would have to appear to be easy to handle.

He retracted the razor blade of the knife, slipped it into a back pocket of his jeans and went to get himself a cup of coffee. He then returned to the garbage bins lined up near the door and waited.

The staff began drifting out, one at a time, or in pairs. Joel returned their adieus, patiently sipping his coffee. Security personnel did not seem to monitor staff departures as closely as they did arrivals. A larger group, some of whom rode together to and from work, began migrating

toward the exit. Joel set his coffee aside and preceded them through the doors carrying a bulky collection of garbage bags. Setting the bags aside, except for the one he'd loaded with goodies, Joel casually fell into conversation with Pam, strolling along beside her as she and the others made their way toward the designated alternative parking.

Joel scanned the area for security people but saw no one. When the group neared the grove of trees, Joel bade them goodnight, stooping to pick up a scrap of litter that had lodged against the curb as if that had been his intended destination. None of the group looked back as he straightened, then veered suddenly into the trees.

He didn't try to make it to the alcove. When he was far enough into the trees to believe that his movements would be obscured, if not shielded from view, he drew the razor knife from his back pocket. Glancing nervously around the grove of pine trees, he slit the belly of the doubled bags and dumped the contents into some low shrubbery at his feet. He was turning to head back when he saw him. The shadow was coming through the trees toward him at a dead gallop—hours ahead of schedule!

Joel almost bolted, but he mastered his fear and forced himself to walk at an even pace to the edge of the grove. There, he turned to look back. The shadow had disappeared. Joel was beginning to think he was imagining things when the bear's little face appeared around a tree a few paces from the cache of treats. Joel smiled. He started back across the pavement toward the hotel, glancing back over his shoulder to see that the animal had wasted no time diving into his supper.

"Excuse me, sir?" A security guy had suddenly materialized not a dozen feet ahead of Joel, halfway between him and the garbage bags he'd set outside the kitchen door. Trying not to look or sound like he had almost jumped out of his skin, Joel kept walking.

"What can I do for you?" he said, giving the man a friendly smile.

"May I see your clearance?"

"Yeah…" Joel said, fishing out his wallet. He dropped the scrap of litter, while juggling the wallet and empty garbage bags. Stooping to pick it up while stealing a glance back at the trees, he was horrified to see the shadow moving almost in plain sight!

"Is that what you need?" he asked the man, passing him the documentation. He stepped closer to the hotel, thus directing the guy's field of view away from the trees.

"You're just arriving for work?" the man asked suspiciously.

"No…" said Joel. "I got here about an hour ago."

"So…" The guy was obviously about to ask Joel what he was doing out here.

"I was just picking up some garbage," he volunteered. "Bag blew away on me," he added, gesturing to the clump of bags waiting beside the door.

The guy seemed satisfied with this. "Thank you," he said, handing Joel back his clearance papers.

"No problem," Joel answered, as they started back toward the kitchen. "I'm going to be in and out of this door for a bit with the garbage," he volunteered.

The man seemed to be grappling with the significance of this news.

"I usually prop the doors open, until I get everything outside," Joel added.

"I'll wait," the man said, nodding. He moved to the side of the door and took up a stand-easy pose gazing out over the parking lot.

From here Joel could barely make out the outline of the shadow moving in the trees.

If security had seemed excessive up to this point, it was nothing compared to what lay ahead. As the two days of the actual conference came upon them, the variety and numbers of security personnel cluttering the hotel, and grounds, and village, and surrounding area, grew exponentially.

Joel had to give up the hope of a smoke break entirely—he'd even given up lunching outside on the loading dock, as the level of scrutiny there rose to constant and uncomfortable proportions.

Bootlegging contraband treats to the little black bear was completely out of the question—not that the animal, or any animal, could possibly make it through the net of police, riot squads, SWAT teams, army and Secret Service anyway. They scrutinized the kitchen, the lists of staff, the halls and banquet rooms of the wing—all over again! They scrutinized the grounds—including Joel's dumpster, the parking lots, the trees and skies above the trees, as if expecting at any

minute to be attacked by an opposing army of equal or greater strength.

Joel was sure he had witnessed security personnel checking the security clearance of security personnel. But that did not surprise him since they seemed to have nothing else to do. The hordes of protestors, which the army was waiting to repel, had simply not materialized. The media were reporting that protest organizers were planning to confine their main assault to the streets of the nearest city, which was down on the prairie miles away.

Still, there was the possibility—or hope, as Joel read the desires of the media, now massing to cover what was shaping up to be a colossal non-event—that some lunatic group would charge the net, now bristling with armaments of all sorts. Having run this gauntlet and somehow remained alive and willing, the lunatics would then be placing the world leaders in danger of having the windows of their hotel rooms exposed to a view of placards decrying some horrific cause, while decrying the opinions of the leaders themselves. This, the joint security force was prepared to fight to the last man and woman to prevent. If they, like the media, were disappointed that no one seemed willing to test their joint mettle, Joel couldn't tell. On the whole they seemed a humourless lot, as if the act of breaking into a smile or a belly laugh was strictly forbidden by protocol. By the end of the first day of the conference, Joel had begrudgingly accepted their omnipresence, consoling himself with the fact that it would soon all be over and things would return to normal.

His work routine had been all but obliterated by the occupying forces now in control of the kitchen. But garbage,

at least, remained as a constant. Joel didn't bother sorting it at all, dumping everything including paper and cardboard into the same bags and bins, which he then wheeled or dragged out to the dumpster.

Two security people were posted outside the kitchen door, a man and a woman. Soldiers in uniform were visible, scattered here and there over the grounds. Radio checks, status reports—all in codes foreign to Joel's ears—merged into a constant murmured cacophony of suspense-filled vigilance. No one spoke to Joel.

The expressions on their faces, as the man and woman watched him loading the dumpster, would lead a casual observer to guess that he was probably a prisoner loading atomic waste. He wondered what time it was, guessing that it could be getting close to the time he took his lunch break—but probably not. The hours seemed to be dragging by at a...

Something was up. The man next to the kitchen door had suddenly stiffened, clapping a hand to his earpiece as if struck by an electric charge. The woman, who didn't seem to be wired to the same communications channel, started to ask the man what was happening but was unceremoniously silenced by an abrupt signal. In the stillness of the night, Joel could hear the echo of electronic voices melding with the shouts of the men on the grounds, obviously sounding an alarm. Soldiers were running through the trees. The man and woman had already stepped through the open doorway to the kitchen, and were in the process of closing the doors behind them when they remembered Joel.

"Inside!" the man said. Joel, pausing to toss in the garbage bag he held in his hands, began to comply but too slowly for the woman.

"Step inside the hotel now!" she said. Joel quickened his pace, pausing to look back only when he was well inside the second set of doors.

"What is it?" the woman asked the man, who was still glued to his earpiece.

"We've had a breach," said the man. The woman seemed to receive this news with all the solemnity of one who has just been handed a declaration of war. The tension emanating from the pair was palpable, as Joel, who they had again forgotten, wished he could step out for a smoke. The man's posture now seemed to relax. He cocked his head, as if waiting for confirmation, then heaving a sigh of relief said, "It's okay—it's only a bear in the army camp."

In the army camp, all hell had broken loose. It was like an anthill that had been trampled on by some passing monster. Sentries stared through the dark at their fellows pouring from their tents to join in the confusion. Orders were shouted, only to be countermanded by fresh orders, as those on duty demanded confirmation of what, exactly, their duty was.

When the news began to circulate that the camp was being attacked by a bear, the frenzied counterattack grew

dangerously close to panic, as reports of bear sightings began to proliferate throughout the camp.

In actuality, the lone attacker had not moved since first being discovered—he couldn't. The army's fresh food cache—as per the guidelines set out in the official handbook—was suspended from a wire strung between two trees. The little black bear, having somehow eluded detection as he made his way through the camp, had climbed one of the trees. He had then started out, hanging upside down by all fours, to make his way along the wire, when he'd been discovered.

As the shouting grew into all-out mayhem below, as the generators sputtered to life and searchlights leapt up at him from all directions, the bear had found himself in an impossible fix. Unwilling to proceed with his plan to rob the cache, unable to turn around, he could not move backwards on the wire to the relative safety of the tree.

So there the cub hung in painful indecision, while the army pursued his own lack of options—the handbook was, apparently, unclear as to what to do with a bear on a wire. The special bear-dog team was brought in—in accordance with protocols in effect—as were wildlife officials, environmental spokespersons and a small group of entirely unwelcome media.

When the barking bear-dog team had failed in their attempt to ameliorate the situation, the next team was consulted, and the next, until having been fired upon with blanks, firecracker bullets, rubber bullets and beanbag bullets, the little bear finally lost his grip and fell from the wire.

The media, with little or nothing else to cover on the subject, made much of the "breach of security." Details of the bear's assault on the army camp, complete with pictures of the poor creature hanging upside down from the wire, were flashed around the world.

The army was calling it an "accidental death" insisting that the animal had been fatally injured in his fall from the wire—and thus had to be put down. Joel had no trouble recognizing his friend.

"I killed him," he said—but just what was the bear supposed to do, give up eating until all this noise had packed up and moved on? Maybe he should have gone to stay with relatives until the army was ready to give the valley back?

How could they be so stupid?

Joel decided that he couldn't face spending another night in the hotel as long as it was occupied by idiots—he'd phone in sick—but even when they'd finally cleared out, Joel realized lunches on the loading dock would never be the same again.

Jack'O's Luck

As partners, Jack O'Grady and Ralph Pellerin were well matched. Ralph was a worker. Indeed, physical labour was his religion, his calling, his reason for rising and his dream when resting. On the other hand, Jack'O, as he was called, was an "ideas" man. In a different place and time, Jack'O could have invented the hula-hoop, the self-cleaning oven or the printing press. Ideas came to him out of the mundane surroundings of their lives as if by magic.

Jack'O could see things that to him were obvious while others, blinded by skepticism, couldn't imagine what lay before them even when it had been pointed out. A case in point: on a recent fishing trip, camped by a fast-flowing stream, it was Jack'O who had noticed the black sand on

the head of a gravel bar. "There's gold in that creek," he'd told Ralph. Ralph, like everybody else in the area, knew that such was not the case. But the next time he went down to the creek to do the washing up, he couldn't resist putting Jack'O's idea to the test.

Patiently sloshing sand and gravel through the frying pan, Ralph had eventually proved up a few colours—tiny grains of what was undeniably gold showed that Jack'O was right. Ralph had pointed out that, at best, he may be able to glean the equivalent of 50 cents an hour from the creek. Jack'O had then set to work on ideas to improve Ralph's sluicing methods, insisting that in truth there was a good living to be made there if one had the money to invest in the right equipment.

Money was something that was generally in short supply on the stump ranch that the men co-owned as latter-day homesteaders.

Ultimately they planned to grow grain and raise cattle on the land. They had purchased an ancient D4 Caterpillar tractor toward that end. When Ralph could finally get the machine running and manufacture the root rake that Jack'O had designed, the job of proving up the homestead would begin in earnest. But again, money for the parts and materials required was slow in coming.

Three summers before, Jack'O had hit upon an idea to solve that problem once and for all. Mushrooms, morels to be exact, were popping out of the ground in the thousands and nobody in that part of the country was cashing them in.

"Do you have any idea what they're worth a pound?" Ralph had to admit that he was by and large ignorant on

the subject, but agreed that the local market seemed to be virtually untapped.

"For now!" Jack'O had said. It was vital to his plan that they move on this immediately—before the nomadic pickers who scavenged the edible fungi could horn in on their territory. Ralph was convinced.

They invested in a one-ton cube van, which Jack'O deemed necessary to house and deliver their harvest. He'd located buyers who, he'd been assured, would take all they could deliver. The buyers had also informed him that they purchased the product dry, which necessitated the conversion of the van into a mobile mushroom-drying rack.

It is a fact that forest fires beget mushrooms. And the dry summers they'd been having had produced fires of spectacular proportions. With the aid of maps, which Jack'O had procured at the local Forestry office, the men had set out to make their fortunes. For days on end they had tramped the blackened earth. When one location would fail to deliver the mother lode, they would pack up and travel on to the next. Up the hills, through the muskegs and into the river valleys they went, without discovering "morels in the thousands." Rain, it seems, also begets mushrooms, and the dry conditions that had produced the forest fires in the first place had persisted.

Occasionally they would hit what looked like a promising patch, only to have their hopes dashed as the mushrooms fizzled out. In the end, they made expenses, minus the initial investment of the cube van.

Jack'O had been unrepentant in his enthusiasm for the idea, maintaining that when the weather changed, as inevitably it would, they would be prepared to reap their just rewards.

The following summer, on a tip from someone Jack'O had met at the Forestry office, they had gone into the bush in search of pinecones. The word was that the trees had been "producing cones like mad"—probably owing to the same dry weather that had produced the fires. Apparently, when the general health of a tree is threatened, it signals its reproductive processes to go into overdrive.

All the men had to do was walk through the clearcuts stripping the cones from the discarded tops. But in many locations the tangle of deadfall and trampled limbs were almost impassable or bulldozed into mangled heaps. When they did hit a good plot, it didn't take as long to fill a sack as it did to pack it back to the van. Pinecone picking, for sale to the tree nurseries, was a labour-intensive business.

Still, they had done better in cones than they had in mushrooms, perhaps making wages over their input expenses—minus the hefty payments still owing on the van.

The van had become something of a white elephant, an albatross hanging around their fiscal necks. Over the preceding winter, Jack'O had developed yet another plan to rectify this situation.

The oil patch was booming, and hotshot services were cashing in making light deliveries to the rigs. All one needed was a vehicle—usually a pickup truck equipped with pipe racks—and a name.

Jack'O had invested in a cell phone and business cards proclaiming that "Hot To Trot" would deliver "Whatever You Got" in record time! So far, business had not been brisk. It seemed that their remote location worked against him, necessitating the long deadhead trip to the suppliers before heading out to a rig. He had prudently converted the

van to propane to offset fuel costs, thereby incurring further investment on the conversion. The numbers made sense on paper, but if the cell phone refused to ring, all the planning in the world wouldn't help.

"It takes time for a name to get around," he'd explained to Ralph. Ralph had pointed out that time was running out. Most of the monthly bills were scarred with an ugly red "Overdue" stamp. If they didn't do something about this soon, it would be the repo-man who would be hot to trot.

Jack'O had thought it uncharacteristically negative of his partner to indulge in such a pessimistic view of their prospects, but there was an element of truth in what the man had said. They were due for a break.

Jack'O had secured one regular contract. It involved making weekly deliveries of groceries and other supplies to the "caribou gate." The caribou gate was an operation that even Jack'O could not have imagined. Its very existence incensed him. Only the government, in Jack'O's view, could come up with something as outrageously pointless as the caribou gate. Only the government could afford to waste dollars in such a spectacularly stupid manner.

The mountain caribou, as they were known locally, were disappearing. The herds, once known to number in the thousands, were now down to "fewer than 200" according to estimates conducted by the government. They had migratory habits similar to the more northerly barren-ground caribou, but were the size and general confirmation of the woodland species. They calved and summered in the alpine meadows of the Rocky Mountains, migrating down through the foothills into the timberlands in the winter. Their favourite foods included lichens and mosses like the

"witches' hair" that grew in the old-growth forests. This low-protein fodder is slow-growing stuff, which meant that it was probably no accident that the caribou varied their migratory route from year to year. Obviously, if they moved along the same habitual track annually they would soon deplete this fragile food source.

When clearcutting became the harvesting method of choice for the rapidly multiplying lumber and pulp interests now denuding the land of these same old-growth forests, the caribou number had plummeted. A fire-storm of negative public relations had resulted, aimed at the companies and the government authorities who were supposedly in charge of protecting the general health of the boreal forest and its inhabitants.

The solution to the problem was two-fold. First, a corridor drawn on the map was intended to give the caribou a forested track on which to conduct their annual migration. Presumably, these animals would naturally favour this more scenic route through the vast clearcuts to their habitual wintering grounds—also under pressure from clearcutting—and everything would be fine!

The second part of the solution to the public relations problem was the gate. The powers that be had identified a bottleneck in the corridor, an area that in migratory seasons would presumably see the greatest caribou traffic. This area, although situated in the middle of what appeared on the map to be untouched wilderness, was actually not. A matrix of haul roads, rig roads and cutlines criss-crossed the area, as did a steady traffic of transport trucks, pickup trucks and ATVs.

The government, having identified this specific area as "sensitive," felt it had to do something to protect its "sensitivity."

So, at kilometre 110 of the main haul road leading into the area, they had constructed the caribou gate. The gate, consisting of a counter-balanced pole painted in flashes of red and white extending across the road, was manned 24 hours a day. Industrial workers, headed to their drilling rig or cutblock or whatever, were required to stop at this gate—whereupon the attendant would emerge from his roadside skid shack and inform the driver that there was caribou-sensitive terrain ahead. This having been accomplished, the attendant would then lift the gate, and the truck would proceed on its way.

A First Nations band not far from Jack'O and Ralph's place had got the contract to man the gate, and Jack'O had got the contract to make the once-a-week run out to the gate with supplies. While he appreciated the business, the absurdity of the situation infuriated him. It didn't help that the attendant, to say nothing of the people he stopped, repeatedly, also saw the situation as bizarre. The man had openly confided to Jack'O that he had no knowledge of caribou actually venturing into the vicinity.

Bears, on the other hand, seemed to inhabit the area in good numbers. They had violated the attendant's garbage bin so often that the man had been forced to keep his garbage inside the skid shack—until Jack'O could haul it away as part of his contract. One night, a bear had actually attempted to break into the shack! Jack'O had advised the man on the use of cayenne pepper and a variety of noisemakers concerning

the problem. But the fellow was firmly of the opinion that nothing short of a 30.30 rifle would do.

This solution was fraught with obvious drawbacks in view of the sensitive nature of the attendant's position there. It simply wouldn't do to have government-sponsored wildlife protectors blasting away at wildlife whenever the wildlife got on the contractor's nerves. Also the picture of Aboriginals manning gates to nowhere armed with high-powered rifles was one that could be subject to damaging misinterpretations.

Jack'O had pointed all this out to the fellow, over an extended coffee break, and had been successful in getting him to try a couple of variations on the cayenne solution. Jack'O maintained that "one good snort" would be all it would take. But, should the problem persist, he had offered his customer a compromise solution to the 30.30 in the form of the loan of a Webley pistol. Jack'O sympathized with the man's situation, as he himself had obtained the high-powered handgun mindful of the bears he and Ralph had expected to encounter while picking mushrooms. One needed both hands free for that kind of work, and packing a heavy rifle on your back, just in case of a chance encounter with a bear, would have been impractical. Although no situation had arisen to necessitate the use of the gun, the peace of mind it provided made it worth having.

On the drive back that evening, Jack'O had sighted no less than five bears—a sow with two cubs, a little black bear—probably a young one still getting used to living on its own—and a beautiful cinnamon boar that would probably weigh in excess of 400 pounds.

A few days later, Jack'O was in town attempting to drum up business. He'd dropped by the hardware store, the farm implement dealership and the Greyhound Bus depot, which was situated in the back of a gas station out on the highway. At each place, he'd chatted up the manager on the instant availability of "Hot To Trot" stressing its capability of delivering "Whatever You Got." The managers had all taken his card and assured him that if they ever discovered a need for his services, they wouldn't hesitate to call.

In the afternoon, Jack'O headed to the Pagoda for lunch and a beer. The owner and manager of this Chinese restaurant and lounge was a friend of Jack'O's—a man after his own heart—although he was probably old enough to be Jack'O's father.

In addition to the Pagoda, Ping owned the convenience store on the town's main street. He was also known to dabble in a variety of other concerns—not the least of which was a legendary poker game rumoured to have seen local real estate change hands more than once.

Jack'O passed through the restaurant, waving to the afternoon coffee clique, on his way to the dark little lounge in back. Ping greeted him enthusiastically from his stool behind the bar.

"How's business?"

"Could be better," Jack'O confessed as he took a seat at the bar. There was only one other customer in the lounge,

a stranger seated at a corner table. The man seemed absorbed in some paperwork, which competed for space on the table with the remains of his lunch.

"You wanna see a menu?" Ping asked.

"Nah, just gimme yer elk sandwich and a beer."

"No, no, no elk," Ping protested. "Jus' steak—grade A."

"I got nothin' against elk," Jack'O chuckled.

"No elk…" Ping insisted, pushing through the swinging doors that led into the kitchen. There was some kind of tuberculosis scare on, which had resulted in bans prohibiting the sale and processing of commercial elk. Some ranchers were threatening to shoot their herds in the face of it. Local gossip had it that Ping was doing a back-door business with a local elk rancher, buying the meat at firesale prices. Jack'O actually had no idea whether the gossip was true or not, but he couldn't resist teasing Ping.

Ping came back through the kitchen doors, coffee pot in hand, and headed for the table occupied by the stranger.

"Anything else?" he asked.

"Oh," the man said, pushing his paperwork aside. "Yeah, just a half a cup." As Ping poured the coffee, the fellow rose and entered the washroom. Ping gathered the lunch plates from the table and deposited them in a trolley parked next to the kitchen door.

"Who's he?" Jack'O asked.

Ping said that the stranger had become something of a regular of late, lunching in the lounge and making use of the place to do his paperwork.

"What's he do?" Jack'O wanted to know. Ping believed the man's work had something to do with the oil patch.

When the guy returned, Jack'O immediately introduced himself as the owner/proprietor of Hot To Trot hotshot services. The man confirmed that he was in an oil-related business, but not one that was likely to require Jack'O's services. Jack'O deposited a short deck of his business cards on the table anyway, saying that the stranger could feel free to pass them on to anyone he felt might make use of them. The stranger said he would, and Jack'O returned to his stool at the bar.

"Business no good?" Ping asked.

"I wouldn't say that," Jack'O answered, evading the point, "but it could be better." He went on to inform Ping that he had landed a "big contract" delivering supplies to the caribou gate. Not surprisingly, Ping had never heard of a caribou gate—and seemed mystified by Jack'O's attempts to explain what one was.

"It's a money-disposal program." Jack'O sounded bitter. "It's run by the government."

"Ahhh," Ping said, as if finally getting a grasp on the concept.

Jack'O's steak sandwich was ready and Ping went to fetch it. When he returned, Jack'O decided to change the subject, and began describing the bears he'd seen on his way back from the gate.

"Ahhh, bears," Ping said, obviously impressed. "Big money!"

"No…" Jack'O said, "I'm talking about bears; wild bears."

"Yes," Ping insisted. "Big money."

It was Jack'O's turn to be mystified. "Whaddaya mean?"

"Penis..." Ping said, apparently searching for more words, "ah, hands, ah... Paws! Bear's paws!"

Jack'O munched on his steak, looking at Ping as if waiting for him to get to the punch line. "What about bear paws?" he prompted.

"Soup!" Ping said earnestly. "Very good for you."

"Bear paw soup?" Jack was skeptical.

"Gall bladder!" Ping cried, as if finally finding the words he was looking for.

A light dawned in Jack'O's mind. Bear parts. Of course. Asians used bear parts in the preparation of their aphrodisiacs and other herbal medicines! "Big money?" Jack'O was intrigued.

"Big money," Ping repeated. "In China, big, big money!"

"Mmmm..." Jack'O pondered. "They still got bears in China?"

"No..." Ping said, "not very much."

A picture began forming in Jack'O's brain, clouded somewhat by phrases like "illegal trafficking," and "out of season."

"So...what would your average gall bladder be worth?" It never hurt to ask.

Ping shrugged. "Maybe...five dollars ah ounce... maybe more?"

Jack'O's mind boggled. Five bears times four paws each, five gall bladders, two penises—at least. How many pounds was that? (It didn't cross his mind that Chinese apothecaries probably dealt in dried bear parts.) He calculated that the paws alone would have to average a pound or two each—how many ounces were there in a pound? Jack'O

couldn't remember. "How would a guy go about selling this stuff?"

"In the city," Ping said. "People looking for this stuff all the time."

The idea would not leave Jack'O alone. Visions of the haul he could have made on his way back from the caribou gate kept him awake at night. The calculations were complicated, involving speculations on the average weight of a bear's penis and so on, but even conservatively the numbers added up to quite a windfall.

There was an ethical question: Was it right to kill a bear just for its paws and a couple of other parts? "Harvest a bear," Jack'O said aloud, correcting himself. And he could probably also market the hides through a friend who had a licensed trapline, and he and Ralph could smoke a haunch or two—the meat was reputed to taste like pork. And why not harvest a few bears? They were obviously in good supply—over-supplied, in fact. The Fish and Wildlife guys were constantly having to relocate bears that had achieved "nuisance" status.

In the end Jack'O was able to rationalize the ethical considerations—which left the question of risk.

It was obviously illegal. But how could you possibly get caught? You shoot a bear, out in the middle of nowhere, take it out back of the homestead to skin it and harvest the rest of the stuff…and let the coyotes do away with the evidence.

It wasn't as if the game wardens were patrolling the bush on the lookout for bear poachers—it wasn't even hunting season—the game wardens weren't patrolling the bush at all!

By the time the next caribou delivery date rolled around, Jack'O was convinced. The only hitch he'd been able to identify in the plan was a small one. It had occurred to him that, having never actually dissected a bear, he couldn't be sure that he could identify the all-important gall bladder among the other bladders and plumbing fixtures. To harvest the various items successfully, he would have to enlist Ralph. But he held off discussing the project with his partner. He was confident that Ralph had the skills required—Ralph routinely butchered the deer and moose that kept their freezers full. Ralph was adept at this kind of work, whether combing through fish guts, looking for signs of chemical pollution in the livers, or pointing out the underdeveloped eggs in the entrails of a goose they'd popped for their supper. But Ralph would probably prove to be a little squeamish on the subject of the illegalities of the endeavour. Jack'O did tell Ralph that he would need his help on the run to the gate, and that he would pick him up on his way back from town.

"What for?" Ralph wanted to know.

"I've got something to pick up on the way back—I'll need you to give me a hand loading it," was all Jack'O had said, and Ralph didn't inquire further.

In town, Jack'O collected the groceries and a bottle of propane, then stopped by the Pagoda. The restaurant was busy with lunchtime traffic. There were customers at a half-dozen tables in the lounge—including the table in the corner occupied, once again, by the stranger.

Jack'O told Ping that he only had time for a "quick coffee" because he was just on his way back to the caribou gate.

"You what?" Ping asked, setting up a tray of drinks.

"I'm headed back to that place I told you about—remember, the bears…?" Jack'O gave Ping a nod to indicate that he required a private moment.

"Oh, you going to get bears?" Ping asked, hefting the tray, and heading out from behind the bar to deliver the drinks. Jack'O tried to pretend that he hadn't heard him. When Ping returned, he set a cup and saucer on the bar in front of Jack'O and reached for the coffeepot.

"Listen," Jack'O said, using a tone he hoped implied the need for privacy. "If I happen to…run over a bear or two on the way…"

"Better to shoot them," Ping advised, a little too loudly for Jack'O's liking.

"Listen!" He leaned over the bar and motioned to Ping to do the same. "If I did come up with a few, paws and whatnot…"

"Gall bladder…"

Jack'O cut him off; the man didn't seem capable of speaking quietly. "Could you hook me up with the people in the city?"

"City…?" Ping looked confused.

"To buy the stuff!"

"Ahhh," Ping said, and leaned closer to Jack'O. Finally, it seemed, he had caught the private nature of what Jack'O was trying to communicate.

"You think you get a bear?"

"Guaranteed!" Jack'O said, and believed it.

"You come see me."

"Big money?"

"You come see me," Ping repeated, and smiled.

With Ping, Jack'O decided, that was as good as a contract. They could hammer out the fine print later.

The road to the gate was in fine shape. They were making record time. Ralph had not questioned Jack'O on their itinerary until now.

"So, what are we doing?"

"I'll have to see," Jack'O said, "after we drop off the groceries." It was an evasion, but it was true that Jack'O did not expect to sight any bears until later in the day. It was a hot afternoon, and he believed the game would be bedded down for a siesta.

"But, what is it; what are we picking up?"

The moment didn't feel right for a lengthy explanation. "I told the guy out here that we might haul his garbage bin in for repairs. Or maybe replace it with a whole new one— he's got a bear problem eh? There's bears all over the place out here—they're over-populated."

Come to think of it, Jack'O thought, *it wouldn't be a half-bad idea to actually sell the guy a bear-proof garbage bin. There'd probably be a market for something like that— summer cottages... rig camps...*

"What did you bring that for?" Ralph had noticed the Webley pistol that Jack'O had shoved into the side pocket of his bucket seat.

"Oh…this guy wants to borrow it. Bear's got him spooked."

"It's not registered!" Ralph objected.

"Yeah, I know. I'll probably just tell him I forgot to bring it. All he has to do is pepper the place; I told him that."

"You get caught with that thing you'll lose it—probably get a fine to boot!"

"Who's gonna catch me?"

"You never know…" Ralph seemed to be in one of his pessimistic moods. Jack'O's brain was locking onto the idea of a bear-proof garbage bin manufacturing business.

"So, what could we charge this guy for a new bin?"

"Depends on what we make it out of. How big does it have to be?"

"Not very big. Maybe it should include a covered rack to store propane bottles in."

"What about angle-iron and some heavy gauge tin?"

"Yeah, that'd work. I'll show you the one they've got—bear ripped the lid off it."

"I could probably build one for 30 or 40 bucks…"

"I'll quote him a hundred," said Jack'O.

They arrived at the gate, packed in the groceries and packed out the garbage. A conference was held over the garbage bin. The thing was made of eighth-inch plywood screwed to a two-by-four frame. Ralph was not surprised that it had failed to keep the bears out. Although the attendant had no new attempted bear break-ins to report, he had noted fresh tracks around the shack. He asked about the hand gun and Jack'O told him that he'd forgotten to bring it.

"But I brought you some more cayenne," he added.

The guy was not confident that the pepper was taking care of the problem.

"One good snort is all it will take," Jack'O repeated.

The conversation cycled back to the idea of a metal bin and Jack'O quoted the guy 150 dollars, "installed." The guy said he'd pass on the quote to his superiors. A truck pulled up to the gate and honked for the attendant. Jack'O said they had to get going, thereby declining the standing offer of a coffee.

On the road back, the conversation centred on bear-proof garbage bins. Each passing mile saw innovations to the original design including spring-loaded lids, self-locking latches and metal legs that could be driven into the ground and anchor-bolted to the frame of the bin.

"We should be writing some of this down," Jack'O declared, and Ralph began rummaging through the glove compartment for a pencil and something to draw on—without success. "There's gotta be a pen in there," Jack'O said, and leaned over to paw through the debris himself.

"Watch out!" Ralph said, bracing himself.

Jack'O glanced up to see the cinnamon bear he'd seen earlier standing in the middle of the road, and hit the brakes. The garbage bags rolled forward and hit the back of their seats. As the van skidded to a halt, the bear decided to give up the road—but not its dignity. It ambled slowly off into the ditch to their right, sending warning glances back in the direction of the van as it did.

Ralph leaned out his window for a closer look. "Who do you think you are?" he said, admiringly. At the sound of

the man's voice, the bear turned toward them and stood up on its hind legs, sniffing the air.

"I think he wants a piece of us…" Ralph said. He started to turn his head toward Jack'O, and found he was sharing the open window with the Webley pistol!

"What…!"

The gun went off a couple of inches from Ralph's nose—temporarily deafening him. The bear's head snapped sideways and it keeled over backwards.

"What the hell!?" Ralph yelled, shocked by the distance between himself and the sound of his own voice.

"Come on!" Jack'O shouted, bailing out of the van.

"What in the hell do you think you're doing?!" Ralph demanded.

"Hurry up—before somebody comes," Jack'O yelled back.

"Are you crazy?" Ralph answered.

Jack'O turned on him. "Get out here!" He still held the gun—the smoking gun—the bear lay in plain sight on the far side of the ditch—the van was almost blocking the road—there was no time to argue.

"Stupid bastard…" Ralph muttered, bolting from the van.

They each grabbed a hind leg.

"Look at the size of those paws!" Jack'O said excitedly.

"Shut up and pull!" Ralph said, leaning into the work.

The bear was heavy. The men nearly powered out dragging it up the slope onto the road bed. It slid more easily on the gravel. Jack'O threw open the back doors of the van. "Maybe if we got a rope on it we could…" he said, studying the step up into the van.

"Just lift!" Ralph said angrily, throwing his arms around the bear. Somehow they managed to wrestle the animal into the vehicle, slamming the rear doors closed on Jack'O's prize just as a pickup truck appeared on the road behind them. The driver slowed to get around the van, casting a curious glance their way as he passed. The man looked vaguely familiar.

Jack'O cradled the pistol in the crook of his arm, shielding it from view, and jammed it back into the side pocket as he took his seat behind the wheel.

Ralph climbed in, slammed his door, and glared at Jack'O. Jack'O checked his side mirror and put the van in gear.

"Have you lost your mind?" Ralph inquired.

"That's a 1000-dollar bill lying back there," Jack'O said, increasing his previous rough estimate by a couple of hundred dollars. Those paws were bigger than he'd imagined.

"That's a 1500-dollar fine and the loss of this van!" Ralph shot back.

"If we'd gotten caught," said Jack'O, elated by his success. "But this ain't even game warden season."

"Hunting season, you mean—and what do you mean a 1000-dollar bill?" Ralph wasn't cooling off.

"Five bucks an ounce!" Jack'O grinned happily.

"For what?" Ralph sounded convinced that his partner had lost his grip on reality.

"Gall bladder, penis and paws!" Jack'O sounded triumphant.

"What in the hell are you talking about?" A bell was ringing somewhere in the back of Ralph's brain—an alarm bell.

"The Chinese! They buy the stuff to make medicine."

"What Chinese?"

"I've got a connection," Jack'O said.

Ralph was confused. He'd heard of the Chinese using gall bladders, but...

"So where's your connection—Hong Kong?"

Jack'O didn't get to answer. As they rounded a bend in the road, the road block came into view. A Fish and Wildlife truck, red and blue lights flashing, was parked cross-wise on the road. The vehicle that had just passed them was parked off to the side.

For two or three seconds Jack'O went into shock; "I don't believe it," he said weakly.

"I do," Ralph said bitterly.

There was no place to turn off; no chance to turn around.

"Throw them garbage bags over it!" Jack'O said. Ralph complied, trying not to make it look obvious.

A uniformed officer was standing in the road, one hand raised in a signal to stop. A second man, dressed in plain clothes, stood beside him. As the van coasted nearer, Jack'O recognized the second man as the driver of the truck that had just passed them. Jack'O also remembered why the guy had looked familiar. He was the stranger who had been camping in the Pagoda lounge.

Jack'O began to brake, off-balancing Ralph who was turned in his seat attempting to pitch the garbage bags and anything else he could find onto the bear. It wasn't going to work. As they crept nearer to the roadblock, Ralph noticed that something very peculiar was taking place in the rear of the van. The garbage bags that he had successfully landed

on the bear were continuing to move. They were not rolling forward as Jack'O checked the momentum of the van, which was now almost stopped, but heaving upwards and off to the side as if the bear was attempting to rise…the bear was attempting to rise!

As Ralph stared in disbelief, the animal began squirming and flailing its legs in the air, obviously intending to roll itself over onto its belly.

"Jack'O…" Ralph said as the bear drunkenly raised its head, and gazed about the van. "Jack'O, the bear…"

"Is it covered?" Jack'O asked, concentrating on arranging his face in a welcoming smile for the approaching officer.

"No! Look at it for God's sake! It's—"

"Calm down," Jack'O growled.

Still dazed, the bear gave its head a shake. Ralph dove for the pistol.

"Leave it!" Jack'O's hand shot out, jamming the gun deeper into the side pocket while Ralph fought to pull it out. "It's too late; he's almost here!" Jack'O hissed through his clenched smile. It was true. The officer was almost at Jack'O's window, followed closely by the stranger.

Ralph looked back to see that the bear was getting to its feet.

"Afternoon, officer," Jack'O grinned.

"Could you step out of the vehicle, please sir?"

It was at this precise moment that the bear, apparently having regained a critical degree of consciousness, locked eyes with Ralph. Ralph, apparently able to read the bear's mind, suddenly screamed "Look out!" and bailed.

Jack'O's first reaction was to duck—the officer at his window had a similar reaction—but as the bear let out a roar and charged the inside front of the van, Jack'O had no problem sorting out the subtleties of his partner's advice and followed his lead.

The bear, having hit the inside of the windshield at full tilt, now began tearing wildly at the inside of the van— while Jack'O clambered behind Ralph up over its stubby hood onto its roof. With the partners looking down from above, the enraged animal finally fought its way out of the cab via Ralph's open door and galloped through the ditch to disappear among the trees.

For a moment, all was quiet. The warden and his partner, who had done some galloping of their own, now stared after the bear from inside the truck with the flashing lights. The truck doors opened, and the officer and the stranger got out. They walked slowly toward the van, which they regarded cautiously, then looked up at Jack'O and Ralph.

"Could you step down here, sir?" The officer seemed a little edgy. Jack'O complied immediately, followed, more slowly, by Ralph. Jack'O did the talking, eventually advancing the theory that the bear "must have sneaked in there after the garbage while we were parked at the gate..."

The officer (or more correctly officers—apparently the stranger also worked for the department) didn't seem inclined to believe that the bear had been a stowaway. They searched the van and found the gun—which they confiscated—and fined Jack'O for being in possession of it. They also found small quantities of blood, which they took samples of. Jack'O continued to deny that he and Ralph could

have been responsible for the blood, maintaining that "the bear must have banged itself up!" while tearing the van apart.

In the end, the officers did not confiscate the van or pursue further charges related to poaching—having personally witnessed the evidence galloping off into the bush.

All in all, Jack'O thought he and Ralph had come through it very well. Ralph failed to see it that way.

It was just Jack'O's luck that the rumours of Ping's illicit trade in elk meat had eventually found their way into the ears of the local Fish and Wildlife guys. The tip had been duly passed on according to department procedures and protocols, to provincial head office where the undercover officer had been assigned to investigate. Having been unsuccessful in coming up with a sample of contraband elk, or any other evidence to implicate Ping, the officer had been pleased to overhear the plans for Jack'O's bear-poaching expedition.

The fact that the Pagoda had been under investigation was old news by the time Jack'O made another visit to the place. Jack'O really didn't want to talk about it. (Ralph, it seemed, didn't want to talk about anything these days, at least not with Jack'O.) But Jack'O couldn't resist knowing exactly how much he would have made.

"So, how much would you gimme for a gall bladder?" he demanded of Ping—there was no one else in the lounge. Ping hummed and hawed. "How much—gimme a number." Ping finally caved in.

"Twenty-five dollar, at least!"

"Twenty-five bucks!?" Jack'O was outraged. "What happened to 'big money!'—what happened to 'five bucks an ounce'?"

"Yes!" Ping said, "Five dollars an ounce! Gall bladder very small, very dry!"

Jack'O didn't feel like arguing; the bear-parts business wasn't one that he was likely to explore further. Bear-proof garbage bins…there was an idea with a future.

The Consultant

The kid wasn't saying anything. Everybody knew who he was—the contractor's stepson. And everybody knew he was there doing penance for unspecified sins. Speculation ran the gamut from drug infractions to stealing cars. The more conservative gossips among the crew asserted that the kid was guilty of nothing more than a premature departure from high school and repeated assaults on his stepfather's liquor cabinet. The boss/contractor had complained openly about the latter two infractions within weeks of his recent marriage to the kid's mother.

The kid was big for his age. Standing off on his own, head shaved to a close-cropped stubble, earring in one ear, dressed in the bright orange overalls he'd been handed

upon arrival, he looked like a member of a chain gang. In fact, "chain gang," considering the work day that lay ahead of us, would be a very apt description of the men assembling in the yard.

It was spring breakup. The yard was plugged with the Caterpillar tractors, graders, big rigs and other equipment the contractor usually employed clearing rig sites, roads and cutlines in the oil patch.

The men in the yard usually earned top wages as operators of this equipment. But today they were reduced to labourers' wages (10-hour days at 10 dollars an hour) for doing a job they would normally consider beneath them—seismic clean-up.

The winter before, seismograph crews had followed their web of lines through timber, swamp and farmers' fields exploding their buried charges of dynamite and recording the subterranean echoes. As part of the easements governing their access to these lands, crews were now dispatched to pick up the shot wires, plugs, chocolate bar wrappers and pop cans that had been left behind. The work had to be done on foot since much of the frozen land that had afforded the winter access was now melted into mud.

Someone hollered, "Safety meeting," signifying the start to the workday, and the men crowded around the back of the shop. A head count revealed that there were more workers than work, and regular employees were given the option of passing up the 100-dollar days slogging through the mud. A few took advantage of the offer, but not enough to cancel the surplus.

"You, you and you—call me tonight and I'll let you know if we'll need you tomorrow," said the foreman. Those

indicated backed out of the circle. The foreman announced that hardhats and fluorescent safety vests must be worn on the job. Someone asked why. "Because," the foreman said, and began dividing us into two-man crews.

It seems that nothing can be accomplished in the oil patch without the constant aid and attention of "The Consultant."

The man began handing out shovels and packs of garbage bags and then directed them to their respective consultant. Perhaps it was assumed that no man who would carry a shovel and pick garbage could read a map, or perhaps it was assumed that we couldn't be trusted to actually collect the garbage unsupervised. Whatever the reason, consultants were the order of the day.

"You're with that guy," the foreman said, and pointed across the yard. A man, probably in his mid-30s, sat on the end gate of a fire-engine red pickup, smoking a cigarette. There was a high-powered snowmobile in the box of the pickup. The man was dressed in racing leathers emblazoned with the same brand as the snowmobile. Shovel in hand, I made my way across the yard and introduced myself.

"Where's your partner?" the consultant asked. If he had a name, he obviously saw no need for me to know it.

I confessed that as far as I knew I was partnerless.

The consultant rolled his eyes and heaved a sigh, obviously vexed at my apparent lack of concern. But I didn't feel guilty. I'd been informed by an acquaintance among the regular employees that the consultants were paid far in excess of the 10-dollar rate. They were also paid an additional hourly rate for the use of their pickups. The man would be making thousands to our hundreds for sitting in

his truck listening to the radio while we did the work. If he actually had to get off his end gate to ask after his second crewmember, that would be fine with me. But he was saved the trouble. The foreman was approaching. He informed the consultant that, "You get the kid."

"Oh, perfect," said the consultant. "Why me?" he added.

"Just lucky, I guess."

I could see the kid making his way across the yard toward us.

"Well, he better be ready to work," said the consultant. "I'm not getting paid to babysit juvenile delinquents."

"Oh, he's ready to work all right," said the foreman, grinning as the kid drew up beside me. "Aren't you…" he added, acknowledging that the kid had to have heard them talking about him. The kid was stone faced.

"Good luck," said the foreman.

"Thanks," said the man in the racing leathers. "Did you pick up some bags?" he demanded of the kid.

The kid turned his blank stare in the consultant's direction, and said, "Whaddaya mean?"

"What do I mean? Did you pick up a package of garbage bags?"

"I didn't know I was supposed to…"

"Oh, you didn't know…you do know you're a garbage picker, don't you?"

"Yeah…"

"Well, what were you planning on doing with the garbage?"

"There's a stack of bags at the back of the shop," I said quietly.

The kid gave me a questioning look then turned toward the shop. The consultant told me to get in the truck. He took my shovel from me and placed it carefully in the box of the truck beside the gleaming snowmobile.

"Wait a minute!" he said, then drawing a package of fresh overalls from the box, spread them over the new leather seat of his pickup. I got in and we swung by the back of the shop to pick up the kid.

The drive out to where the program began was uneventful. The kid still wasn't talking. The consultant felt moved to inform us that if he hadn't been called in on this "stupid job" he'd be snowmobiling in the mountains. He made it clear that we would be "hauling ass" in order to allow him to return to that project as soon as possible. He also provided us with sundry statistics concerning the engine size and the speed the machine in the box of the truck was capable of. When the kid and I failed to express the awe and general interest this information should obviously elicit, conversation lapsed into silence.

Finally the truck began to slow to the speed limit, then coast to a stop as our driver checked the map he'd stashed on the dash in front of him. "That's it," he said, scanning a stubble field to our left. The intermittent line of shot-holes stretched out over the field like regimented gopher holes. "Level the mounds, pick up anything that shouldn't be there," said the consultant, without getting out of the truck, then as an afterthought added, "I'll pick you up down at the highway in an hour."

Not having been privileged to a view of the map, I could only guess that the highway could be as far as three or four kilometres away over uncertain ground and encumbrances.

The kid and I got out and retrieved our shovel and a couple of garbage bags. "An hour?" I said, glancing at the consultant.

"You got a problem with that?" he asked.

"I don't know," I said. "Maybe, if it's all like this…" The field seemed firm, if not dry, and would probably be fairly easy going.

"Just be there," said the consultant, and sped off.

"What a jerk," the kid muttered, unfolding one bag and stuffing a spare into the baggy back pocket of his overalls.

It was a beautiful spring day; the sun warm, the air alive with bird song. Surveying the vista before us, and perhaps attempting to lighten the mood, I made a somewhat unguarded comment to the effect that all seemed right with the world!

"The world sucks…" said the kid. His tone did not invite further discussion on the subject.

A routine soon developed between the two of us. Arriving at a shot-hole, I would locate the shot wire. If the hole was still intact, it was easy to extract the entire length of the wire. Usually, however, the hole had collapsed. In this case, I would dig down to a depth I thought to be below the level of the farmer's plow or cultivator, and cut the wire with the spade. Meanwhile, the kid would be stuffing the plastic shot plug, and whatever other debris was in evidence, into his garbage bag. I'd hand him the wire and we'd be off to the next hole. It wasn't hard work.

At the end of the field we crossed a line of trees to find that the next plot of ground was pasture. The firm sod was even easier to hike over than the soft stubble. We were making good time.

Alas, as we crossed the fence line onto the next plot of ground, we hit mud. This field had either been summerfallow or the farmer had worked it up after the harvest. Each step we took buried our boots well past the ankle. The effort required, drawing one foot after another out of the muck, soon had us sweating.

"I should have grabbed a water bottle," I said, thinking of the bottles I'd stuffed into a small cooler along with my lunch. The kid nodded, grimly surveying the pond of black mud surrounding us.

"You wear a watch?" I asked. The kid shook his head. I guessed we'd been going for about a half-hour. The highway was nowhere in sight. The mud ended, thankfully, in another pasture—or rather a succession of meadows between groves of scraggy-looking aspens. We hadn't gone far when we were joined by a pair of donkeys. Three more fell in behind us as we entered the first clump of trees. On the other side of the trees our growing procession attracted the attention of a half-dozen more. One began braying loudly to those ahead and all were soon gathered around us as we stopped for a shot-hole.

"What do they want?" the kid asked nervously.

"Nothing," I said. "They're just curious—probably bored." One craned its neck to gingerly nibble at the elbow of the kid's orange overalls.

"Take off!" he said, taking a swing at the offending jackass with his bag of garbage. Startled, the herd took a jump and then stared as one at the kid, as if demanding to know what his problem was. I had to smile.

As we moved on, the donkeys fell in behind us in single file. When we stopped, they would crowd around to watch

us work, nudging one another this way and that until everybody had a clear view.

Through the trees ahead, I could see the outbuildings of a farmstead I took to be the donkeys' home. The seismic line seemed to be aimed right at the place, and I wondered whether the hole we were on would be the last in the line—presumably the crews would have stopped dynamiting a safe distance back from the farmer's waterwells and residence.

One of the donkeys began braying and was joined by a second, then a third. The volume was incredible! The kid, who had yet to relax in the animals' company, became increasingly agitated by the racket. As if seized by an attack of donkey-phobia, he suddenly joined in the braying himself, shouting "Heeeyah!" and heaving his bulging garbage bag in a roundhouse swing at our assembled audience. Once again the donkeys took an involuntary jump, colliding with each other in the process. Once again they turned to stare at the kid as if questioning his sanity—certainly his manners.

"Get lost!" the kid yelled, with another swing of the bag. The donkeys, who seemed to be getting used to this maneuver, responded with a toss of their heads, but little more.

"Hey!" A voice from the direction of the farmstead startled us all. I looked up to see an older man, whom I took to be the farmer, striding through the pasture toward us. "What do you think you're doing?"

The kid let his garbage bag fall to his side and stepped back. It was clear that I was elected to do the talking.

"Hi there!" I called out, as the man bore down on our position in his pasture.

"What are you doing here?" he demanded.

"We're just cleaning up the mess the seismic guys left behind," I said pleasantly.

"You're with that oil company!" The statement was voiced as an accusation.

"Ahh…contractor, actually…local company, maybe you know…"

"Who told you you could come on my land?"

For a moment the question stumped me. "Well, like I said, we're just cleaning things up a little, we…"

"Who asked ya?"

Stumped again.

"Damned oil companies think they own this country—think they can do whatever the hell they want!"

"Actually, I tend to agree with you," I said. The kid gave me a questioning look.

"What?" said the farmer, still fuming.

"I agree with you."

"Well…then what are you doing working for them?"

I'd just been wondering the same thing myself. Obviously I could use the money, and seismic clean-up didn't seem like the worst thing I could be doing, but actually being identified as one of "them" had led me to wonder if I wasn't selling a little corner of my soul for 100 dollars a day.

"How far's the highway from here?" I asked, deciding that a change of subject might be best for all concerned.

"'Bout a mile south—what's that got to do with anything?"

"We've got to meet a guy there—would it be all right if we carried on south?"

"South, north, I don't care where you carry on to as long as you get off my land!"

"Thank you," I said, and giving the kid a nod started walking. A few paces on I glanced back to see that the farmer had stayed with his donkeys. He seemed to be inspecting them for garbage bag damage.

I decided to give the farmstead a wide berth. I didn't fancy the idea of taking up the discussion on the subject of our trespass with whatever members of the farmer's family might be hanging around the yard. The man was right. No one had invited us onto the property no matter how good our intentions. Still, the encounter was something of a shock. I'd been coming onto farms and ranches all my life, invited or not, and couldn't recall a single instance when I'd received a similar reception. Whether lost and looking for directions, or stuck and looking for a tow, one could usually expect to be received with a modicum of hospitality.

We squeezed through the barbed-wire fence, crossed the ditch and headed down the road in the direction of the farm, scanning the hayfield to the south for the seismic line. The sun was getting hot. Again I regretted not having had the sense to bring some drinking water along. We spotted the line adjacent to the farmer's driveway. I could see the man returning to his yard. Normally I would have asked for a drink from the pump, which I guessed would be used to fill a water trough somewhere in the barnyard, but this wasn't the time.

"How late do you think we are?" I asked the kid.

"Who cares…" he said sullenly. I could think of one person who probably did.

At the first shot-hole, the kid tied off his full bag of garbage and unfolded the spare. We still couldn't see the

highway. The hayfield was bordered on the south by a line of willows. Pushing though the willows, we were greeted by news both good and bad. In the distance we could finally see the high-speed traffic that indicated the location of the highway. But between it and ourselves lay a field of mud that turned into open water near the highway. We started into the mud, which grew deeper with each step as we moved in the direction of the water. Ducks and geese, preening in the sun, blanketed its surface. It soon became clear that we were going to have to abandon the line to detour around the worst of the mud. We were already sinking about mid-calf, the kid dragging the full garbage bag behind him, me using the shovel as a staff as the field sucked at my sodden boots.

We turned west, but the field was flat and conditions didn't change much as we staggered through the swampy muck. It was slow going. I was at the point of considering a return to the line of willows when finally the ground seemed to be firming up. Ten minutes on, it seemed to improve enough that we struck a line south towards the highway. Twice we blundered into bog-holes, invisible on the black surface of the field, but eventually waded victoriously onto the grasses of the ditch bordering the highway—mud nearly up to our belt lines—and sat down for a well-deserved breather.

The screeching of tires skidding to a halt on the pavement cut short our break. The consultant, as he burst from the cab, did not look happy. "So, who told you it was nap time?!" he said, glaring down at us from the shoulder of the road.

"Actually," I said, "we just got here."

"Oh, you did. What are you doing here, anyway? You're a half mile off the line!"

"Well, the line is under water," I offered.

"Get in the truck!" snarled the man in the racing leathers. But as we rose from the grass, he suddenly seemed to be of two minds on the subject. "There's no way you're getting in my truck like that!" he declared, horrified at the sight of the wet mud plastered over our lower extremities.

"Yeah? Well, there's no way I'm getting rid of my pants!" I countered. The kid actually smiled.

"Shit!" said the consultant, spinning with rage. "Get in the back!" he ordered.

The kid and I looked at each other, then, resigned to our fate, stepped toward the gleaming red vehicle.

"No!" screamed our driver. The kid, who was in the act of heaving his muddy garbage bag into the box of the truck, checked his swing.

"What do you think you're doing?"

"What do you want me to do?" the kid asked calmly. For a moment, the consultant didn't seem to know what he wanted him to do, then reaching into the box of the truck, ripping a new garbage bag from the package, which he threw in the kid's face, said, "Bag it!"

The kid's expression went blank, but I noticed a slight tremor in his hands as he began unfolding the plastic.

"You get any mud on that sled and you'll be spending tonight in the wash bay on your own time!" warned the consultant. "And hurry it up!" He climbed into the driver's seat, slamming the door behind himself.

"Maybe we should just run behind…" I suggested. The kid's face remained blank.

The ride in the box of the pickup was not an unpleasant one. The drinking water was still cool, although the

cooler had been sitting in the box of the truck exposed to the heat of the mid-day sun. I passed the kid one of the bottles, which he accepted with a grim nod of thanks, but declined the offer of a sandwich.

"You sure?" I asked.

"I'm good…" he answered, staring sullenly out at the passing scenery.

"Have an apple," I said, tossing it to him.

He hesitated, but seemed to decide that apples weren't worth arguing about, and bit into it. The truck was slowing down.

"C'mere," ordered our consultant, as he emerged from the pickup unfolding the map, which he spread out on the hood of the truck. "We're here," he said, jabbing a finger at the map. I leaned over to take a look. "You see this line?" I said that I did. "It ends here…" The finger moved diagonally over the grid of fields to intersect a road to the southwest. "Do you think you could manage to follow it this time?"

"What's this?" I asked, pointing out a section of the map next to where the finger had stopped. What looked to be the better part of a half-section of land had been crosshatched in black ink, and a bright red line had been struck through it. The seismic line seemed to dissect the crosshatching, ending at the road the consultant had indicated as the point of our next rendezvous.

He leaned over for a closer look. "What's the difference?" he said angrily. "I asked you if you could follow the line."

"Looks okay from here," I said, gazing off to the southwest. "Depends on how much water is out there I guess…"

"Do you see any lakes or rivers?" he demanded.

I glanced back at the map. "No, but…"

"Then just follow the damned line!"

He scooped the map off the hood, angrily crushing it into a crude fold before tossing it into the truck. "And take this," he said, extracting a leather-cased walkie-talkie from behind the seat and shoving it into my hand. "This time call before you get lost!"

"We weren't lost," I said, but the guy wasn't listening.

"…Save me burning up a tank of gas looking for you." He reached into the box of the truck for the shovel, which he threw on the ground, cursing the mud on his hands. "Pigs…" he muttered. "You got your bags?" he asked the kid.

The kid discarded what was left of his apple core and went for the bags. We'd both kept our water bottles.

"Well?" said the consultant, glaring at us. "What are you waiting for?" I picked up the shovel and we moved into the ditch.

"Two hours, tops!" shouted the man in the racing leathers, "or I'll leave you guys out here!" The tires spun in the gravel as the pickup sped off toward the east.

"He's going to town for lunch," the kid said, staring after him.

"You're probably right," I said.

It really was a beautiful spring day, and I resolved not to let the consultant's attitude spoil it. Following the line from shot-hole to shot-hole, we soon found ourselves mingling with a large herd of cows and calves. The latter frolicked in the sunshine while their mothers stared at us stupidly, sleepily chewing their cud. The kid seemed more at ease with cattle than he had been with donkeys.

The land sloped gently to the south and was, therefore, relatively dry. We moved along at a leisurely pace. Neither of us was in any mood to impress our boss by setting a new record for seismic clean-up. About an hour into the hike, we stopped on the edge of a large hayfield for a break. Lounging in the afternoon sun, lulled by the sound of insects lazily buzzing through their day, I was tempted to take the nap we'd been accused of taking earlier. Off to our left, the hayfield turned into an open swamp ringed with cattails. The clamour of geese mingled with the song of red-winged blackbirds and drifted over the hayfield in waves. The seismic line angled through the field skirting the edge of the swamp, and disappeared into a stand of spruce trees. I guessed that while it might get a little soggy passing the swamp, the sod would probably bear our weight.

Sudden movement overhead startled me from my thoughts. I glanced up to see a lone Canada goose speeding past us in the direction of the swamp. Shielding my eyes from the sun, I saw that the goose was not alone at all but had a bald eagle on its tail.

"Look at that!" I said, but the kid was already watching.

The eagle, though it seemed to be flying at a more leisurely pace than its prey, slowly overtook the goose, but did not strike. It overflew its target, passing a metre above it. Then, just when it looked as though the goose might be allowed to make the safety of the swamp, the eagle arced skyward in a loop-the-loop that culminated in a power dive. The arc of the dive actually brought it under the fleeing goose where, incredibly, the eagle flipped upside down, clutching upwards to bury its razor-edged talons into the belly of the goose! An explosion of goose feathers marked

the beginning of the end. The bird's wings flapped awkwardly once or twice before folding. It tumbled once before turfing into the hayfield in a lifeless heap. The eagle, which had righted itself after contact, now banked to glide to a landing next to its prize.

The kid and I watched silently as it tore into its lunch.

"I've seen lots of eagles," the kid mused, "but I never seen one do anything like that…"

"Me neither," I said.

The eagle, which was losing no time filling its belly, ignored us as we rose to resume our hike. We seemed to be running out of prairie. The row of shot-holes became a cutline as it entered the spruce trees, and the land rose and fell over gentle hills and hidden hollows. A few hundred metres into the trees we came to what would normally be a lazy creek wandering over the forest floor. But at this time of year, it was swollen into a rushing stream that did not look inviting. At the point where it intersected the cutline, it was a couple of metres across and, I guessed, chest deep. With only two options before us, I chose to turn upstream—the kid didn't seem to care what we did. Fifteen minutes of hiking brought us to a place where the stream forked into its two smaller tributaries. A hundred metres past that, we found a place where the first channel narrowed, gushing wildly between an old stump and a rocky bank. We tossed the shovel and garbage across, burning our bridges so to speak. Then, taking a short run at the situation, I took the first leap. I made it, but just barely, splashing feet first into the shallow waters above the bank before scrambling into the rose bushes beyond. The kid cleared it easily.

We were gratified to discover that the second tributary was the narrower one of the two, and we could almost step across it.

"Crew one, are you by?" We'd almost forgotten about our consultant.

"Clean—up—crew—are—you—by?"

The kid had adopted the walkie-talkie since shovelling demanded both hands and I had complained that I was probably going to set the thing down somewhere and forget it. He'd fixed it to his belt through a side-slit in his overalls, which made things awkward at the moment. He fumbled with the belt, hurriedly trying to free the squawking box.

"Crew one! Answer me!" The consultant was quickly working himself into one of his little tantrums.

The kid finally passed me the radio.

"Crew one—go ahead…"

"Where the hell are you guys?"

"Beats me," I said, smiling at the kid, then depressed the talk button and answered, "We just had a bit of a detour—hit a flooded creek here in the bush. We're just coming back onto the line now…"

"Where?"

"Where what?"

"You're coming onto the line, where?"

"On the other side of the creek."

"There is no creek!" said the consultant, obviously believing the map.

"Well, actually, there is. It's in a big stand of spruce," I offered.

"Do you remember where you're supposed to be?" the voice sneered.

"Of course," I answered.

"Well, how far from here are you?"

"I can't see much in this bush," I said, "but I don't imagine we're too far."

"You don't imagine…in other words, you're lost—again!"

"Are you really as stupid as you pretend to be?" I said, giving the kid another look, then pushed the button. "Give us a few minutes to get out of this bush and we'll call you back with a landmark."

"Well, hurry it up!" advised our consultant.

"Oh yeah, we're runnin' now boss, we're runnin' now…" I said, passing the radio back to the kid. We sauntered on through the big spruce trees. The cutline came out of the trees on the brow of a cutbank of clay. To our extreme right, we could see open water—probably the creek we had just crossed backed up by a beaver dam or maybe the distant roadbed. Alders and willows obscured our view in that direction. Ahead of us, the line crossed what looked like a natural meadow. It then seemed to disappear into a dense jungle of alders, willows and stunted swamp spruce. From where we were, I could see no sign that the cutline carried on into the jungle. I decided to take a closer look before reporting our position.

We crossed the meadow to find a woven wire fence well over a metre high separating the meadow and the bush. I looked back to see that we were still on line with the shot-holes we'd been following, but no cutline was in evidence through the willows. "No Trespassing," "No Shooting," "Private Property" signs alternated down the line of fence.

"I think we better consult the consultant," I said. The kid handed me the walkie-talkie.

I reported our position, giving the man a detailed description of what lay ahead of us. He responded that he was waiting for us on the other side of the identical fence, which ran along the road he was on, and ordered us to get on with it.

"I'm not sure that's a good idea..." I ventured.

"Oh, you don't—and why is that?" The voice oozed out of the radio, dripping with sarcasm.

"Well, I really don't think this guy's going to want us here."

"So what?"

"In fact, it looks like the seismic line actually quits here!"

"Well, it doesn't," snapped the man with the map. "Just get out here—now!"

I looked at the kid, who looked back with his usual blank stare. There's an old saying that goes "the boss may not always be right, but he's always the boss." Pondering this, I heaved a sigh and began climbing the fence. Picking up my shovel on the other side, I felt more convinced than ever that we were making a mistake. Muddy little trails ran this way and that through the undergrowth. It was dark under the dense canopy of willows and alders. I led the way, feeling every inch the trespasser I was. On the other hand, I guessed that it would be very unlikely that we'd be discovered in here, unless the owner happened to be wandering around the place on foot. But there seemed to be no reason for anybody, including ourselves, to be out here—there was no sign of the cutline.

"What is this place?" the kid asked quietly. I confessed that I really had no idea. I began scrutinizing the black mud of the trail for tracks, and found them, in profusion: cloven hoofed, too small for cows, or buffalo, or even elk…

"Maybe this guy raises deer," I guessed, but the picture didn't fit.

We followed the winding little game trails as they twisted around willow crowns, or dipped through boggy hollows, choosing those that led in the southwesterly direction the line had followed. Bit by bit, the land began to rise and patches of rip-gut and wild maize began to make room for themselves among the wild roses and devil's club.

Through the trees I could see an opening bright in sunlight, and thought we might be coming to the other side of this gloomy little jungle. But as we drew closer it turned out to be a small meadow of tall tawny grasses surrounded on all sides by more bush. I stopped suddenly—unsure why. The kid, coming along behind, almost bumped into me. "What is it?" he whispered.

"I thought I saw something," I said.

The kid was stepping up beside me when I saw it again.

"There!" I whispered, nodding to my left.

"Oh, yeah…" said the kid. "Think it's a bear?!" His tone implied that the possibility did not please him. But it didn't look like a bear. It didn't look like anything at all—a dark patch of grizzled hair gliding silently between the leaves and branches of the understorey. Whatever it was seemed to pass us by. We moved on.

Our first step onto the sunlit edge of the meadow set off the alarm. The ground came alive with creatures the colour of the moving patch of hair, squealing like the demons of

hell as they dashed through the grass in all directions. We'd stumbled onto a nest of wild boar basking in the sun!

The piglets ran, tails straight up, like little train cars behind the sows galloping stiff-legged, like short buffalo, into the surrounding dark. In seconds, all had vanished; the meadow was silent. But before the kid or I could gather our wits, the counterattack began.

Flickers of movement to our left, and right, set the hair rising on the back of my neck. Then, directly across the meadow, we got our first look at the animal straight on.

Through one of the tunnel-like trails that led into the clearing, we could see the bulging shoulders and ugly head swaying from side to side as it advanced. When it broke into the sunlight, the thing seemed to grow in size, its tusked jaws, beady eyes and massive hump swaying from one front leg to the next with each step.

"Oh, god…" said a small voice at my side.

"Don't move…" I whispered back. My throat was dry, my voice hoarse.

Having gathered their piglets behind themselves, the hogs had obviously drawn their line in the meadow. The first hint of aggression on our part would bring them down on us in a frenzy, which I had no trouble imagining would end very badly. I thought of an old farmer who'd had the bad luck to have been killed and partially eaten by his own hogs—domestic hogs—not the wild variety stalking us from the other side of the clearing! At the same time, I sensed that it would not be wise to turn our backs on the situation and try to outrun it.

Slowly I raised the shovel above my head. The animal stopped, its black eyes drilling into us—then charged! It

halted not two metres in front of us, pausing for two or three heart-stopping seconds, before recommencing its step-by-step swaying action, in reverse. Taking this as our cue, we also began backing slowly down the trail that had led us into the clearing.

The animal offered two more mock charges—and sundry verbal insults in some form of pig-latin that was not difficult to catch the drift of—but did not pursue us beyond the edge of the meadow.

It didn't take long for our careful withdrawal to turn into flat-out retreat. We turned tail and ran, the kid easily out-distancing me to be the first to bail over the woven-wire fence. Having joined him, I felt strangely elated—fuelled, I supposed, by residual adrenalin. The kid, on the other hand, was not amused.

"That idiot could have got us killed," he said, as we hiked back north along the fence line.

"But I don't think he did it on purpose," I said, half joking. "I mean, I don't think he had a clue this guy was raising wild boar."

"I don't think he's got a clue, period," said the kid. "What if that thing had actually got us—whose fault would it be?"

"Well, it would make for an interesting day in court," I said, still riding the wave.

The kid withdrew into his more typical silence—but his mind, as it turned out, was still analysing the merits of the case in detail. When we got to the end of the fence line and looked west, toward where the road should be, we were not surprised to see that that ground lay under water. We'd already observed that most of the lands north and west

were flooded. A line through the bush had been cleared for the fence; the Cat had bulldozed the brush into a windrow along its length. This we attempted to use as a bridge to the road, but were frequently reduced to wading through the icy water before we got there.

When we did, the kid immediately threw down his garbage, hardhat and vest, and began kicking off the orange coveralls he wore over his regular clothing. He then released the walkie-talkie from his belt and handed it to me.

"I shut it off," he said, matter-of-factly.

"You shut it off?"

"I'm outta here," he explained.

"What?" I wasn't getting it.

"I'm leaving," he said. "See ya." And with that began hiking north down the gravel road.

Our consultant would still be parked, presumably, somewhere along the fence line to the south.

Watching the kid go, I began to guess at the gist of his argument. He'd been press-ganged into a job he hated, with no way to escape, and the recent events offered a plausible excuse for him to quit. On the other hand, I doubted whether he cared about the plausibility of his excuses at all. Whatever his reasoning, he'd obviously crossed a line and was committed to open revolt.

A battered old pickup passed me coming from the south, its driver eyeing me suspiciously as he coasted by. Hearing the truck, the kid turned and stuck out his thumb. The truck's brake lights came on, it stopped and the kid climbed in.

I turned the radio on and raised the consultant.

"Where in the—why haven't you guys answered me?"

"We couldn't," I said. "We were too busy with the hogs..."

"What are...where are you?"

I told him where I was. The fire-engine red pickup appeared in minutes, drifting to a halt in the loose gravel. The consultant was spitting mad. "You dumb bastards couldn't...where's the kid?" he demanded, staring at the gear piled beside the road.

"He left."

"What do you mean, he left?"

"He's gone," I said with a shrug.

There seemed to be several aspects of this simple statement of fact that the consultant needed to ponder. While he was doing that, I broke the news that the fenced paddock contained a large number of wild boar.

"Wild what?"

"Boar...like, razor-back hogs? The kind that take people who mess with them apart."

"So...?"

"We ran into them back there—it might have had something to do with the kid taking off."

The consultant swore, then once again seemed to feel the need to think. Perhaps he was pondering the meaning of the red line that had been drawn through this property on his map. Perhaps he was figuring out how to explain losing the boss's kid. Whatever it was seemed to inspire a great deal more swearing.

Downwind

Spring had come early to the grasslands and coulees of Cottonwood Creek. To the Hutterian Brethren whose cattle ranged over vast leaseholds in the area, it was a mixed blessing. For the boys who were pulling calves, the shirt-sleeve weather was made-to-order. But the land was dry. All that was left of the scant snows of winter were the remainders of drifts lining the leeward rims of the coulees. The pastures already bore the green tinge that traditionally would not be expected for two or three weeks. Without rain, or a late snowfall, the green would turn brown before it was time to turn the cattle out onto the open range. But nobody in cow-camp was looking for rain just yet—certainly not snow! Even the youngest among them had done

his time rescuing newborn calves from the punishing winds of spring blizzards.

The crew totalled six in all—not counting the two dogs and four horses. Eli was the youngest, at 17; big Dan the eldest at 26. They stayed in the line shack—a one-room shiplap affair with a lean-to addition built off the back for sleeping quarters. It wasn't luxurious but its tarpaper walls kept out the wind, and the big wood/propane heater, which also served as a cook stove, kept the place warm whatever the weather.

Big Dan was the boss in camp. Jake was the official Cow Boss of the colony, but he didn't usually stay at the shack. Jake made visits to the place at frequent, if irregular, intervals ostensibly to keep the boys on their toes. Generally they needed no prodding.

There is something about calving season, something akin to panning for gold, which gets in your blood. Every healthy calf is a win; every unhealthy calf a challenge—and every dead calf a blight on the record of the crew. (Twins are a bonus.) The ultimate goal would be to turn out every cow in the herd with a calf frisking at her side. Of course that would probably never happen. At peak times the colony ran up to 1200 head of cows, and only a miracle of God could ensure a perfect score. The real goal, almost as unattainable, was to beat the previous record—and the way the warm spell was going, this might just be the year to do it.

The pecking order among the crew was such that Eli and Zeke drew the night shift. Zeke was two years older than Eli, but tended to be on the quiet side. Eli was a talker. Despite his tender years, he was known to have opinions on everything, continuously.

The bulk of the heavy work took place during the daylight hours. Men from the colony often augmented the day crew by hauling feed, spreading straw for bedding or penning and treating the cattle. Not that the night shift wasn't work. Babysitting a maternity ward the size of the Cottonwood Creek cow herd involved more than simply keeping awake. Knowing when a cow was about to go into labour, and convincing her that she'd be happier seeing the blessed event through in the relative comfort of the calving sheds, was a task that could keep a man on his feet. (And on the run if the expectant mother happened to be a rangy old range cow.) When a half-dozen or more calves decided to make a race out of it, the night could pass very quickly for Eli and Zeke. If a major problem developed, big Dan or somebody else from the day shift was on call.

The herd was divided into two. The main complex of corrals and calving sheds was about a half-mile up the creek from the shack in the shelter of the wide valley. The second herd was up on the flatland to the east, about a half-mile from the first. It was generally understood that Zeke would mind the valley herd and Eli the herd up top, but usually they spent the night commuting between the two together. The old pickup they rode in was also a comfortable place to warm up on cold nights. Several of the calving sheds were equipped with portable propane heaters so it wasn't that the boys would be left in the cold, but the truck felt more like a command vehicle.

Big Dan was not one to revel in the role of overseer anyway. The truth was that for the past few days, Dan had been doing a little moonlighting. A black bear had been sighted in the area. Speculation was that it had worked its way

down the creek, feeding on poplar buds. Dan had seen signs that the bear had discovered their carcass dump. (Dead cattle were pushed over the edge of a deep ravine located downwind and out of sight of the shack, in the opposite direction from the cattle. The dump drew the coyotes away from the herd, reducing the risk that they may be tempted to start making dead calves out of live ones.)

Having studied the signs, tracking the bear's movements over the past days, Dan had become convinced that the bear had decided to become a regular patron at the dump.

Dan hadn't shared the details of his study with the boys. When he did mention that he'd seen evidence that the bear had visited the dump, he did so in such a way that it left the impression that the animal had just been snacking on its way by. It was not uncommon that Dan would rise at random times through the night to make rounds. It was not as common, but not rare that he would take a rifle with him. If any of the boys had noticed that Dan had been leaving the shack armed, at regular pre-dawn and pre-dusk intervals, nobody mentioned it.

Colony members were granted a small allowance. The amount was not intended to reflect a dividend or share of income; certainly it was far too meagre to represent a wage. The needs of all the members of the commune—food, shelter, clothing, etc.—were intended to be met equally. But given the tendency any of us has to prosper beyond our needs, it was not surprising that a modest underground economy existed within the colony. Those wishing to indulge in some of the basic luxuries found ways to augment their allowance. A bear hide, when added to the coyote hides Dan

had already salted away, would make a very welcome addition to his modest treasure trove. Besides, coyotes hunt in packs but bear hunters tended to work alone. To even approach the dump—reading the wind correctly, choosing invisible access and holding a vigil, silent and motionless hour after hour as the cold crept into the very marrow of your bones—these were tasks made more difficult by adding to your number. Once the bear discovered that it was being hunted, the hunt would be over.

It was a busy morning. The day crew was assembling whatever gear the men expected the demands of their day would require. Eli and Zeke, back from the night shift, were reporting the tally: five new calves alive and well, no casualties among those whose health the boys were monitoring.

"That calf outa' that brindle heifer up top…?" said Zeke to no one in particular, "…it still won't suck." He went on to report that he had milked the heifer out just before coming off shift and that the calf had had no trouble accepting the milk secondhand. The heifer, he noted, was not easy to milk.

"It's your own fault, spoiling it like that," Eli said. "That calf's gonna be a pail-bunter all its life."

"It won't suck," Zeke said simply.

"Course it won't," Eli argued. "Not as long as it don't haf'ta—just stop feeding it; it'll suck when it gets hungry."

"I'll check on it," said Big Dan.

Two of the boys had saddled horses. Dan had announced that they would be sorting today, cutting the dry cows and some cows that had slipped their calves out of the bunch in the valley. The two dogs, a border collie and a blue heeler, sat in front of the shack, anxiously following the movements of the men with their eyes.

"You guys go ahead," Dan said to the boys holding the horses. As they mounted up, the blue heeler moved to follow. The collie looked to Dan. Dan snapped his fingers and the heeler returned.

"You gonna turn them culls out?" asked Eli. He was sitting on the step, more or less in the middle of the traffic.

"We might be shippin 'em," Dan replied.

Eli took a sip from the coffee cup cradled on his drawn-up knees. "When?"

Dan shrugged, intent on the pages of the log sheets he was sorting.

"We gonna ship 'em all?"

Dan didn't seem to hear the question.

"We gonna ship all them culls?"

Dan scowled at the pages before him, flipped ahead, then back.

"Is Jake coming out today?"

Dan didn't reply.

"Dan?" Eli persisted.

"What?"

"Is Jake comin' out today?"

"No," Dan said, "he's in town seein' if he can make a deal on them culls."

"Are we gonna ship 'em all?"

"How would I know?" Dan tossed the log sheets through the open window onto the seat of his pickup, and began stripping off his heavy black coat—the day was warming up quickly. The dogs fidgeted, nervously imploring Dan not to leave them behind. They needn't have worried. Dan maintained that "a good dog is worth three riders" and got few arguments on the subject.

He glanced at the dogs and gave a nod in the direction of the truck box. The dogs were in the box before he could reach for the door handle. The remaining member of the day shift was climbing in on the passenger side as Dan got behind the wheel. The motor sparked to life and Dan looked back at Eli still sitting on the step.

"I'll be back in a while," he said. He didn't say that he'd come in hours after dark and risen before sunup, returning to the shack not long before Eli and Zeke got off shift. Dan was badly in need of a nap. In lieu of this information, Eli was left to ponder the many possible reasons for Dan's returning, as the pickup cruised out of sight.

It was a glorious spring morning. Somewhere, out over the prairie, a meadowlark was diligently setting the scene to music. Eli lifted his cup to his lips to find that the coffee, or what was left of it, was cold. He rose, swirled the dregs around in the cup and dumped them beside the step.

Inside, the shack felt musty and close. "It's stuffy in here," Eli said. "It smells like wet boots."

"It smells like it always smells," said Zeke. He was sitting at the table leafing through a Canadian Tire flyer, which he'd pulled from the box of fire-starter next to the stove.

Eli reached for the big camp coffee pot, testing its weight. "You want some more coffee?" he asked.

"It'll keep me awake," Zeke said.

"So?"

"So it'll keep me awake."

The coffee was still warm. "You sure?" Eli asked, holding the pot aloft.

"No, I don't want none," Zeke confirmed.

"Dan's comin' back—maybe he's got somethin' for us to do…"

"No, he don't."

"How do you know—he said he's comin' back."

"He'd of said if he had somethin' for us to do."

"Then what's he comin' back for?"

Zeke didn't answer.

"You wanna take a ride and see how the creek's doin?" The idea seemed to have entered Eli's mind at nearly the same instant it came out of his mouth.

"I'm goin' to sleep," Zeke said, heading for the back room.

Eli set his cup down on the table and spooned in some sugar.

"Them horses could use a stretch," he said, glancing around for the cream. "Maybe we'd see that bear…"

Zeke wasn't listening. The cream was not on the table. Eli went outside to the cold-storage cupboard mounted on the front of the shack, and returned with the large mason jar. He twisted the lid off and took a sniff. The cold cupboard was obviously not keeping cold enough in this warm weather—the cream was starting to sour.

Eli started to replace the lid, intending to return the cream to the cupboard, then thought the better of it. He tossed the lid into the washbasin and set the jar down next to the door. He'd take the sour cream with him out to the horse shed where he'd mix it into the dogs' bowls. (The dogs made their home in the straw bales next to the shed.)

Retrieving his coffee, Eli went back into the fresh air and sunshine and once again took his seat upon the step. He did not feel sleepy. It was true that if Dan had a job for

them he'd probably have said so. So why was he coming back? Should Eli wait for him? For the moment, he decided, he was content just soaking up the sunshine on the step.

Something peeked around the corner near the base of the shack to Eli's right, and then drew back! Eli had caught only a glimpse of movement. He stared, motionless, at the corner of the shack and waited. There it was again. The creature had stolen a second peek at Eli. It was bigger than a gopher...*Badger?* Eli said to himself, and waited. What would a badger be doing sneaking around the shack? Badgers in general were not sociable. A minute went by, then another. Eli was slowly setting his cup down on the step when the animal peeked again—almost too quickly to be seen.

Eli had an idea. Quickly and quietly, he rose from the step. Snatching up the old corn broom that leaned against the doorjamb, he tiptoed along the front of the shack to his left and around the corner. Once out of sight, he broke into a run, sprinting along the side of the shack and along the back to the next corner, where he pulled up short. Holding his breath, Eli leaned out just enough to give his right eye a view of...nothing. His eye darted quickly along the side of the shack then scanned the adjacent prairie. The hard-baked ground, tufted here and there with dry grass and sprigs of green, didn't offer enough cover to hide a mouse.

Puzzled, Eli stepped around the corner, and holding the broom at the ready, began making his way along the side of the shack. About halfway, he paused to look back. If the badger had made a run for the horse shed, Eli would have seen it. That only left the unlikely possibility that...Eli tiptoed

to the front corner, took a deep breath, then stepped boldly into the open ready to do battle. His coffee cup, waiting for him on the step where he'd left it, was the only thing remotely out of place.

Eli was certain he had not imagined it. Only minutes before, an animal had been playing peek-a-boo with him around the corner of the shack. He stooped to examine the ground, looking for tracks.

The base of the shack had been banked with dirt to keep the wind from whistling under the floorboards. The bank was hard and dry and did not offer much of a surface for recording the movements of small animals. But glancing back along the side of the shack, Eli saw where the surface of the bank had indeed been disturbed.

A loose pile of dirt spilled out of a clump of dry weeds and down the face of the bank. Parting the weeds, he saw the open mouth of a tunnel! The animal had obviously set up housekeeping in the warm dry space under the shack. But it wasn't a badger. A badger would have heaped a mound of dirt around his hole, a sort of front porch from which to take the sun or keep a lookout. It was way too small for a coyote den, and a coyote would never den-up under a shack full of men armed with guns anyway. But what would?

The answer came to Eli in a flash of inspiration that made it all clear—the musty smell he'd noticed earlier, the animal's homesteading ways—the tunnel was the work of a packrat! Eli had never actually seen a packrat, but he had heard about them. They stole things, which they packed back to their stinky nests.

What to do? It would obviously be pointless to try digging it out. The rat would have the run of the whole underside of the shack. Trapping it made sense, except that Eli didn't have any traps—there were some old traps somewhere back at the colony but… Maybe if he laid a loop of wire around the mouth of the tunnel, he could wait and snare it the next time it poked its head out of the hole. On the other hand, why not just shoot it? There would be no point in preserving the pelt—whoever heard of somebody skinning out a stinking old packrat?

That was the plan. Eli would get one of the rifles and sit over the hole. The rat's next game of peek-a-boo would be its last.

Skipping up the step, Eli paused to put the broom back and was distracted by the sight of the sour cream spilled across the entryway.

"What…?" Eli was sure he'd set the big jar flatly and firmly on the floor beside the door. Zeke was asleep in the…

A skunk stepped into view, as if to own up to having spilled the cream. For a second the two stared at each other—Eli in shock, the skunk, tail straight in the air, defiant.

"Your move," it seemed to say.

Eli's first, and unfortunate, reflex was to take a swipe at the animal with the broom. He missed. The skunk did not. Even as he retracted the broom, Eli was engulfed in the spray. He staggered backwards off the step, choking in the atomized fetor, eyes streaming as if dosed with pepper-spray. The skunk, indignant, emerged onto the step, then lowered its tail and jauntily made its way along the front of the

shack to disappear around the corner and, presumably, into its tunnel under the shack.

By the time big Dan pulled up, Eli had procured the washbasin, a pail of water and the dish soap. He was kneeling on the ground before the basin in a lather of suds, moaning a sort of mantra of curses upon the skunk, while spitting, sudsing, rinsing and sudsing again.

Zeke was standing a ways out on the prairie, upwind, in his long-johns. Having been awakened by Eli's howls of outrage, Zeke had then been evicted by the fumes. Once outside, he had become ill.

Big Dan had no trouble detecting and identifying the odour. He stepped from the pickup, reluctantly, and demanded to know how they could be "so stupid as to go messing with a skunk!?!"

"Wasn't me. It was him," Zeke said bitterly.

"I wasn't messing with it!" Eli howled.

"Well, you sure smell like you were—where did you find it?"

"I didn't find it—it found me!"

"Where?"

"In the shack."

"In the shack!" Whatever humour Dan may have found in the situation drained from him now.

"Go get the creolin," he said to Zeke, referring to the disinfectant they used in the treatment of livestock, "…and dump a good dose of it in the rain barrel."

"I can't go in there—it makes me sick," said Zeke.

"So you're just gonna stand out here in your underwear and wait for me to scrub out the place?"

"But…"

"Just get the creolin—and the kerosene and a scrub-brush," Dan added, turning to the pathetic figure on the ground. "That dish soap ain't gonna do nothing—you could scrub your ears right off with that stuff and they'd still stink."

Eli looked up, blinking angrily through the suds. "So jus' what am I supposed to do then?" he demanded.

"Burn them clothes for a start—and maybe if you soak in the rain barrel long enough, you'll be able to stand yourself—as long as you don't get too close."

Eli rinsed his face and looked back at Dan. "It's livin' under the shack." The news was imparted like the final gong of doom.

"What?" Dan's ability to absorb bad news seemed to be exhausted.

"I seen where it dug its hole under the shack."

Dan just shook his head. "Well, don't, for pity's sake, go messin' with it—just leave it alone—do you understand me?"

It seemed a needless warning.

Dan later thought that the skunk smell was maybe just what he'd needed. Maybe the taint of it, which he'd picked up deodorizing the shack and consorting with young Eli, would be just the thing to camouflage his own scent. The bear, Dan had begun to fear, had grown suspicious. No matter how he approached the dump, no matter what

hours he chose to lie in wait, the bear seemed to show up before, or after him.

Dan was well rested. He and Zeke had made beds of straw for themselves out back until the air freshened in the shack. Eli had stubbornly refused to let the skunk evict him from his bunk, which was all right with Dan and Zeke, because even after rigorous scrub-downs, with everything from the creolin to the kerosene, Eli was still a bit gamey.

Dan had decided that only an all-night vigil would net him his prize. Giving the ravine as wide a berth as possible, he had driven around to its far side and parked out on the prairie. In addition to his rifle, he'd brought a couple of old woolen blankets, as well as a bit of sausage and cheese to snack on through the night.

The sun was still bright on the western horizon as Dan hiked over the prairie to the edge of the ravine. The open prairie, he'd decided, was the only route that the bear would definitely not use to approach the dump.

Close up, the crevice eroded into the face of the ravine appeared to be an even better hiding place than Dan had imagined. He eased himself over the edge and into the "V," skidding on his rump a dozen or so feet to where the crevice veered off of a big chunk of sandstone. It was perfect! The bait lay opposite not more than 140 yards. The faint odour of rotting meat wafted on the slight breeze, competing with the skunky flavour of the wool blankets, as Dan wrapped them around himself from his shoulders to his knees.

The sun burned itself out, briefly setting the valley ablaze before it fell into shadow. Coyotes sounded off from all points of the compass, heralding the rise of the moon—

which was almost full. The stars came out nearly as bright as the moon, and the baked clay walls of the ravine shone like porcelain in their combined light.

Somehow Dan knew the bear would come. He felt it looming out there in the dark. It may be circling in the valley below at that very moment, lifting its nose to sample the breeze for a hint of man smell.

Dan imagined the black form ghosting slowly out of the dark valley. That's where it would come from. It had probably spent the day dozing in a willow thicket along the creek. Now it was hungry, greedy for the free meal it knew waited for it up the ravine—that would be its downfall. Even after discovering that a man was keeping tabs on the place, it had persisted. True, it had out-smarted that man—up until tonight. Tonight it was in for a surprise.

Dan tensed…he had heard something. He stared wide-eyed at the dark blot on the opposite side of the ravine, which was the pile of carcasses. Nothing moved. He lifted his head to look below. Nothing seemed out of place out on the valley floor. The silence was overpowering. Even the crickets were listening as time itself seemed to pause.

A dark form broke the line of sky along the rim, moving above the bait. It was moving quickly—too quickly—joined by a second…coyotes. Dan watched as they stopped to sniff the air. One whined nervously. The other plunged over the side as the whiner stayed on guard staring directly at Dan, or so Dan imagined, until the animal decided to join its partner.

Good, Dan thought. He was invisible in the dark woolen blankets, and his scent disguised. He watched as the coyotes became shadows and were swallowed by the dark

blot of the carcasses. The sounds of their gurgled growls drifted across the ravine.

Suddenly, they stopped. Dan could see the outline of their heads erect against the lighter backdrop of clay. They were listening to something he couldn't hear. It seemed to inform them of impending danger as they bolted in unison for the rim. One disappeared over the edge while the other paused to sample the air. It trotted along the rim toward the valley, then stopped abruptly, once again poking its nose into the breeze. The yips it gave into the night sounded to Dan's ear like warnings—warnings that a black bear was approaching the dump.

The coyote took off at a gallop. Silence returned to the ravine.

An hour passed, and then another. The night's chill had descended on Dan as he lay on his back in a semi-upright position along the "V." His legs, braced against the sandstone, had begun to cramp. He lifted his right knee, working the stiffness out of the leg and then did the same with the left. He sat up to rewrap his legs in the blanket, then leaned back to tuck the top blanket tightly around his waist, and was just pulling the remainder up around his chin when he froze…something wasn't right! His eyes darted along the rim—his mind strained to replay the last few seconds; a sound, no louder than a mouse, or a pebble tumbling down the "V" toward him? Tilting his head back, he saw the bear calmly looking down at him.

Exploding against his woolen wraps, trying to free the rifle, his arms, his legs—skidding on his knees and one hand as he scrambled to raise the gun—cursing as he scanned the stars through the open gunsights…the bear

was gone. The man clawed his way up the crevice and onto the prairie to find nothing to pull the trigger on but blame. At the precise moment of the bear's approach, Dan had been occupied making himself cozy!

But why would the bear have come from that direction, over the open prairie? It didn't make sense! The bear was breaking the rules—it wasn't fair…But the hunt was over. The bear, Dan knew, wouldn't be back.

It wasn't my fault, Eli told himself. It could have happened to any one of them—and probably would yet if they didn't do something about it. Dan, who that morning had been in a particularly grumpy mood on the subject, was wrong about leaving the skunk alone. It was only a matter of time before somebody else, or one of the dogs, would find themselves in the same situation Eli had been in.

The boys had all made up beds in the straw stack out back, refusing to even consider entering the shack unless it was absolutely necessary. They had also avoided being in close company with Eli—especially Zeke, who had insisted they tend to their jobs separately on the preceding night's shift.

The smell wasn't as bad as they all made it out to be. In fact, it was almost gone. Eli, sitting on the step in the mid-morning sun, took a sniff of himself, and his surroundings, to confirm the fact. *You could hardly smell it at all,* he told himself, poking his nose into his coffee cup. The coffee

aroma drowned out the skunk smell completely—they still didn't have any fresh cream. He found himself glancing repeatedly at the corner of the shack to his right. Dan had said that the skunk had probably taken off after its dust-up with Eli, but it hadn't.

Before going on shift the night before, Eli had braced a couple of dry weed stalks across the mouth of the tunnel. This morning, when everyone else had gone, he'd checked the tunnel to find that the stalks had been pushed aside. Random ideas for murdering the evil creature began wandering into Eli's mind—Zeke had already gone to bed out in the straw and was probably already asleep.

Skunks liked eggs. Maybe a bowl of cracked eggs set before the mouth of the tunnel would draw the varmint out far enough for Eli to get a bullet into it. But if he missed, or just wounded it, the little devil would probably retreat under the shack and really stink up the place! Even if he blasted the stink-bomb to smithereens, the result would undoubtedly be the same—the same as snaring it, or trapping it...poisoning it? The idea had some very attractive possibilities. The more Eli thought about it, the more poison seemed like the only way the deed could be safely accomplished. He pictured the skunk crawling away to slowly breathe its last, with nothing to trigger its dreaded cannon...

There was a box of Warfarin in the shack, if he could find it, which they set out for mice. Would a skunk go for something like that? Did they eat the same stuff as mice? The more he thought about it, the less likely it seemed. The Warfarin would be an experiment at best, and it might take

days. How much of the stuff would Eli have to feed it to get results? Skunks were a lot bigger than mice.

What else was poisonous? Exhaust fumes came to mind. He thought of the flexible hoses they used to vent exhaust while working in the colony's shop—but the exhaust would rise through the floorboards to pollute the shack and besides, Eli had no vehicle at his disposal, much less a hose...propane! The idea hit him with such force that he rose to his feet and began to pace. Propane, as he had often been told when handling the stuff, was heavier than air. It would pool under the shack like water—and propane was something Eli had in good supply; there was a spare bottle of it leaning against the shack, already equipped with the hose they used to hook it up to the heaters out in the cow sheds! It was perfect!

Eli launched himself into the work, gleefully assembling the things he would need. Cautiously, he leaned over the hole and looked in, just in case the skunk was lying in wait at the entrance—it wasn't.

Slowly, he inserted the hose, pushing it down into the hole as far as it would reach. He then packed rags around it, stuffing up the mouth of the tunnel to prevent the gas from blowing back his way. Solemnly, almost ceremoniously, Eli reached for the valve. A thrill ran through him as he heard the gas hissing into the line. He opened it all the way; then, picking up his coffee cup, stepped back a few paces and sat down cross-legged on the ground. How much propane should he let go? It would spread throughout the space beneath the floorboards, but how thick did it need to be to poison something? Best just let 'er rip, Eli decided. The irony of gassing a skunk occurred to him, and he smiled...

For a while Eli couldn't figure out what had happened, or why he was being dragged backwards along the ground by Zeke dressed in his long-johns. Zeke seemed to be yelling at him but Eli couldn't hear him—he couldn't hear anything over the ringing in his ears. The shack…had vanished!? A rubble of splintered boards and trash lay smouldering around the bank of dirt. The big iron heater and propane bottles—the propane bottles seemed to be what Zeke was yelling about, insisting that they were "gonna blow!" as he continued dragging Eli in the direction of the straw bales.

Only when they were hunkered down behind the bales did Eli began forming more complete thoughts, and the picture of what had happened began to dawn on him. It was the sight of that old heater standing cock-eyed amidst the rubble that tipped him off. Eli had forgotten about its pilot light, which flickered eternally near its base. Zeke continued yelling about a leak, a leak in the lines which he surmised "musta set 'er off!" Eli had regained consciousness sufficiently to not enlighten him. As he leaned back in the straw to let his bones reassemble themselves, Eli couldn't help wondering what had become of the skunk.

Respect

"Poppa...Poppa wake up..." Mr. Schimelpenik's murmured response sounded as if the gentle prodding he was receiving from Mrs. Schimelpenik somehow fit pleasurably into his dream. "Poppa!" The gentle prodding progressed to painful poking, as Mrs. Schimelpenik began stabbing her fingers into her husband's ribs. "Wake up!"

He moaned and began to roll over in search of a more comfortable position.

"Poppa, you—must—wake—up!" she insisted, laying hold of his nightshirt and giving him a violent shaking.

"What...? What time is it?"

"Never mind what time is it—there is somebody in the bakery!" She was speaking as loudly as she dared, given the circumstances.

"No…" Mr. Schimelpenik groaned. "There is no one in the bakery—go back to sleep." It was clear that he intended to follow his own advice.

"There is!" It was also clear that Mrs. Schimelpenik was not going to allow it.

The beleaguered baker reached out from beneath the covers, drew the windup alarm clock from the nightstand and studied the phosphorescent dial. "Mama, I still have two hours before I have to start the bread."

The sudden clatter of bread pans and cookie sheets hitting the floor of the bakery below brought Mr. Schimelpenik bolt upright in the bed.

"There!" said Mrs. Schimelpenik indignantly. "There is your 'no one in the bakery go back to sleep'!"

"Hush!" said Mr. Schimelpenik, kicking free of the bed-clothes. He swung his feet over the side of the bed and onto the floor, in search of the carpet slippers he'd parked there upon retiring.

Something heavy hit the bakery floor with a thud. "Who would dare…?" muttered Mr. Schimelpenik, as he crept to the head of the stairs. All was quiet below.

Taking one step at a time, the baker descended the dark stairwell. A board creaked under his weight and he froze, listening. A faint scuffle confirmed that the intruder was still on the premises. It occurred to Mr. Schimelpenik that he would find it comforting to have something in his hands—like a baseball bat. But there were no baseball bats handy; only the push-broom that leaned against the wall near the bottom of the stairs. Mr. Schimelpenik shifted his weight, taking the pressure off the creaky board, which croaked back into place.

The scuffling, snuffling sounds persisted, leading the baker to believe that he would be taking the intruder by surprise. Who would dare break in upon he and Mrs. Schimelpenik while they lay asleep in their bed...? What kind of person would do such a thing?

The kind of person who was there in the dark, helping himself to the bakery supplies, knocking things over, perhaps damaging the equipment—was he drunk?

As his temper arose and his right fist closed on the broom handle, Mr. Schimelpenik almost began to relish the moment: he would give this trespassing swine a lesson in respect that he would never forget! Having located the light switch, holding the broom aloft, the baker braced himself and flicked the switch.

"Buster!?" The tone of Mr. Schimelpenik's exclamation was an equal blend of disbelief and disappointment. Buster, who was sitting on his rump in the middle of the broad bakery workbench holding a jam-pail between his front paws, gave the baker a dirty look and poked his nose back into the jam pail.

"Why you...you..." Words failed him as the baker wound up and let loose a roundhouse swing with the push-broom which, if it had connected, would surely have ended the bear's life right then and there!

Buster, who now seemed to feel that the jig was up, dropped the pail and launched himself off the workbench in the general direction of the back door. But Mr. Schimelpenik was one step ahead of him and cut the big bruin off with a second swing of equally murderous intent. Buster saw it coming and reversed direction, skidding and

slipping on the wooden floor—now littered with flour and a tasty variety of sugar, syrup and jams.

A chase ensued with the bear spinning out in the corners, slamming into cupboards and racks, inches ahead of the deadly push-broom slamming this way and that in relentless pursuit! Rounding the last turn, Buster gained enough of a lead to bound through the screen door—literally, for he did not take the time to open it first—and made good his escape.

Mr. Schimelpenik followed as far as the back porch, impotently sounding his threats and promises concerning retribution. If only he could have landed one good lick with his broom. He lowered the weapon and turned to face the mess.

"Poppa?" He kicked the mangled doorframe and screen out of his way and stepped in to survey the chaos, the waste, to calculate what was left of his once well-ordered little bakery.

"Poppa? Is that you?"

"Yes, Mama, it's me."

Mrs. Schimelpenik emerged from the stairwell with a cast-iron frying pan held at the ready. "Are they gone?"

"Yes."

"Are you all right?"

"I'm all right."

"My stars…" she said, taking in the state of things. "What a mess."

"Yes," said Mr. Schimelpenik. "What a mess."

"Who would do such a thing?" demanded Mrs. Schimelpenik, as anger replaced her fear.

Mr. Schimelpenik heaved a sigh. "Buster," he said sadly.

"Buster?"

"Yes, Buster."

Mrs. Schimelpenik's gaze fell upon the remains of the screen door. "I told you you shouldn't be leaving the door open like that!" she said.

"I didn't leave it open."

"Yes you did."

"No, I didn't."

"You did."

"I checked it; it was hooked when I went to bed."

"The screen door…"

"Yes, the screen door!"

"I'm not talking about the screen door—you can see the good of hooking the screen door…"

But Mr. Schimelpenik was not listening. "I don't understand…" he said, his voice tinged with anger.

"What don't you understand?"

"Buster; he's never done anything like this, ever!"

"What's not to understand; he's a bear, why shouldn't he do something like this? Leaving the door open—you might just as well go out and invite him in."

"Then why in all these years—he's never even come up on the porch before this…"

"He's a bear," said Mrs. Schimelpenik, setting down her frying pan.

"And what were you going to do with that?" asked Mr. Schimelpenik.

"I was going to use it on the head of anyone who tried to come up those stairs—but that wouldn't include the bear—look at you with your broom; are you crazy, fighting a full-grown bear with a broom? You think you are Superman?"

"Next time I won't miss," vowed Mr. Schimelpenik.

"Next time?! Next time I'll shut the door myself and there won't be any next time—crazy old man…"

"Enough…" sighed Mr. Schimelpenik. "I will need to scrub everything before I can start the bread."

"I'm not likely to sleep now," said his wife. "Give me your broom. You can run the wash water."

The war was on, and Jasper, like every other town and city in the country, was feeling the pinch. Salt and flour, beans and pork, even clothing and gasoline were being rationed. So Mr. Schimelpenik's problem of replacing his supplies was not just a simple matter of placing an order. Even if there had been a surplus of available flour, which there was not, Mr. Schimelpenik's money would do him no good without the coupons to show that he was due an extra allowance.

He'd salvaged enough to supply that morning's bread orders, which left him scraping the bottom of the barrel. After making his deliveries, he took his problem to the grocer next door.

Mr. Fonger owned and operated one of two grocery outlets in the town, with the help of his 19-year-old daughter Mary—Mrs. Fonger having passed away some years before. The Fongers were relatively new to town. Upon their arrival, they had made friends with their neighbours, the Schimelpeniks, and over the ensuing few years had

ingratiated themselves to much of the rest of the community, from both personal and business perspectives. In short, they liked their adopted community and their community seemed to like them.

Slowly, they had built a clientele whose patronage would have reflected a modest degree of prosperity had it not been for the war. It was not uncommon that, having placed an order for a case of canned peaches, they would receive three or four cans. The grocer would then be placed in the position of having to "dole out" the goods. Mr. Fonger tried honestly to maintain a first-come, first-served policy, but inevitably some customers would do without, whatever ration coupons they may have in hand. Sometimes, in the eternally enigmatic ways of government, a shipment would contain an inexplicable largesse of something like sardines, or dried apricots, or molasses. But the offer of a deal on canned sardines was usually small compensation to one whose mouth was set for canned peaches.

At the moment, Mr. Fonger was in the storeroom doing an inventory of flour and the other basic items on Mr. Schimelpenik's list. Having totalled the goods in hand, the grocer then had to anticipate the needs of his regular customers. It was a delicate balancing act. In the end, he went for broke, gambling on the hope that his next shipment would arrive on schedule, containing most of what he had on order. If it did, and as long as no one else's larder was wiped out by Buster, there should be enough to go around. If it didn't, well, if it didn't, Mr. Fonger would wind up in a similar position to the one Mr. Schimelpenik was facing. But it just wouldn't do seeing his neighbour put out of business, even temporarily, just because of the bear. If the

situation were reversed, the baker would certainly do what he could for him.

Mr. Fonger began assembling everything he thought his customers could spare in hopes that it would be enough to see the Schimelpeniks through.

The baker was out front at the grocery counter waiting for the verdict and receiving Mary's commiserations, such as they were. "Well, he is a bear, Mr. Schimelpenik."

"Yes," said the baker. "Mrs. Schimelpenik has already informed me of that. But the point is that he is a bear who has never done anything like this before, ever!" Mr. Schimelpenik was leaning against the counter, sipping a cold orange crush.

"First time for everything, I guess…" said Mary, rather absentmindedly as she was concentrating on assembling an order Ma Airns had just phoned in.

"First time for everything!" scoffed the baker. "Why? That's the question: why, for the first time, would he decide to mess up my bakery?"

"Oh, I don't think he would have done it on purpose," said Mary. It had been Mary who first began calling the animal Buster Bear.

"You should have seen the place; you should have seen what he did!"

"But he probably didn't mean to…"

"Oh, so it was just by accident?"

"Not by accident exactly, he's just a messy eater, that's all—he's a bear."

"Again the news that the bear is a bear."

"You know what I mean."

"What you mean is that bears are bears the same as every other bear, but they are not. Your Buster, for an example, was never a dump bear."

"A dump bear…?" said Mary, checking Ma Airns' grocery list.

"The bears at the dump, the nuisance grounds, the ones they take the tourists to see—fighting over the garbage— filthy! Buster has never been a dump bear."

"No, I don't suppose he has."

"Even my garbage barrel he stayed out of!"

"That's because you leave scraps out for him."

"Well, why not? What's of no use for anything else why not leave out?"

"Mrs. Schimelpenik says that's what started it."

"So better I mix the scraps in with the trash and make him a garbage bear?"

"That's not what I'm saying."

"You and Mrs. Schimelpenik both—when he shows up tonight, you make sure to watch. I'm gonna show that son-of-a-gun what happens when you don't treat others with respect!"

"Well, now Mr. Schimelpenik, I think I do agree with Mrs. Schimelpenik."

"How's that?"

"Well, she feels that Buster could be dangerous, after all…"

"If you're going to tell me that the bear is a bear…"

"No, that's not what I was going to say…"

"You just make sure you're watching for him tonight— we'll see who thinks who is dangerous."

"I don't know, Mr. Schimelpenik…"

"What, you think I should just let him ruin my bakery and say nothing about it?"

"No, but…"

"You gotta teach him his place or he really will become dangerous."

The tinkling of the chimes that hung over the front door announced the arrival of another customer. It was a young man in army uniform, a corporal to be exact, a stranger.

"Hello…" said Mary, with a welcoming smile.

"Hello," said the stranger, and paused to survey the store.

"Was there something I can help you with?" Mary asked.

"Ah, yes," the corporal said, and approached the grocery counter. "I'll have one of those," he indicated a Fat Emma candy bar, "and a Coke."

Mary went to the pop cooler, reached in for the cola, which she dried on the towel attached to the front of the water-filled cooler, and asked if the soldier would like it opened.

"Yes, please," he said.

"Anything else?" Mary asked.

"Not really…" the young man said.

Mary rang in the items, counted out the change and thanked him.

"Thank you," he said.

Mr. Fonger emerged from the back packing a sack of flour, which he flopped onto the counter saying he had put together an order he hoped would suffice.

"Are you sure you can spare it?" the baker asked.

"We'll be fine," said the grocer with a quiet smile, and turned back for another load. "Just don't go feeding it to the bears," he added, disappearing into the storeroom.

"You can be sure we won't be doing that!" the baker called after him, "but you're not going to run yourself short?" he asked as Mr. Fonger returned.

"No, we'll be fine," said the grocer, and continued to stack the order up on the counter.

"…And full price," asserted the baker. "I don't want to hear any talk of wholesale or anything like that."

"Oh, I think a certain volume discount would be fair considering the…"

"Then I don't want it—you can take it back!" declared the baker.

"You drive a hard bargain, Mr. Schimelpenik," said Mr. Fonger, flipping open the invoice book.

"…And cash! There's no need for you to be carrying my inventory on top of everything else, right Mary?"

"The customer is always right, Mr. Schimelpenik."

"That's right!" The baker's tone changed considerably as he continued. "I can't tell you how much we appreciate this," he said.

"Glad to be able to help," said Fonger.

"Well, it means a lot. That damned Buster is going to get his, let me tell you!"

"Well now, you want to be careful, Mr. Schimelpenik," said the grocer, still working on the invoice.

"Oh, I will be—don't worry about that—in fact, Mary here is coming home right after the dance to supervise, eh Mary?"

"Well, I haven't decided if I'm going to the dance, but..."

"Of course you're going to the dance, isn't she?" he said, turning to her father for confirmation of the fact.

"Oh, Mary will do what she thinks best about that, I guess..."

"Well, why wouldn't she?"

"I didn't say I wouldn't..."

"But you must." It was apparently clear to Mr. Schimelpenik that Mary represented an asset the dance could scarcely do without. "What do you think, young fellah? Do you think this beautiful young lady should go to the dance?"

"Mr. Schimelpenik!" Mary was aghast.

"What? I'm just asking this young gentleman's opinion on the subject."

The stranger had been browsing through the store while he munched his Fat Emma and sipped his Coke. He looked at Mary, blushingly trying to avoid looking at him, then at the baker, and smiled.

"Well, sir," he said, "I can't say that I know what dance it is that you're referring to, but I would have to agree that it could only be improved by her attendance, yes."

"Mmm," said Mr. Schimelpenik, "watch out for this one, Mary—he seems to have a silver tongue in his head."

With that, the baker tipped up the remains of his orange crush while at the same time reaching for his wallet, and turned his attentions to the business of settling up with Mr. Fonger. He seemed impervious to the withering look he received from Mary, as her hands became busy boxing Ma Airns' grocery order.

Will Sykes, Corporal William T. Sykes to be exact, had stepped down from the train with nothing more in mind than the idea of stretching his legs. The conductor had told him that they would be departing in exactly one hour, and that he should not be late or his duffle bag would go on without him. Sykes had paced the length of the busy platform, circled the station and decided he had time to explore the picturesque little town.

Aimlessly window-shopping his way through the streets, he had spied Mary. By hanging around the grocery store, he had learned her name and had taken an opportunity to impress her with his frank and open assessment of her charms. He had also learned that a dance was to be held in the community that very evening—a dance that Mary, apparently, was reluctant to attend unescorted.

The corporal had hung on hoping for an introduction, whereupon he intended to humbly offer himself as escort—he'd assumed (correctly) that his uniform would make him welcome at the community hall, or wherever the townspeople gathered to dance. No opportunity for an introduction had presented itself, however, when the corporal's gaze had fallen on the store's big wall clock, which brought Mr. Sykes' attention to the immediate problem of retrieving his luggage from the nearly departing train!

Having accomplished this feat more or less in the nick of time, the corporal then set out at a more relaxed pace to

gain further intelligence concerning the night's objective. He would also have to give some attention to the problem of a place to hole up, as well as confirming the departure time of the next day's train.

"I just felt like throwing something at him!" said Mary.

"Well, I would imagine—" said Ma.

"I mean, a perfect stranger, somebody we don't know from Adam, and he says that—talks to him like I'm not even there!"

"Exactly! Never mind bringing a perfect stranger in on it—honestly!"

Having delivered Ma Airns' groceries, Mary was receiving tea and the sympathies of that venerable lady at her kitchen table. Ma Airns, as she was known to the young people who treated her kitchen as a sort of hangout, ran a boarding house in a great barn of a place just off the main street. In addition to taking in boarders, she let out rooms by the night or week to tourists.

"I got on one side and fell off the other!" Mary said with a laugh. She was explaining the real reason for her reticence concerning dancing. "The horse didn't even move!"

She'd explained that she and Phyllis, Billy Tompkins and Billy's girlfriend Belle had hiked out to Ted Burns' cabin the previous day. Burns had offered her a ride on his horse, whereupon she'd performed the aforementioned acrobatics, landing hard, rump first, on rocky ground.

Mary had no concern over having done herself serious harm—she had been able to hike back to town—but she had bruised some prominent muscles. They were feeling tender enough that the prospect of several hours of non-stop dancing failed to hold its usual appeal. Besides, it was getting so that a dance or social was cropping up about twice a week, and a girl could count on putting in a full shift.

A canteen of sorts (soft drinks only) had been set up in the church basement, ostensibly for the boys who were shipping out—or returning on leave—or just passing through (as was Corporal Sykes).

The simple fact was that Mary was feeling more like she needed a night off than a night on the town.

"Well, you have every right to do as you please!" said Ma.

"Oh, I know," said Mary, "but Phyl wants me to go with her—Dad's probably going to go along with the Schimelpeniks...if Mr. Schimelpenik just hadn't made such a big deal about it!"

"Well, you don't worry about Mr. Schimelpenik or any-body else. You just go ahead and do what you think is best."

They were interrupted by a knock at the front door. Ma began hoisting her creaking arthritic frame out of her chair.

"I'll get it," said Mary, and darted off through the din-ing room. She threw open the big front door to find Mr. Schimelpenik's silver-tongued stranger standing on the step.

"Well..." said the stranger, his face breaking into a broad grin.

"What do you want?" Mary blurted out the question without thinking.

"The sign says you rent rooms," said the stranger.

"I don't know," said Mary. "I mean, I don't know if there's one available—you'll have to talk to Ma—would you mind waiting a moment?" she asked, recovering a semblance of manners.

"Not at all," said the stranger, still grinning like the Cheshire cat as Mary closed the door.

"It's him!" she said, returning to the kitchen.

"Who?" said Ma.

"The fellow from the store!" said Mary, carrying her cup and saucer to the sink.

"I see…"

"He wants a room—I asked him to wait," Mary's hand was already on the handle of the back door. "Thanks for tea, Ma. I really should get back, anyway."

"I understand, dear," said the older lady, and smiled.

The soldier was still smiling when Ma opened the door. She informed him of the availability of a room and its price, which he readily accepted. The smile faded slightly as Ma informed him that Mary, whom he'd enquired after, had had to return to work at the store.

It was Mr. Schimelpenik's long-established habit to sleep in two shifts. Having shared a lunch with Mrs. Schimelpenik, he would retire for the afternoon while she manned the front end of the bakery. The bakery closed at

six o'clock, whereupon the baker would rise to enjoy the evening listening to the radio, or socializing. Often the day would end with him sitting out on the back porch smoking and sipping a glass of schnapps, before returning to bed until it was time to start the bread.

That day his afternoon sleep had been a series of fitful naps. He'd been kept awake by thoughts of Buster's unprecedented attack on the bakery. How many years had it been now since the bear had started coming around? In the early days of summer, before the berries began to ripen, there were a few weeks that would see the bear's visits become a regular, almost daily, event. It was true that Mr. Schimelpenik had encouraged the habit by leaving the bakery scraps out. But it was not true, in his opinion, that there was anything wrong with doing this. Indeed, the baker felt that the bear's patronage actually helped keep the alley clear of stray dogs and cats and other unwanted scavengers. He felt that a trust had developed between him and Buster, which Buster had now broken. Why?

The baker, like everyone else in these lean times, had adopted his own austerity program resulting in less waste, and therefore less of a share for the bear. Mr. Schimelpenik had long suspected that he was not the only one in town contributing to Buster's girth. The bear was well known and there must be others who set something out. Perhaps these offerings had also shrunk, or disappeared altogether, as waste became a luxury few could afford. Whatever the reason, the bear needed to be disciplined. The line would have to be reinforced between what was acceptable and what was unacceptable. Buster wasn't stupid. He would quickly learn, or remember, the natural aversion he'd displayed in the past to encroaching on someone else's territory.

The bakery shared a back porch with the grocery. It was divided by a low railing that went all the way around the narrow porch. Staircases, intended as fire escapes, angled up from the porch to small landings on the back wall of each building. There, the back door of the respective living quarters let out onto the landings.

Having eventually given up on sleep, Mr. Schimelpenik was puttering about the rear of the bakery. Contrary to his usual practice, he dumped the spoiled flour, sugar and jams into the empty wooden barrel he used for trash. He then pulled the big barrel over on its side, and rolled it up against the porch. Stepping back into the alley, he studied the situation, climbed the four stairs leading up onto the porch and studied it again from there. He entered the building, returning moments later with the push-broom, which he extended over the railing, measuring the distance to the mouth of the barrel—it was a comfortable reach. Setting the broom aside, the baker then began a series of tiptoed steps between the back door of the bakery and the railing. His head was cocked as though he was listening for something.

He was still engaged in this curious pursuit when Mrs. Schimelpenik appeared in the open doorway behind him. "What in the world? Have you lost your mind altogether?"

Startled, Mr. Schimelpenik declined to explain that he was sounding out the creaky floorboards in search of a silent route between the door and the railing. Instead, he assured her that she need not trouble herself on the subject of his mental state as he knew exactly what he was doing, and asked when supper would be ready.

"What supper?" she said, and asked if he had "forgotten completely" that they planned to participate in the potluck dinner and dance at the church.

He argued that it was impossible for him to have forgotten about the dinner as no one had informed him about that aspect of the evening in the first place.

"You're hopeless," she said simply, and left him to resume his tiptoeing.

Mary turned down the potluck dinner, telling her dad that she and Phyl would be coming along to the dance later. She was sitting out on the landing above the alley, smoking a cigarette. It was becoming quite fashionable for young ladies to smoke, although Mary did not feel comfortable doing so in public—or in front of her father. Her dad smoked and didn't mind that she did, as long as she didn't do it behind his back. He'd said as much shortly after she and Phyl had begun experimenting with the habit.

Mary was very glad that her dad had seen fit to help restock the bakery, and wished that there had been some secret way for her to pay the bill out of her own money—she was paid a nominal wage for working in the store. Deep down, Mary feared that the whole thing was probably her fault.

She had been sitting out on the landing peeling an orange about the time Buster had ambled by to lick up his bakery scraps. When he had finished, just for fun, she had

tossed a handful of orange peels down to him. Buster had sniffed over the peels, decided they were edible and gobbled them up. Feeling that it was a little unfair that all he got was the peels, Mary had begun tossing him a wedge or two. A bad throw had landed one of the tasty temptations on the Schimelpeniks' porch. When the big bear had begun cautiously mounting the steps in pursuit, Mary had risen from her chair, admonishing him to "stay down!" He had backed off but not given up on the wayward wedge until Mary had thrown the remainder of her orange out into the alley. A car had turned into the alley waiting patiently for the bear—squinting in the headlights—to finish what it was doing before waddling out of the driver's way. When the car, and Buster, had gone, Mary had descended the stairs to retrieve the temptation from the porch, tossing it into the alley as well, and given no more thought to the incident until the next morning. She'd felt sick hearing the news.

Now she didn't know what to think. Was it really her fault the bear had returned to make a pig of himself? Maybe she should just sit her dad down and tell him the whole story. He'd understand—he understood everything—and maybe he'd be able to help her figure out what she should do. Or, maybe she should just drop it.

The dance was in full swing when she and Phyl arrived. They were immediately whisked onto the floor, waltzing and two-stepping their way through the community. The evening's events included a rousing sendoff for Bernie Bjornson. Mary didn't even know Bernie had joined up. She couldn't quite picture him in the army—Bernie was a quiet boy more at home seated in front of a piano conjuring up the works of Strauss and Chopin. He was a regular at Ma Airns'.

The stranger, who had informed her that he had taken a room at Ma's—as if she cared—was everywhere. He'd cut in shortly after she'd hit the dance floor, and proudly introduced himself. Mary did not want to snub him—he seemed nice enough—but she couldn't find a way to let him know that she just wasn't interested, as he bought her drinks, offered her smokes, hounded her for dances and generally made a nuisance of himself. She couldn't turn around without finding herself, once again, in his company, and began to fear that people would start to talk.

Before she knew it, the dance was winding down. The Schimelpeniks and her dad had already left. In a brief aside, Mr. Schimelpenik had reminded her not to forget about Buster. In the gay din of music and laughter, she had actually been able to do just that. She really wished Mr. Schimelpenik would listen to reason and leave well enough alone, but she knew that was not likely to happen.

Generally speaking, Buster was harmless enough, but he was a bear. There was the hope that he'd stay away from the bakery until the baker had cooled down and given up on the idea of…doing what? Mary really didn't like to think about the very real possibility that her stubborn old neighbour was going to get himself into a fracas he couldn't handle. She would just feel awful if he did. But Mary had warned him. Her dad had warned him. Mrs. Schimelpenik had nagged him. There was really nothing more Mary could do—except take in the show, and as much as she was of two minds on the subject, she did intend to do that.

Phyl and the gang were carrying the party on to the Bjornsons. Mary declined, saying that she was "pooped." They offered her a ride, which was silly as it was no more than a block and a half from the church to the store. She'd waved them off and started walking when the stranger, who had finally seemed to disappear, popped out of the evergreen hedge bordering the sidewalk.

"Why, it's Mary!"

"Oh!" she said, a little startled, "it's you." She kept walking.

"Yes!" he said, confirming her good fortune. "I just stepped out for some fresh air—but you're not leaving?"

"Everyone is," she said, still walking.

"But the night is young—where do you people go, after hours?"

"I'm not sure I know what you mean." She suspected he'd been drinking.

"Well, how about you? Surely you're not ready to call it a night?"

"Oh yes I am." Her feet were killing her, her bruised posterior reminding her of the reason she hadn't felt up to dancing in the first place.

"All right," said the stranger. "Then the least I can do is walk you home."

"Thank you, but that won't be necessary. It's just…"

"Seriously," said the soldier. "It's not safe."

"What's not safe?" Mary demanded. She paused to allow an oncoming vehicle to pass before crossing the street.

"Being out here alone…"

"Since when?" She began to fear that the stranger might be a bit funny in the head.

"I was just out back there, you know, talking, and one of the guys said there's a bear on the loose."

"Oh," Mary said with a snicker. "That's just Buster."

"I didn't catch the guy's name, but he'd just seen it—not more than a half hour ago—up by Mrs. Airns' in fact."

"I'm not going to Ma Airns'—maybe you need someone to walk you home." She continued up the street at a determined pace.

"The point is, it could be anywhere. It's a bear, they move around."

"I told you, it's just Buster," Mary insisted. They were nearing the alley.

"Say, listen, I think we got off on the wrong foot there in the store…"

"Why of all the…" Mary was indignant. "I really don't see that we got off on any foot at all!" She paused in the mouth of the alley.

He squared off with her, barring her way. "It wasn't that bad, was it? All I said was that the dance would be improved by your presence—and it was…"

Mary was looking beyond the stranger into the dimly lit alley. Buster was standing at the back of the Schimelpeniks' porch, puzzling over the trash barrel, which, it seemed, he had just pulled onto its side.

"Mary?"

"What?"

He reached out, tenderly gripping her shoulders. Buster had taken a couple of experimental forays nose first into the barrel, jerking back as if he suspected a trap. "Why not let me see you home and we'll pretend we're meeting for the first time—we'll start all over again from the very beginning."

Having decided he had nothing to fear, the bear had now committed himself head and shoulders to the contents of the barrel.

"Would you like to meet Buster?" Mary asked.

The question seemed to derail the stranger's line of thought. "Buster?" he said, struggling to find the connection.

As Mary watched the barrel swallow the bear up to its bulging belly, Mr. Schimelpenik suddenly emerged onto the porch, and raising his push-broom above his head like an oversized golf club, teed off on the bear's behind. Buster's bulk took an involuntary leap forward, jamming itself tighter into the barrel. Mary's sudden laugh puzzled the soldier further.

"How do you like that?" shouted the baker, winding up for a second swing. The barrel was emitting a muffled roar

as the bear discovered it was stuck. "You think you can just help yourself?" demanded Mr. Schimelpenik—his broom glancing off the barrel.

The soldier was not keeping abreast of the rapidly unfolding events. He turned and stared dimly into the alley, struggling to catch up, while the barrel bumped toward the alley with the baker thumping away in pursuit.

Suddenly the barrel seemed to rise on its hind legs, straight into the air, then toppled over backwards. When it hit, it released Buster, moving so rapidly in reverse that he somersaulted backwards before landing on all fours—in a dead run!

"It's the bear," said the soldier, triumphant at solving that part of the puzzle. Mary had stepped deftly to the side, leaving the stranger on his own in the mouth of the alley.

"His name's Buster!" she called, with ill-concealed glee. She felt no twinge of fear, as it was obvious that Buster had only one thought and that was to flee—which turned out to be the same thought that occurred to the soldier, as the big bear advanced pell-mell toward him. The stranger bolted off down the street, displaying a speed and agility that one could only regard as a compliment to the physical conditioning he'd received courtesy of the army. Buster took no notice as he disappeared in his own direction.

"Did you see that?" the baker called, as Mary stepped back into the mouth of the alley.

"I sure did!" she called back.

"You see…I told you I'd get him back," he said, setting the barrel back in place and clamping on the lid as Mary approached.

"Poor Buster," she said, still chuckling despite her declared sympathy.

"Yeah, poor Buster," scoffed the baker, mounting the steps to his porch. "Say, Mary, I was just going to have a little glass of schnapps; would you care to join me?"

"Well, that might just hit the spot right about now Mr. Schimelpenik, thank you." She followed him onto the porch, and settling herself comfortably in a wicker chair opposite her host, lit a cigarette. Seeing the unbridled joy on Mr. Schimelpenik's face as he poured the drinks, Mary decided that one way or another he'd gotten his money's worth out of Buster and she could forget about the orange peel incident. The neighbour passed her her glass, and raised his own in a toast.

"To mutual respect," he said.

"Yes," said Mary, "to respect."

Epilogue:
The Empty Den

In the neighbourhood of my brother's ranch is an old sawmill next to a grand log house surrounded by forest. Driving by, we routinely point out this property as the site of "the empty bear den."

The ranch itself is at the end of the road on a river. The lands to the south of this river are still wild. The nearest settlement in that direction would be at least 200 miles, though no bridges or high-grade roads exist to link the area directly to these southerly communities.

So the ranch is privileged to receive constant and varied visits from its neighbours to the south, many of them taking up residence on the ranch, as suits their purpose. In spring and early summer, one may encounter small herds of cow

elk and their calves. By early fall, the valley begins to echo with the calls of the bull elk entering the rut. In winter, the herds grow larger as the elk band together, moving over the landscape in search of the best winter feed. The moose favour the alder swales and dense river flats, while the white-tail and mule deer seem at home almost anywhere.

This kind of population density could not exist without attracting the attention of other neighbours: a pack of wolves usually blows into the valley some time in the winter, coming and going on a schedule known only to its reigning executive. Lynx and cougar seem to find sufficient attractions to leave their tracks there in any season. Black bears are perennial favourites, coming out with the crocuses and disappearing with the arrival of the first big snows.

Grizzlies wander through at will. There was much speculation last fall that an uncommonly large boar had denned up just the other side of the ridge that looks down on the ranch house. Those who frequent the area on horseback or on foot have been heard cautioning each other to keep an eye out for signs of this giant's presence. His tracks have been sighted down at the creek-mouth, which is virtually just out the back door of the barn (hidden from sight by tall river-bottom poplars and dense willows).

Of course, there's also the gentler folk of the neighbourhood. Trumpeter swans nest on the old meander scar that winds over the valley floor. To watch 16 or 18 swans lifting off the water in formation as the adults conduct flight training for the cygnets is to know the wonder of flight. Chirruping barn swallows dive past one's ears with such regularity that they're soon forgotten. They build their nests inside the garage and the barn, apparently

counting on the fact that an open door, or at least a broken window pane, will continue to afford them access.

Leaving the ranch, the road climbs out of the valley and winds north as the trees begin to give way to cultivated fields. Preceding decades have seen the bush slowly recede into the swamps and creek valleys, except for islands of aspen or spruce left to shelter farmsteads or difficult terrain.

The land surrounding the empty bear den is an exception. Situated in the midst of fields of canola, barley, wheat and peas, this block of bush has never been cleared. Its owner was not a farmer. Rather, he ran the sawmill, custom cutting lumber for a variety of needs including those of the farms and ranches surrounding him. The old mill-site is still in evidence, through the tall grass and suckering shoots of willow and poplar. The old fellow passed on to glory years back, and there was no one in place to pursue the lumber business.

The main house, which he built of logs, stands as a testament to his craftsmanship. The house is large, a two storey, and features a fieldstone fireplace on the main floor. The fireplace is large enough to include a built-in waterfall trickling down the stone face. The rest of the interior is all natural woods, chopped from the surrounding stands of birch, spruce, diamond willow—whatever the sawyer/builder found suited his needs.

Wild animals do not entirely shun cultivated farm lands. But neither do they tend to linger on open ground—they prefer the cover of the bush, especially during the hours of daylight. So the island of virgin forest stretching back from the old mill-site offers a sanctuary of sorts for animals on the move through the settlement.

Many years ago—our eldest son was no more than a toddler and is now a grown man out on his own—we were invited to Thanksgiving dinner by the sawyer's widow. The feast was as remarkable as the setting. The lady of the house seemed to favour the natural—today we say organic—fruits of the land. Even the home-baked dinner rolls were made with whole-grain flour milled on the land that had grown it.

I need not go through the menu. Suffice to say that the lady's culinary skills were matched by her success as a gardener. It was in all respects—the hospitality of the hostess, the gentle humour of her family and the sumptuous repast—the perfect celebration of Thanksgiving.

Not long after dinner, the lady, as seemed to be her custom, suggested that we might like to accompany her on a walk through the trees out back. It was late afternoon, perhaps early evening. The cool air was scented, here with mint, there with the pungency of wild cranberries. Some in the party, like ourselves, were just starting their families. All of us were young, except for our white-haired guide. The small children ran ahead or fell behind, as it suited them.

Like the universal grandmother that she was, our guide would stop to point out a nest entangled in a dense shrub of red willows. She would describe the tiny eggs it had held and the tiny family that had emerged from them. No question from the little people attending her was trivial enough to receive a trivial answer.

The land was more or lest level, swampy in its lower extremities and firm and dry as we progressed into the timber. In a stand of aspen, the forest floor rose to form a small knoll. Some seasons back a black bear had taken advantage

of this dry mound to dig itself a winter den. The entrance was clearly visible, open to view on all sides.

The children were fascinated, wanting to know if the bear was "home." The guide explained that, no, the den was empty, the bear had moved on. The den had been empty for many seasons, except for a family of coyotes who had spruced up the place to raise its litter of pups there the year before.

I don't know how long our stroll through the neighbourhood lasted, exactly. When we got back to the house, there was the offer of a second round of desserts. The evening passed in songs of thanks-giving and general conversation. When we left, we took with us a feeling of having been touched by the serenity abiding in the forest, home and heart of our gracious hostess.

It was a couple of years after our visit, perhaps a few weeks more advanced in the season, when the story broke. I didn't pay much attention at first. The media tends to go into a frenzy on these occasions, hounding the family with merciless demands to replay the event in graphic detail. Within hours, it seemed, the story had gone national.

My ears pricked up when I heard the location. Close to home, these stories have a legitimate relevance that I don't believe they can have on the pages of some tabloid in the hands of curious strangers.

When I heard the names, I was shaken by the horrific vision of the scene described in relentlessly expanding detail, as reporters probed deeper. I knew these people! I felt helpless, incapable even of imagining the scope of what they must be experiencing, much less seeing what I could

do that would be of any help. I offered a feeble prayer for all concerned.

It seems that on that fateful day a family dinner had taken place, more or less identical to the one we had attended. The dinner had been followed by the usual after-dinner walk in the forest. When the party had reached the empty bear den, a girl just entering her teen years had hopped into the mouth of the den to "see how deep it was on her." The den was not empty.

The cornered bear lashed out with teeth and claws—to the unfathomable horror of all present. The girl's father leapt into the den to free the girl, fending off the bear with his feet and legs. Someone else had set off running back to the house for a gun.

By the time the father had extricated the girl from the den, an artery had been severed. She did not recover. The father's recovery took months of treatment in hospital.

Knowing these people, I can only surmise that it was their faith in God and his Creation that sustained them through their loss. Only that would be sufficient to ban the ever-beckoning question, "Why?" Only those who have seen the smallness of our lives, relative to the mystery and timeless grandeur of Creation, can see the vanity and hope-lessness of attaching blame.

Yet there were others who, with perfect hindsight, won-dered aloud how no one had seen the fresh tracks. Others yet who questioned the wisdom of allowing children to be exposed to the dangers of the forest.

There were those who argued the conventional wisdom that bears never reuse a den and opined that it was just a freak of nature that such would be the case. There were

those who pointed out the power of habit to blind us to what lies before our open eyes—but none of these people had been there. They could not know, as I knew, that any one of us could have done exactly the same thing.

Our children have always had free range of places like the ranch. The story of the empty den has been told and re-told in the hope that it will instill a healthy fear and respect for all that we cannot control.

One should never go gamboling about in the wild without seeing what is written on the ground, just as one would not go gamboling through the streets of the city without seeing the traffic lights. But we all recognize that the exercise of caution and due diligence on our streets and highways is not an absolute guarantee against the untimely death of the innocent.

Bears do not deliberately set themselves in enmity with man. Generally they exhibit a fear and respect of us which usually provides for a live-and-let-live coexistence.

I cannot explain the apparent rise in clashes between people and the dwindling bear population any better than the self-proclaimed experts I've heard attempting to do so.

But perhaps many of us have somehow un-learned our relationship with the living world around us.

The End

About the Author

Jim Nelson lives in Grande Prairie, Alberta, where he works as a freelance writer. Much of his work has been for the stage, film or radio, including everything from a heritage series of musicals, *The Ballad of Knobby Clarke*, to political satire in a cowboy poetry series for CBC radio, *Bunkhouse Breakdown*. His first book of short stories, *Horse Laughs and Hard Knocks*, was published by Lone Pine in 2000.